Plundering Egypt

Plundering Egypt

A Subversive Christian Ethic of Economy

G. P. Wagenfuhr

CASCADE *Books* • Eugene, Oregon

PLUNDERING EGYPT
A Subversive Christian Ethic of Economy

Copyright © 2016 G. P. Wagenfuhr. All rights reserved. Except for brief quotations in critical publications or reviews, no part of this book may be reproduced in any manner without prior written permission from the publisher. Write: Permissions, Wipf and Stock Publishers, 199 W. 8th Ave., Suite 3, Eugene, OR 97401.

Cascade Books
An Imprint of Wipf and Stock Publishers
199 W. 8th Ave., Suite 3
Eugene, OR 97401

www.wipfandstock.com

PAPERBACK ISBN 13: 978-1-60608-663-6
HARDCOVER ISBN 13: 978-1-4982-8869-9

Cataloguing-in-Publication Data

Wagenfuhr, G. P. (Gregory P.)

Plundering Egypt : a subversive Christian ethic of economy / G. P. Wagenfuhr

xvi + 258 p. ; 23 cm. Includes bibliographical references.

ISBN: 978-1-60608-663-6 (paperback) | ISBN: 978-1-4982-8869-9 (hardback)

1. Economics—Religious aspects—Christianity. 2. Economics in the Bible. 3. Political theology. 4. Christianity—Economic aspects. 5. Economics—Moral and ethical aspects. I. Title.

BR115.W4 W143 2016

Manufactured in the U.S.A.   03/29/2016

All Scripture quotations, unless otherwise noted, are the author's translation.

Some Scripture quotations contained herein are from the New Revised Standard Version of the Bible, copyrighted, 1989 by the Division of Christian Education of the National Council of the Churches of Christ in the United States of America. Used by permission. All rights reserved.

For Ainhoa
Ξένοι καὶ παρεπίδημοί ἐσμεν ἐπὶ τῆς γῆς.

Contents

Preface | ix
Introduction | xiii

1 The Theology of Relationship | 1
2 A History of Economic Relationships | 15
3 The Creator-Creature Relationship | 86
4 Estrangement: Creating Cosmos | 121
5 Reconciliation: Subverting Economic Relations | 151
6 Plundering Egypt: Ethics | 197
7 Conclusion: The Great Commission | 232

Bibliography | 237
Name Index | 243
Subject Index | 245
Ancient Document Index | 253

Preface

This book came out of my reflections on the place of money in the church in light of the work I did for my PhD on revelation as desacralization. In so few places in the church is the contrast of Scripture and contemporary belief and practice more evident than in economics. There is no shortage of Christian financial pundits who have supposedly biblical principles for economic thriving. This is amazing when one considers that the writings referenced by these pundits were written in entirely different social and economic situations to our own. There is a profound ignorance of the history of money, evident even in many popular translations of the Hebrew Scriptures, which translate "silver" or *kesef* with "money," so inviting the reader to import modern economic theory into an ancient society that had never seen a coin, let alone a financial institution. Supposedly God is there as an economist, like Adam Smith's invisible hand of providence, ensuring that the natural economic laws he established at the creation continue as intended. God is seen as the source of money such that Christians can be stewards of God's resources. And it would be somewhat understandable if popular Christianity had made a few minor mistakes in the way it thinks about money, erring a little too often on God supporting their chosen careers and blessing their investments. Most all peoples have bartered with the gods. But the problem is just as prevalent, perhaps more so, in professional theology. And this is seriously concerning for the future of academic theology, not to mention a post-Christendom church.

Only recently has a transactional atonement come under scrutiny, but for the wrong reasons. Postcolonial interpretation has helped confirm a contemporary hatred of violence and hierarchy. But postcolonial interpretation, child of Marxism, is itself economic and based in our own modern postmonetary economic system. So attempts to make the atonement non–transactional are still motivated by, and use the logic of, economics. Instead of a hierarchical atonement, an egalitarian atonement is now emphasized. It often goes unspoken that hierarchy vs. equality, that long-standing social debate going back to ancient Greece, is itself a product of economic thinking and relationships.

So it is not surprising that many Christian attempts at economic ethics work from principles divorced from a robust biblical theology, and so end up basically affirming a version of the contemporary liberal economic agenda. Socialism, communism, and capitalism are all narratives that depend upon a certain perspective of human ontology, what human thriving means, and how it can be achieved. These narratives all have roots in civilizations deeply influenced by some more or less rudimentary reflection on the Bible. As we will see, the idea that humans are naturally self-interested is a secularization of Augustine's vision of original sin, invented in the Renaissance, that removes any notion of original sin from the narrative. Self-interest is supposedly neutral and natural. It is not evil, but is often misdirected. Such a perspective, necessary as it is to economics, creates a Pelagian theology. If what is wrong or dangerous about humans can be harnessed by right and just government, the common*wealth* can be ensured and humans can thrive. We can fix what is wrong with our societies if only we discover the right system or theory of how to deal with this ontologically real thing called "The Economy." After reflecting on the actual history of money as given by archeologists and anthropologists, and not the invented stories of mainstream economics, what if we find that the Bible narrates an alternative story to that given by all possible economic theories? What if we find that this story suggests that economics is a human invention in response to our rejection of God and is not an essential part of our nature? What if we find that Jesus is being deadly serious and profoundly intellectual when he says that God and money are entirely separate and contradictory masters? How then can God be in support of our economy? How then will we create an ethic of money that does not call for a simple rejection?

By taking the biblical revelation seriously, which means not treating it as a collection of timeless ethical principles, we must go through the hard work of reading in context, understanding the sweep of the whole story. We can then form a theology from which we can derive ethical applications. If we short circuit this process, Christian ethics will always and everywhere be but a feeble echo, heard long after the original call to action given by those who take a more active hand in forming the world we inhabit. Christian ethics will continue to eviscerate the church by arriving too late with nothing new to say, save for adding some proof texts to what conservatives or progressives have already long believed without reference to the Bible.

I remain resolute that the gospel of Jesus Christ has unbounded power in all possible contexts, not because it affirms or condemns this or that practice of this or that people, but because it subverts all possible worlds and values that people try to create. This book is a call to Christian ethical action. It can find no support outside of the church, because it does not pursue commonwealth, but reconciliation. Reconciliation, as we shall see, subverts any and all past, current, and future theories of economic relations.

I would like to thank all those to whom I am not indebted, but who graciously supported me in this project, expecting no compensation: my wife Ainhoa, my grandparents Brigadier General Philip Caine USAF (Retired), PhD, and Doris Caine, who proofread this work, my parents Kolin and Barb Wagenfuhr for their continual support, and the Triune God revealed in Jesus Christ who took the first step in reconciliation and has bid me do likewise. This is my attempt at telling the gospel of reconciliation with economic implications.

I thank Robin Parry of Wipf & Stock for taking on this project.

Introduction

In Egypt the Hebrews were an economically oppressed people. They lived under hierarchical, racial, and classist violence. As slaves they existed in an economic relationship with the Egyptians, always seeing them through the lens of their separate and subservient lives. A man named Moses, spared from a genocidal-infanticidal campaign of the Pharaoh by the machinations of his mother and the grace of the Pharaoh's daughter, comes to despise Egyptian oppression. Not having been a slave himself but of the aristocracy, he did not live with the fear of repercussions for disobedience or spreading subversion. One day Moses saw an Egyptian beating a Hebrew slave and interceded to the point of killing the Egyptian. His indignation at a system turned to an uncontrollable rage focused on a representative of that system. And so Moses tried the first path of resistance—violence. Moses retreated into a forty-year exile living with remote Midians and building a life there. Called back to his former family and tribe, Moses and his brother Aaron begin the second attempt at resistance and change—nonviolent protest. As the protest is not heard, Moses performs signs and wonders. He does not incite the people to violence or to rise up. These signs and wonders are able to be performed by the Pharaoh's court magicians as well, at least for a time, invoking a cosmic battle to show the supremacy of the Hebrews' God. Which cosmology will prove superior? This is an outright battle, so although there is no direct violence, the battle is located on the spiritual plane with material results.

The Pharaoh's gods prove inferior, and yet he will not relent. Property loss to the extremely wealthy is relatively less catastrophic and, as usual, the owner is able to outlast the slave or striking employees due to accumulated wealth and alternative sources of labor and supply. It is only when the Pharaoh experiences personal and irreplaceable relational loss, with the death of his firstborn son and heir, that he relents to liberate his slaves. This is only temporary, however. Filled with vengeful wrath he will pursue the Hebrews even to his own destruction. The loss of the source of his wealth is a significant blow to his identity in the eyes of his own people. He is an image of the gods, representing the gods on earth. The cosmic battle he has lost could be the loss of the entire Egyptian cosmos.

As the Hebrews depart Egypt, the Egyptian women give their gold and silver jewelry and clothing to the Hebrew women. The Hebrews do not go away empty from their time in slavery, ending up with worldly riches. But these riches are entirely useless for a long wilderness journey—gold and silver having no use value. Eventually they come to Mount Sinai where, feeling abandoned by Moses and his God, the Hebrews turn to Aaron and create a golden calf out of the plunder of Egypt. Aaron stood up and proclaimed "Behold these are your gods who brought you out of Egypt."[1] And so the Hebrews were led astray by their own plunder, turning their gold into their gods and believing that they delivered them from Egypt.

This is a hopeful and tragic story all at once. The oppressed Hebrews are released from captivity but so earnestly desire to be mastered that they must create their own gods out of their plundered wealth. But it is not an unusual story. Money transforms those who use it into its own image. The Hebrews so valued their gold that they turned it into a god, a projection of what they thought had saved them. Because value is created in the self and in the community, and this was a wilderness community ostensibly not engaged in any trade or production of its own, the gold was entirely useless. Nevertheless, it was given great value as a representation of divinity. The Hebrews create their own gods and worship them, deceiving only themselves in the process.

Though they did not escape Egypt by violent revolution, nor did they stay in support of the Pharaoh, the Hebrews did not carry through in the plundering of Egypt. For they took away something far more important than treasure, they took away a system of economic value so that the plunder of Egypt ended up corrupting them. This book tells a larger story, and one that does not end so disastrously. The Christian is called to plunder Egypt, not by taking its valuables or inheriting its values, neither affirming Egyptian economics nor rising up in revolutionary violence. The Christian ethic of economics is a third way, obeying the letter of Egyptian law while subverting its economic structures by the love that refuses to acknowledge material wealth as determinative.

1. Exod 32:4.

INTRODUCTION

Outline

This book tells two stories: the history of human economic relationships, and the story of reconciliation in the Bible. By juxtaposing these stories, we find that the two are profoundly different from the very beginning. The first chapter sets forth that this book is one example of a particular kind of theological method, a method that prioritizes relationships over metaphysics. The second chapter then recounts an anthropological history of economics, dividing human economic history into three kinds of society: premonetary, monetary, and postmonetary. Metaphysics itself is seen to have its genesis in the new invention of coinage in the monetary society. This introduces a difficulty for economic ethics. The Hebrew Scriptures were broadly written in a premonetary society, and the New Testament was written in the monetary society, but we now live in a postmonetary age that has significant differences to these former eras, which makes direct application of economic principles from Scripture problematic.

The third, fourth, and fifth chapters examine the three kinds of relationships that people have with God in the narrative of Scripture: the Creator–creature relationship, estrangement, and the Reconciler–reconciled relationship. Each of these is examined in some detail for their relation to economic concerns. We learn that God is not an economist in his relationships as the Creator, but engages in these relationships for the purpose of subverting them, leading to reconciliation. Estrangement creates new ways of thinking in the absence of a relationship with God. The economic relationship is one major outcome of this estrangement by its transformation of human epistemology.

The sixth and seventh chapters address the application of this theology to a few ethical concerns. Throughout we find that God's mission in reconciliation is a subversive one that is neither a divine "Yes" or a divine "No." It is a divine engagement in human systems for the purpose of liberating individual people from these systems and stories for reconciliation with himself, creating reconciliation with others and his creation, forming a community of the reconciled whose mission it is to continue this work of subverting the stories and values of human *cosmoi*.

Special Terms

Along the way the reader will encounter a few terms of my own that require a little explanation. The first is *cosmos* and its plural, *cosmoi*. These terms refer to humanly created worlds, acknowledging that, in estrangement from

God there is no one world or creation. Indeed, the creation is marred beyond recognition as such by worlds that people groups create. People do not create one world, our world is continually shifting. We are integrated into a world from birth until death, but it is a world of our construction and a world we are continually constructing. So in order to avoid confusion I speak of a single *cosmos* to mean a humanly created world, often in story form, and its plural *cosmoi* to refer to the many worlds that have been created throughout space and time.

A second term or concept that is important to identify is the economic relationship. "The Economy" is a reification no different than the golden calf of the Hebrews. It is a major construct of the postmonetary age. Instead I refer to economy as a kind of relationship in which personal relationships are mediated through material wealth. In this way we can identify similarities throughout human history, enlightened by the vast differences of human economic expression.

A third term to note is estrangement. In keeping with the prioritization of relationship over metaphysics throughout this work, I do not refer to the event of original sin as *the Fall*, but as *the Estrangement*. For I will argue that humans do not undergo metaphysical transformation but break a relationship with continuing repercussions that are amplified in our own time.

Though this is mainly an academic work I conclude with a call to action. Indeed, this entire book is a call to action and is itself an example of the action of subversion. As Christians, the false dichotomies presented by our cosmos must be rejected, for the cosmos itself must be re-narrated. Thus, the terms of our problems must be challenged and restated. Christ has nothing to offer a preordained economic system, for Jesus came to love individuals, not to offer his own cosmology. And so we see that Christ is the second and better Moses. Moses's people were led astray by plundering Egypt, exchanging reconciliation with God for slavery to idolatry and the worship of economics. The people of Jesus—not necessarily the actual history of Christianity, but those who follow the living Christ—devalue economic relationships by loving subversion.

The problem of economics for the Christian is eminently theological. A proper theological ethic that addresses economics must engage in a cosmological subversion, for economics lies at the heart of our present relationships with each other, the gods, and the nonhuman world in our very conception of each of these things. If we desire to engage with economics as Christians we must start again at the beginning of a story. In this book we trace two stories, a history of economics and the biblical history with an eye towards economics. We will see that the power of the gospel is not in direct opposition nor in affirmation but in subversion.

1

The Theology of Relationship

What is presented here is a brief outline of the theological method that lies at the heart of this book. It is a newer method that is as original as any other idea can be. This means that it has influences, some that are readily apparent and others that are not. The clearest influence is Jacques Ellul (1912–94), the French theologian, sociologist, and professor of the history of institutions in Bordeaux. Though I see Ellul's most important theological contribution as being a pioneer in a theology that highlights relationship while downplaying the importance of metaphysical questions, what follows here is not a summary of his work or ideas, but a development of some of the hints and minor points that Ellul makes throughout his work. Ellul did not develop a theological method based on this notion. His own method involved a similar juxtaposition of sociology and theology, but without significant theological development. Intimations in his work have helped lead me to this theology of relationship.

THE PROBLEM OF METAPHYSICS

Who are we? What does it mean to be human? What is it that unites things and gives them meaning? Such questions are what metaphysics attempts to answer. Metaphysics answers these questions by exchanging or sacrificing relationships for a universal definition. Relationships must be exchanged, or traded, in order to have universality. For it is only by abstracting particulars that one can have universals, and yet the particulars are what make relationships meaningful. Pornography is an excellent example of this troubling exchange. By depersonalizing sex and turning what is an expression of a relationship into an expression of individual desire, one pursues technique and method—categories of behavior that elicit feelings of power and pleasure. The concentration on method, on categories of activity, and on types of objects, means that the woman is only important as an aesthetically pleasing machine. She, like a statue, is important only for what she represents, and what she represents is partially the responsibility of the man himself. One cannot express love mediated through universal categories. In doing so it is turned into self-love, a projection of the self. Pornography is often said to objectify women, and this is very true, but it also makes the man become a subject. The lone viewer of pornography enters into a solipsistic world in which women exist for his pleasure in creating his identity. But such women do not really exist at all, except in his eye and mind, for the image replaces the person. The addiction of pornography is like the addiction of metaphysics and the addiction of money. The more one desires the universal and finds it, the more unreal individuals and relationships become. Individuals have been exchanged for universality, love of another exchanged for love of the self. This is an economic relationship, as are all kinds of metaphysics, for they operate on the law of scarcity, on equilibrium, and so demand sacrifice to maintain balance. A relationship with one person cannot last long if it is done for the sake of individual pleasure because one is seeking an experience of universality and by definition experience of one particular cannot lead one to universality.

This is the problem of metaphysics: it is economic. When we return to more fundamental questions, like "Who are we?" or "What is being?" the lessons learned from pornography carry over quite well. In order to define a universal, we must take away particularity. Consider human ontology or human nature, what-it-means-to-be-human. We must begin with concrete relations that we have with other people and other animals, then abstract the concrete to form a universal. In doing this we exclude what is not like us, ever refining the process and excluding more subtly. Animals are excluded by means of rationality, for example. This eventually proceeds to excluding mentally disabled humans from true humanity. Rationality values itself and creates a solipsistic world in its own image. Rationality loves itself. Aristotle's God thinks itself. In the end, human metaphysical rationality might be nothing more than an exploration and love of itself.

Creating universals in this way tends toward a certain political philosophy. It is not inconsequential that Aristotle was an enemy of the demagogues and the tutor of Alexander the Great. Nor is it inconsequential that virtue was his ethic, as this is an ethic based in attempting to achieve an ideal notion of what-it-means-to-be-human through the achievement of *eudaimonia*.[1] Virtue and self-discipline tend inevitably toward mysticism because they are aimed at an achievement of an ideal that is difficult, if not impossible, to fully instantiate. By creating an abstract ideal Aristotle renders humanity something that must be obtained. We might say Aristotle's metaphysic is virtuous, godlike, aspirational, or aggressive in that it strives after an exclusive human ontology. Another classic example of this would be Nietzsche for whom the word "human" carries a dirty connotation when he describes the herd as "all too human."

An opposing definition of human might be called populist, democratic, inclusive, and passive, thus endowing all with equivalent rights, extendable in many cases to nonhuman animals. This again is based in an abstracted ideal rather than in a concrete particular set of relationships. The ethic of this sort of metaphysic is observable in liberal society, an ethic of entitlement and affirmation.

In either case we have extreme visions of what-it-means-to-be-human that necessarily produce an ethic that judges people in terms of their relation to an ideal; though this is an ideal that has been created by a person observing and analyzing actual relationships in a deeply historical context, building on the received metaphysics of generations. In this way metaphysical speculation begins to look less like speculation and more like Feuerbachian projection. The real problem of projection is not with God. The concept of the One, or God is simply the culmination of metaphysical inquiry. The real problem is metaphysics. The mechanism of projection is no less real for metaphysical universals than it is for God.

The building blocks of "reality" are people and things. But these two must inevitably merge into one by seeking unity or oneness. People and things become contained in nouns, in subjects and objects. They are "real" insofar as the description corresponds to "reality." Metaphysics is problematic because it seeks after the real, presupposing the real to be found in or through nouns, thus finding an ultimate reality contained in an ideal person-thing, which usually happens to be called "God." This ideal person-thing has all the features of both things and people, serving as the source of both. In this merging of people and things, any possibility of relationship is either excluded or is made essential, so that some theologians speak of a relational ontology. But what if our conception of metaphysics, and thus of God, is fundamentally problematic? What if we prioritized relationships over nouns? What if people and things were understood not only as forming

1. A Greek term with a somewhat debated definition. A literal etymological definition is "good spiritedness" but it is usually taken to mean "thriving." Traditional translations of Aristotle say "happiness."

relationships, but also as being formed by relationships? This would, of course, militate against a seeking for the One. It would also prevent turning a living God into a set of propositions or ideals. And it would force us to abandon any concept of essential similarity to God. This would force us to reassess how metaphysics leads to economic relations, how metaphysics as a subject was partly created by money, and how metaphysical thinking inevitably results in a divine legitimization of human economies. The problem with metaphysics, as we shall see with economics, is not that it is inherently violent or hierarchical, for egalitarianism depends equally on metaphysics and economics, but that it is a symptom of loneliness and estrangement from the Creator, his creation, and from his creatures.

THE PROBLEMS OF EPISTEMOLOGY AND ETHICS

The problem of metaphysics leads us to particular epistemological and ethical problems. Virtue ethics, and a maximal or aggressive notion of human ontology, go hand in hand, just as a populist or minimal human ontology goes hand in hand with a rights-based ethic, as we've said. Ethics depends on ontology for the source of knowledge of the good. We must distinguish between ethical method and values. Ethical methods, for example, agent-based virtue ethics, act-based deontology, or consequence-based utilitarianism, do not provide value data. That is, we might know *how* to attain the good, but we do not yet know *what* the good is. This good has often derived from the situation in which the ethicist has lived, whether supporting it or providing the terms for rebellion against it.

If we try to disentangle ethics from metaphysics we inevitably destroy its universal appeal and thus its power. Ethics must fit behavior into categories. Kant's categorical imperative is the most obvious example. The purpose of ethical reasoning is to establish and encourage right action, action in accord with rule, principle, and nature. But ethics without ontology is highly relativist, that is, based in particular relationships rather than in universal ideals or rules, and so somewhat impotent.

Epistemology is also problematic if we prioritize relationships, because we end up focusing, not on how a universal "we" know, but on how individuals know. Indeed, relationship knowledge is quite different from factual or ontological knowledge. Relationship knowledge comes in narrative form, not propositional form. Romantic languages preserve this distinction much better than English. The difference in French of *savoir* and *connaître* attests to this. In English we say "I know that" to refer to factual or ontological knowledge, and we say "I know so and so" to refer to relational knowledge.

As we will see in the biblical narrative, relationship determines epistemology and epistemology becomes problematized when people become estranged from God. Metaphysics can only explain epistemological problems in terms of the limitations or corruption of rational human nature. Metaphysical theology thus presupposes that human rationality is not limited or so thoroughly corrupt that it cannot grasp the divine or analogies of the divine. I will show through the biblical narrative that it is systematically impossible to know the divine if there is relational estrangement, because God reveals himself only in relationship and not in ontological similarity.

PRIMACY OF RELATIONSHIP

As will be seen in the course of this book an anthropological history of economics and the influence of money on the development of Greek philosophy and metaphysics will help demonstrate the primacy of relationships. The character of relationships determines metaphysics, epistemology, and ethics, not vice versa. The development of coinage radically transformed relations in premonetary debt-based societies, with consequent changes to their cosmos.

Theologians and philosophers must deal with relationship before considering being, and after thinking about relationships it will usually turn out that being is a superfluous concept. Heidegger talks of a "thrownness," the experience of being always-already within the world. This is an experience of previously established relationships. But instead of trying to find what lies behind or beyond these relationships, as Sartre attempts to do, perhaps accepting the fact of relatedness and examining it would prove far more fruitful than an investigation of what can never be known: being in itself. Relationships are not part of, or subordinate to, what-it-means-to-be-human, simply because this is unspecific. Humans are not uniquely social animals. Instead of describing what-it-means-to-be-human, relationships preexist questions of being. And it seems to me that it is not possible to transcend actual relationships by positing a notion of "relationality" that lies at the heart of human ontology, or ontology in general.

Granted, we can form a relational ontology, but such concepts are at best meaningless, and at worst highly self-deceptive. For what can be gained by notions of a social ontology, except an ethical imperative to be "more fully human" by relating to each other in this or that way? Indeed, most ethical arguments tend toward this end. The argument runs something like this: (1) x is what it means to be human; (2) it is an ethical imperative that humans be humans; (3) therefore, we as humans ought to do/be x. In this argument the second proposition is generally unstated. This second proposition, a tautological ethical imperative, enables ethicists to find or project an ethical agenda onto human nature without observing the absurdity. If I am human then I ought to act like a human, which requires me to look at a species identity, choose the aspects that are ideal and attempt to form my life around those ideal aspects of the species identity. Human flourishing, it is said, is most well achieved when we live up to our species identity. But it is just as easy to find another aspect of human nature to emphasize, perhaps conquering power, perhaps the ability to make enemies and overcome them through strength of mind, will, and body. Those who are weak are thus less than human, and are rightfully killed as abominations to the shrine of human nature. It ought to be clear that the form of ethical argument based in human ontology is absurd.

But countless philosophers and thinkers of various fields have followed in this tradition. Adam Smith is exemplary. He taught that humans are uniquely economic animals. After all, "Nobody ever saw a dog make a fair and deliberate exchange of one bone for another with another dog."[2] Humans are, by nature, creatures prone to "truck, barter, and exchange one thing for another."[3] And so it is a moral imperative that the government not get in the way of human flourishing by the enabling of free markets. Mercantilism was inimical to proper human thriving, because it went against the grain of human nature. Smith's arguments are largely disproven by anthropological investigation of human societies that did not really engage in barter relationships, as we shall see. Nevertheless, Smith attempts to derive an economic and ethical theory from human nature, that great *carte blanche*. Such a move ought to be regarded as rhetorical and political rather than serious ethics.

Discrediting this kind of argument is necessary to the establishment of a theology of relationship, because most who encounter such an argument will make objections based in established knowledge of human ontology. They will thus fail to see that their own nexus of relationships forms their notion of human ontology, and thus they imprint a world construct of their own upon human nature before magically deriving their preconceived idea from human nature. Possessing knowledge of human nature that is unmediated by preexisting relationships, and therefore possessing disinterested knowledge of human nature, is impossible. Not only is it impossible, it is undesirable, as we shall see.

    2. Smith, *Wealth of Nations*, 5. Not only did Smith use this example, but Al-Ghazali (1068–1111) and Al-Tusi (1201–74) both use this exact example. See Hosseini, *Smith's Division of Labor in Medieval Persia*, as noted in Graeber, *Debt*, 279 n84.

    3. Smith, *Wealth of Nations*, 5.

Some will also object that our relationships are formed by our nature. And this may be true as well, but we cannot transcend our concrete and particular relationships, nor should we want to. A mystical ascent to the world of the forms or the mind of God, or to nirvana, is not possible, or even desirable. For such an ascent implies the conjunction of the self with the whole, or the great One, that eliminates any principle of individuation. As a Christian theologian, I believe one of the great strengths of the Christian narrative is that God does not expect us to become enlightened through self-negation or transcendence of individuality, but by embracing a reconciled relationship with God, and thus with others, thereby highlighting individuality-in-relationship rather than diminishing it. Indeed, what can be a better principle of individuation than the kind of relationship one has with God, the one who can know our hearts and loves us all the same?

Theologians ought to glory in this inescapability of relationality, and it is strange when one considers the endless submission of relationality to ontology in theology. No matter what source we have for divine revelation, it is still implicit in the need of revelation that there must exist some kind of relationship through which this revelation is mediated. Reason, tradition, history, nature, or Scripture all require some form of relationship to something outside of being in itself.

This book is one example of an applied theological discourse that examines the relationships between God and people throughout the narrative of Scripture, and compares those relationships to those we observe between people and nature, and between people themselves. Economy is a kind of relationship. Referring to a "kind of relationship" does not require a realist ontology of relationship. Instead what is being attempted is a discourse that submits questions of being to questions of relationship. Instead of a "relational ontology," an attempt to fit relationships under the guise of being, this is a discourse on relationships. Every relationship is unique because it involves different characters. Nevertheless, there must be similar characteristics of the Creator-creature relationship, the estrangement between God and his creatures, and in the Reconciler-reconciled relationship because they all involve a relationship or lack thereof with God, who is constant. This sort of discussion is not an easy task with the current state of our language, or even with how our language has developed over the last few millennia in Western society. Our vocabulary and syntax is always-already ontological, even economic.[4] But this does not mean that we cannot perceive the limitations of our language, especially by consideration of ancient languages and

---

4. Kevin Hector seeks a therapeutic way out of the linguistic debt to metaphysics, holding a possibility that language is not necessarily metaphysical by a proper theology. Hector, *Theology Without Metaphysics*.

culture. We can learn the walls of our linguistic expression, and even proceed somewhat beyond them, aware of the great difficulty that this presents.

Our own language has great difficulties going beyond metaphysics. English standard word order: subject–verb–object, prioritizes being because the subject is of primary importance. Furthermore, because English verbs are not inflected—the subject cannot lie within the verb as in Romance languages—the subject is propelled to even greater significance since it must be explicitly mentioned apart from the verb. Because speech requires time, the first utterance is that upon which all other words must rest. In contemporary colloquial English the addition of "so" at the beginning of a sentence softens a strong statement or question by reducing the presence of the self and thus the perceived violence of the statement. Interrogatives place the question word at the beginning, thus altering the remainder of the sentence in tone and meaning. But the standard sentence begins with the subject and so it carries priority. I don't mean to imply that sentence syntax is determinative of the human mind and the questions we ask, only that it is one influence, and one that is not always acknowledged.

But in classical Hebrew, for example, a language that we might call pre-ontological, the word order prioritizes the verb and thus it prioritizes the action. Verbs relate because all action requires a subject and an object, even if the subject and object are the same. Verbs also locate the action in time, and thus provide, at a bare minimum, a relationship between a subject and time. Thinking does not really require space, but it does take time, and this places us in a whole complex set of relationships. The time of day at which I think of something may change what I am thinking about or how I think about it. Thinking about sleep when I have to wake up early is very different than thinking about sleep at ten in the morning after a bicycle ride. But there is a larger sense of time as well. Thinking about slavery in mid-nineteenth-century America is very different to thinking about slavery in early twenty-first-century America. The terms, conversations, and socially acceptable opinions have all changed. Verbs lead us to consider these things in a way that concentration on nouns do not. Verbs situate the subject. A properly constructed sentence requires a finite verb, that is, a verb that is limited to a specific subject and time. Not all verbs require objects, but the majority do, and this places the subject in relation to an object in time.

What all this means is that, for a native speaker of English who has no knowledge of foreign languages, or even of English syntax, the priority of the subject, and most notably "I," makes questioning the priority of metaphysics in philosophical or theological reasoning to be absurd. After all, isn't theology itself just thinking about God? Yes, what but goes unspoken in this definition is the relationship of the subject of the sentence to its object.

Theology is *our* and *my* thinking or account of God. It is not accidental that theology is a Greek term, given to us by a people who were enamored with metaphysics. For a *logos* is an account, a reckoning, a term derived from economic considerations. And, as we shall see, economic relationships, especially those which are aware of money, tend toward quantification, then to abstraction, and thus toward metaphysics and notions of correspondence between truth and reality. So in this sense it is not surprising that theology has been dominated by metaphysical considerations. But we can begin to repair this problem. God may be *a se*,[5] and if this is the case, he is unreachable, and thus theology is nothing but metaphysical speculation. Christian theology must begin, as Karl Barth does, with revelation. Because *we* are the subject of theology, the ones who are doing theology, who are writing an account of God, the object. If we forget that we are the subject of the action of theology our theologies tend inevitably toward unifying the subject and object: gazing at ourselves in a celestial mirror.

A theology that prioritizes relationships over metaphysics will inevitably give us a different perspective on economics and this book explores the implications of just such a theological method. But this is a theological method that requires quite a lot of self-study. This book is profoundly mine. I am its author, and it will naturally bear witness to my own personality. I'll not give my biography, but my own life story is important. This book, and my theology, rest profoundly within all the various relationships that I have with a number of influences. It also rests upon the lack of relationships I have had, that others may have had. For example, a lack of a strong mentors throughout my childhood, a lack of intellectual masters throughout upper education and my postgraduate work of whom I could be a disciple, has helped instill and confirm a suspicion of authority. And many of these things need to become explicit in the course of doing theology. It is essential then to combine a study of theology with sociology, anthropology, psychology, and other human studies. Not because these social sciences have infallible methods or true theories. But because they lead us to the understanding of how the act of doing theology is related to the subject of such a theology—ourselves.

REVELATION AS RELATIONSHIP

Revelation is itself a relationship. God has revealed himself to people in a time and in a place. He does not reveal some kind of absolute truth from the perspective of one who lives in the world of forms. Such a revelation could

5. Latin: "in himself," i.e., self-sufficient.

not be given in speech or writing in any case. But God does not reveal some kind of a-perspectival truth, because God himself does not occupy such a place. The God of Jesus Christ is always in relationship with his creation, though there be an infinite qualitative distinction, as Kierkegaard and Barth following him are so keen to say. This is not an ontological relationship. There is no metaphysical connection between God and his creation. But there is a chosen, personal relationship. Therefore, God has a perspective, and one that is not fully communicable because it can only be understood in the particular relationships that he has, which are nearly infinite. However, God can and has revealed stories of a few of these relationships, which comprise the majority of the Bible.

God reveals himself. But this is not a revelation of the being or essence of God, but a self-revelation in relationship to people. We cannot know God except as he has revealed his relationship to us. Our attempts to find God through metaphysical enquiry have always been met with very predictable results—various kinds of self-projection. The metaphysical method of doing theology is nothing but a language game. We look at the structure of our language, its spatiotemporal aspects, and abstract these things from it. We consider what it must mean to be a subject without an object. This is why Aristotle's God is disinterested. In order to consider what "God" means, Aristotle must abstract every kind of relationship except the one that is necessary, the first cause. Because he has abstracted every possible relationship, it is no surprise that his conclusion is that God cannot be in relationship. His conclusion is implicit in his method. This is the economy of metaphysics.

But God is in many, innumerable, indeed, nearly infinite personal relationships. What this means is that all of his self-revelation must be characterized not only by himself, but also by those to whom he is revealing himself. Thus divine revelation is necessarily contextualized. It takes on the character of the people to whom it comes. But, like all relationships, it does not leave people unchanged. Thus we have the spatiotemporal aspect of revelation. It is characterized by time and change, by the births, deaths, sins, and faithfulness of those with whom God is in relation. God is known in these relationships, not in spite of them.

THEOLOGY AS RELATIONSHIP

Theology itself is a relationship, though this is often unacknowledged. Even for atheists, who, though they do not believe in God still define themselves by the concept, there is an implicit relationship in their doing theology. The atheist is in a kind of relationship with at least the idea of God. There are many personal influences that go into the doctrinal belief that there is no God. And this creates a relationship, albeit a negative one. It has often been observed that atheism depends, just as all negative concepts do, upon the positive. Atheism only lives and survives by the thriving of theism. And so we can say that the atheist doing anti-theology is still in some kind of relationship with God or the idea of God.

Theology is my or our talk about God. Therefore, we need to ask not just "Who am I?" and "Who are we?" but also "Who are we in relation to God?" Theological enquiry is not a static enterprise. If there is a living God, then doing theology places us in a kind of relationship with God that changes our theology. Theology is always undergoing revision, just as any relationship cannot remain static for it to be living. And this means that our talk about God inevitably undergoes shifts as our lives change.

All of this means that the kind of relationship we have with God radically determines what form our theology will take. This is why Augustine's idea of faith seeking understanding is so important and perceptive. A living and actively reconciled relationship with God cannot but have a major effect on one's theological method and conclusions. Likewise, a relationship estranged from God will necessarily construct a different account of who God is. And so we can see that revelation, even the static text of Scripture, is not of itself sufficient for knowledge of God. God, through the Holy Spirit, must transform the dead text into something living and active.[6]

This has profound implications on how theology is done. Academic theology that attempts to bracket off this relationship necessarily begins to speak of an *idea* of God. Though there is still a kind of relationship here, and such a theology will undergo some changes based on the author's life circumstances and new learning, it will itself only ever talk about an idea of God rather than God himself. Thus it should be no surprise to us that theology has become a subject relegated to the back corner of the humanities department, or subsumed under departments of religious studies. The idea of God cannot transcend humanity, and so this sort of theology is nothing but a kind of self-deceptive psychology masked in empowering and grandiose language of eternity. As a further consequence we should not be surprised when students of theology and religious studies "lose their faith," because there is a category error occurring. These students believe that they are talking about God, when they are merely talking about themselves and about our contemporary culture in which the idea of God has fallen on rather hard times.

---

6. Heb 4:12.

These considerations become important for the task at hand of considering the economic relationship and how a Christian ethic might interact with such a relationship. Any kind of ethic that does not take this relationality of theology into consideration will end up following one or another nontheological account of economics with the idea of God there to give infallible justification to the proposed economic system. Such a theological ethic is ultimately meaningless, for it adds nothing to the considerations of the economic system. It is, however, a tool for persuasion and propaganda to influence a broadly Christian social group that is susceptible to this kind of sophistry.

The perceived downside of this relational theological and ethical method is that it can say nothing to influence those who do not have such a living and active relationship with God. But this is only a perceived downside, not an actual one, because Christians already have almost nothing to add to the general ethical debate. There is no genuinely unique Christian position that is shared by the vast majority of Christians. Instead they tend to fall in line with those whose political views they already share. And this also means that Christians can safely dispose of the idea that they are seeking a "common good" that unbelievers will accept. Such Christian pronouncements are often, unfortunately, delusions of grandeur. Pursuing this argument further here will distract us from the main task, and it will become clear as the reader reaches the conclusion of this book why it is that Christians cannot seek a positive systemic socioeconomic order, and so cannot wholeheartedly support the commonwealth.

THE THREE RELATIONSHIPS

As I have said, every relationship is unique because it involves different characters. This is what is so powerful about the consideration of relationship instead of ontology. Rather than considering the nature of species, we consider the relationships that God has with individual people and other creatures. Each will be unique, but because all these relationships involve God in some way, they all will reveal something of God's character.

So although it is a simplification, considering three different kinds of relationships in Scripture creates a neat timeline within which we can place ourselves, helping to produce a portrait of our world and what our hope for the future can be. God is revealed historically, much to the annoyance of all who are looking for timeless principles to live by. And it is therefore of utmost importance to place ourselves in the proper time, rather than trying to abstract principles from time immemorial, from a now extinct kind of relationship that once existed. I am thinking primarily here of Genesis 1–2.

These three kinds of relationships are the Creator-creature relationship (chapter 3), the relationship of estrangement (chapter 4), and the Reconciler-reconciled relationship (chapter 5). The first relationship occupies only the first two chapters of the Bible. This is because, as we shall see, the notion of a creation depends upon the notion of a Creator. And in the relationship of estrangement, this knowledge is, as Paul says, suppressed in unrighteousness.[7] Thus creation and the Creator in many ways disappear. And when people come to reconciliation with God in Jesus Christ, they do not simply revert to the knowledge of Adam and Eve in the garden, but to a more mature knowledge that knows God as an adoptive Father, and as the Reconciler. Thus from Genesis 3 until our own day the latter two relationships have existed simultaneously. There are those who "walked with God" like Enoch (of Seth)[8] or Noah, and these lived within a very basic Reconciler-reconciled relationship, at least as far as we can know. Through the course of biblical history, we come to know more and more about God the Reconciler. Indeed, the very point of Scripture is to reveal God as the Reconciler throughout a long historical period and not just God as Creator or Judge, notions other mythical traditions already contained.

One foundational thesis of this book is that the kind of relationship that one has with God determines the kind of relationship that one will have with oneself, one another, with each of God's creatures, and with God's creation itself. In other words, what role God plays in one's life is the primary factor in determining the shape of other relationships. A relationship of estrangement will lead to estranged relationships with all others. For example, to believe that God does not exist, or to actively rebel against him, will inevitably result in the transformation of the "creation" into depersonalized categories like "nature" or "the universe." These concepts are rather meaningless insofar as they are used to incorporate everything, thus excluding nothing. Both Nature and the Universe are often spoken of as having agency, which is tantamount to saying that everything causes everything, which is either absurd or a tautology depending on how one interprets such a statement. But these super-universal concepts play the same role for most economic perspectives that God or the gods do in more traditional societies. That there is such a thing as the Economy depends entirely upon a depersonalized view of agency. Estrangement from God leads to the elevation of the sum of human economic relations to the status of a universal with agency.

7. Rom 1:18.
8. Gen 5:24.

For there to be a natural law of human economic relationships requires a particular anthropology, and there is no anthropology without a correlative theology. Those who deny this point evince a relationship of estrangement from God and from themselves.

The kind of relationship one has with God determines the kind of relationship that he or she has with everything else. To be reconciled to God leads to a very different perspective of creation and other people and how one is to interact with them in the economic field. An entirely unique Christian ethic will therefore follow this perspective.

ECONOMIC RELATIONSHIP AS A CASE STUDY

The three main relationships seen in Scripture that we are looking at in this book are related to a fourth, the economic relationship. Now, it is somewhat dangerous to say that there is something called an economic relationship because it may lead one to think that the human history of economic relations has not profoundly changed over time. It has, of course. And it is a rather complicated history that mainline economists tend to reduce to a highly simplistic myth of progression from barter to currency to virtual money. The rather complicated history of human economic relationships does not mean, however, that there are too few similarities to speak of a general kind of relationship.

This economic relationship is serving as a case study to prove the merit of the theological method I have very briefly outlined here. Rather than focusing on a reified thing, like the Market or the Economy, it is far more important to focus on the kind of ways people relate to each other that we can call "economic." Because we are not considering things, but relationships, it is important to ask what the economic relationship has to do with the three broad relationships we see in the biblical narrative.

Thus this book forms a genealogy of the economic relationship in the broken relationship with God. This is, of course, entirely impossible to document or consider actual history. I make no claim to establishing historical fact. The importance of this book's argument is not in its verifiability, but in its interpretative power.

2

A History of Economic Relationships

Before we begin to consider how the biblical story and theology relates to economics, we need to engage with a very brief history of economic relationships. Importantly this is not a history of economics or the Economy. Instead I prioritize human relationships and look at the history of how people have related to each other and the world in economic terms. This means many standard questions are not investigated or even mentioned. This chapter produces a purposefully simplified view of the history of economic relations as premonetary, monetary, and postmonetary.

This chapter begins with a discussion of ancient Greece and the origins of money and metaphysics. Surprisingly, these two very important human creations have their birth in roughly the same time and place. Although money was invented in Lydia/Greece, India, and China at roughly the same time (600–500 BC),[1] it is more beneficial to concentrate on the one case that has played the much larger role in Western history. For this section I refer often to the work of Richard Seaford, a professor of classics and ancient history at Exeter, whose book *Money and the Early Greek Mind* offers a thorough investigation of the social and cultural conditions that made the development of money possible.

After this discussion of monetary society, we then go back in time to premonetary societies and discusses relationships of debt and credit. Although this is a prior situation to the invention of money, the three above mentioned societies all largely abandon coinage and return to a system of

---

1. Graeber, *Debt*, 212.

debt relationships around AD 600. For the discussion of premonetary society I will often refer to David Graeber's *Debt: The First 5,000 Years*. Graeber is professor of anthropology at Goldsmith's, University of London. He has written widely about theories of value.

Finally, we travel to our own time when modern money arrangements seem to be a synthesis of debt and currency and the consequent perspective of a universal humanity. Each of these perspectives reveal an implicit narrative that we might call theological. All presuppose an essential problem, a proposed solution that fits the terms in which the problem is expressed, and a way to that solution. For each there is a problem that needs solved, though the nature of this problem is different in different monetary situations. Ultimately we see that the economic relationship, though expressed in different ways in different times, is a constant among human peoples. The solution to the problem is always given in terms that ironically reinforce the problem itself, so that attempts to bridge the gap result in widening the gap.

WHAT IS MONEY?

There are a number of qualities that something must meet to be considered money. Precious metals had long been used in exchange before coinage came about, but precious metal should not rightly be considered money as we shall see. This means that what we see in the Old Testament, for example, is a society in which silver and gold weighed in shekels were used as a measure of value. Nevertheless, precious metal should not rightly be considered money, and the ancient Israelite society, like its neighbors, was a debt-based or premonetary society. Seaford gives a good list of the qualities that make up money, that is summarized below.[2] Not all of them are required, but the more qualities met, the more rightly we call the thing money.

(1) Money is first of all valued not for its use value, but for its ability to *meet social obligations*. In this there is a distinction between exchange and payment. Money for exchange and money for payments of fines, taxes, tributes seem to have distinct origins. This is a point that the common Neoclassical narrative, and that of Aristotle, miss when they put the origin of money in market transaction alone. This power to meet social obligation is a necessary but not sufficient condition for something to be money. That is, there are many things that could meet this condition, and many governments have demanded taxes in a variety of goods. Seaford combines this ability to meet social obligation

---

2. Seaford, *Money and the Early Greek Mind*, 16–20.

with the storage of an object for the meeting of future obligations. This brings an object closer to money, as stored objects lose their use value.

(2) Money is *quantitative*, whether in number or amount, or both. Something can meet a social obligation, say in a public sacrifice, without it thereby being seen primarily for its quantity. We might think of the Old Testament importance placed on the quality of animal offered.

(3) The object under question may be used as a *measure of value*. Again, something can be used to measure value of different things without it being used as money. This measure of value can also function as a unit of account and so it need not be exchanged. Such seems to be the case for cattle in Homer. Cattle seem to be for offering at a sacrifice, and thus they meet a social obligation. Nevertheless, though it may have these aspects, cattle do not seem to actually be exchanged as a currency in Homeric Greece. They function as an imaginary unit of account rather than an actual exchangeable commodity.

(4) *General acceptability* is a crucial qualification for something to be considered money. An object can meet other qualifications, but if it is not generally acceptable, it is not really functioning as money, but more of a direct exchange of goods or barter.

(5) On the other hand, *exclusive acceptability* is also an important aspect of money. Though things can be exclusively accepted in special situations, when combined with *general acceptability* one has nearly identified money there. For example, many premonetary societies exchanged one specific thing for another, and this was an exclusive relationship, x for y, but not for z. So it would fail to be generally acceptable as exchange or value and thus not be money.

Qualities 1–5 are generally sufficient for a thing to be considered money, but there are two others that play a very large part in the development of money, and have major implications in the formation of metaphysics, and thus of much theology.

(6) Seaford uses the awkward term *fiduciarity* to explain how money is abstract. Coins are physical objects with a certain exchange value. But once they are stamped with a seal their value is guaranteed by virtue of the seal, not by the weight of the coin alone. So for a one-ounce gold coin to truly be money, it would need to have greater exchange value than one ounce of gold would in bullion or natural form. If the value of the coin was equal to or less than its constituent metals, they would be melted down and used, or exchanged in bullion form. But fiduciarity is not simply conventional value as though coins were only tokens

with no intrinsic value. Modern money is this way, but only after going through the stage where the coin had a greater exchange value than an intrinsic value.

Fiduciarity, though it is a strange word, is a necessary concept to grasp. To restate it simply, fiduciarity is "the excess of the fixed conventional value of pieces of money over their intrinsic value."[3]

(7) The influence of the *state* plays a major role in the development of money. Though again this is more specific to the origins of money than to its continued existence. The state helps the development of money in a number of ways and Seaford does not mention many of them, because they are not directly applicable to ancient Greece. He notes that a government can guarantee the value of a coin and thus help it be divorced from the exchange value of its constituent elements, or it can stamp a guarantee of purity and weight. But there are many other ways the state encourages an object to be money. Through taxes a government can demand payment in a certain form. If a government demands sheep, sheep will immediately take on a different value than they had previously. If the government coins its own money, it ensures that valuable precious metal reserves return to the government itself and thus the local economy can be boosted while providing some safety net in case of military demand by melting the coins down and trading the bullion internationally, or paying the troops in bullion exchangeable internationally. The so-called state theory of money, often associated with John Maynard Keynes, goes too far in exclusively pointing to the state for the formation of money. But it does have a point that taxes help create markets by enforcing a uniform currency. Nevertheless, many ancient governments did not demand taxes of their own citizens, instead they took tribute from subject peoples.

Fines are another crucial means of developing something into money. Though I will discuss the transformation of justice by money later, we can say here that the establishment of the city-state requires a more objective or mediated justice system and money provides a convenient way to universalize all offenses, making the criminal a debtor to the state instead of to the victim. But this obviously requires that the currency be stored or accessible for the payment of fines.

Now that an object can rightfully be *identified as money* based on the above seven characteristics, we need to consider the *properties of money in itself*. Money is homogenous, impersonal, a universal aim, a universal

---

3. Ibid., 7.

means, unlimited, concrete and abstract, and distinct from all else. This list again comes from Seaford's work.[4]

(a) Money is *homogenous*. Money has equivalent value because its value is conventional instead of based primarily in the object itself. This means that money has no history. It is valuable precisely because its history is unknown. Because money is homogenous it is exchangeable for nearly anything else. But its homogeneity in valuing things tends to spread to those things, such that money becomes the primary mode of valuation and most all things are viewed in terms of it. It is a universal to which all particulars may be compared. This is called *commensurability*.

This homogeneity can and does spread to its users, so that they begin to be valued in terms of money as well. It is worth quoting Seaford on this because it will become an important point later on:

> Firstly, it [money] facilitates the kind of commercial exchange that is disembedded from all other relations: the only relation between the parties to such exchange is commercial, and *from the perspective of this relation* the parties are identical to each other, for all each wants is the best possible deal. Aristotle[5] observes that currency equalises not only the goods but also the *parties* to the exchange.[6]

Money, as Aristotle and Seaford observe, alters people themselves by altering the very structure of social relations. Money imposes its homogeneity on society, a point we will see become very clear in modern society with its emphases on the transcending of difference.

(b) The homogeneity of money requires that it be *impersonal*. The heirlooms so important in gift-exchange or premonetary societies help develop a person's character or personality. This is seen in epic literature, whether from Greece or elsewhere, in the importance placed on these heirlooms, often of a military character. Who is Jason without the golden fleece? Who is Thor without Mjolnir his hammer, or Arthur without Excalibur? Both are significantly named. The impersonality of money is what enables it to be equivalent in value and therefore homogenous.

The impersonality of money means that it is promiscuous. That is, it can be exchanged with anybody for anything. In so doing it ignores all other non-monetary relationships. This was, as Graeber notes, the

---

4. See ibid., 149–72.
5. *Nicomachean Ethics*, 1133a17–21.
6. Seaford, *Money and the Early Greek Mind*, 151–52. Italics original.

utopian vision of Adam Smith. Instead of the inefficiency and trouble that personal relationships bring to exchanges and transactions, having the mutual respect that one dollar has for another, exchanges would take place on an even footing, guaranteed by the anonymity that money creates.[7]

(c) Money becomes a *universal aim* of people who use it. The homogeneity of money suggests that there is something equivalent about the various things of life. That is, people begin to see value only in the monetary value of the thing and thereby abstract the thing from the value, leading to a pursuit of money itself. Aristotle distinguishes this kind of practice, of seeking money as an end in itself, rather than as a means to the end of household management. In typical aristocratic disdain of the market, he derides those who seek money for itself, because this becomes a never-ending process. It is the most unnatural of human activities.[8] Those who use money begin to want to acquire money in itself for the representative stored power that lies within.

(d) Because money is a universal aim, it also becomes the *universal means*. Because people begin to want money above all else in exchange for a good or service rendered, money becomes required to perform all things. Money becomes the foundation, not only of economy, but it can also pervade things like ancient sacred rituals, as Seaford demonstrates from the dramatists Sophocles and Aristophanes. Money not only serves to buy all kinds of products, it is necessary to acquire supreme goods, like public welfare or divine good will. Money also becomes the means to political power.

What Seaford does not point out that is absolutely important to understand is that because money is a universal means and end, it is a self-sustaining cycle of human thought based solely upon itself. The mere use of money transforms all things by the establishment of a new kind of relationship, one always mediated by money.

(e) Money is *unlimited*. That money is a universal means and end requires that money be unlimited in power and therefore in number. Money has no limit, even if there can be said to be a certain number of dollars in circulation, its power and influence are potentially unlimited, for its value is not based on its exact quantity, but relative power. Money is the basis of unlimited desire, as well. For it is only possible to conceive of unlimited desire by reference to an abstract value, as money represents. Having a massive surplus of any goods is unsustainable. They

7. Graeber, *Debt*, 335–36.
8. *Politics*, 1257b.

will rot, decay, lose value, or cost more to upkeep than they eventually become worth. But one can always imagine having just one more dollar and the consequent power that would bring. It is hardly coincidental that the first person on record to speak of the personal virtue of moderation is Solon (c. 638–c. 558 BC),[9] who lived in the first generations of Athenian money society. The principle of moderation requires something that is potentially unlimited. There is no such thing prior to the invention of money that would enable such a view.

And it is easy to see from here how money is deeply connected to metaphysics. If premonetary societies can only consider power to be personal, and thus projected onto gods, monetary societies must consider power to be universal and unlimited, thus impersonal. So Anaximander's *apeiron* or Parmenides's god are each universal and impersonal, as well as all powerful, as I will discuss below.

(f) Money unites opposites. Money enables one thing to be changed into another. We will see how Heraclitus refers back to monetary gold to describe the universal fire that can transform into anything. But money also is able to invert opposites and ultimately homogenize all things. Seaford notes how money can efface the difference between breeding in marriage. It can make a good man bad and a bad man good.

(g) Money is concrete and abstract. This is another way of talking about *fiduciarity*. Money is, during the monetary period but not necessarily during the postmonetary period, concrete and abstract. It is based on something physical with actual inherent use value or exchange value, but it is also abstract and therefore of greater value in exchange than its inherent materials would allow.

(h) Money is *unique*. As universal, money cannot be a particular instance of something else. There is nothing for which money can be substituted in every case. The uniqueness of money ensures that its homogenizing power turns things into itself, and not into a third thing. Thus, when relationships are mediated by money, they take on the characteristics of money rather than some third thing.

Money is homogenous, impersonal, a universal aim and means, unlimited, it transcends former divisions, is concrete and abstract, and is unique. These characteristics have important theological implications when we come to see that money is related to metaphysics. Any God or universal being, mind, or thing constructed through metaphysics is likely to share in most, if not all, of these characteristics. Let us then turn to ancient Greece

---

9. Solon, frag. 4c.3, in Seaford, *Money and the Early Greek Mind*, 197.

and the rise of coinage to see the deep connection that metaphysical thinking has with money. We shall then turn back to premonetary societies and finally to the postmonetary society we see developing today.

FROM MONEY TO METAPHYSICS: ANCIENT GREECE

The Story of the First True Money: Coinage

In Homeric heroic society there is a vital difference between kinds of goods: heirlooms and consumables. These are unable to be traded directly and no third way, namely, money, exists to give them an equivalence in value.[10] This is a situation not at all confined to preclassical Greece, but is fairly universal to premonetary societies.

The glimpses we get of heroic society show a disdain for the exchange of heirlooms for common objects. In cases where Homer gives the value of a set of armor, he does so in cattle, for the reason, it seems, that the sacrificial system provided a means of accounting for values of otherwise disparate objects. Indeed, gifts given to temples around this time are often heirlooms themselves, like armor. In this situation without money sacrifice is what gives value.

Homer is himself dismissive of gifts given to the temple, instead prioritizing the tomb and the heroic deed. Gifts to the temple create relationships and sociality whereas tombs and heroism are particular to the individual. The heroic individualism of Homer is somewhat unique to Greek society and it would play an important part in the formation of money. Homer represents a transitional figure in whom the novelty of gifts to the temple is seen and derided. The Homeric virtues of honor, life, and perpetual fame are vaunted above the reach of wealth.[11]

The other side of this heroic Greek economy was in the distribution of booty. Much of the dramatic tension of the *Iliad* revolves around what Seaford calls "reciprocity in crisis." Achilles and Agamemnon are at odds because of unfair distribution of booty. Though Agamemnon has hurt Achilles's honor and offers extraordinary wealth to cover over the injury, Achilles will not accept any wealth for dishonor, nor wealth for certain death in battle. Life and honor are far more important than wealth. The *Odyssey*

---

10. Though there are means by which things can be valued, like silver, silver itself is not normally exchanged. Likewise, even in societies that have an awareness of money it can be purely imaginary as in the European Middle Ages where the Carolingian system of "imaginary money" ruled. See Graeber, *Debt*, 282.

11. Seaford, *Money and the Early Greek Mind*, 56.

portrays a similar crisis, though on the other side. Nobles who could feast in the house of a lord like Odysseus go too far and turn their welcome into plunder.[12] These crises of reciprocity, of what one can rightly exchange for something incommensurate, are major social battles. Distribution is based on a combination of status and merit. This distribution according to honor we might understand as an equality of opportunity for wealth.

But Homer also shows the peacefulness of corporate animal sacrifice that is pleasing to a deity. These do not tend to happen in a temple in Homer, which is an important fact. Sacrifices are times of communal feasting wherein each person, Homer is at pains to show, receives an equal part.[13] In this way the wealth of a group is redistributed from the wealthy to those without wealth. These sacrifices ensure stability, as they are performed regularly and according to established forms and customs. The sacrifice is redistributive and equal, such that we might say participation warrants equivalent reward, an equality of outcome. That they happen apart from a temple shows that they do not exist for the maintenance of a religious order. In this way no temple tax is extracted from the people, an important distinction between Greek and ancient Near Eastern practice. Ancient Near Eastern temple systems were complex and large. They required large sacrifices to support a massive infrastructure, and so the temple, naturally, was closely associated with a massive, imperial state. This hindered the formation of money in the ancient Near East because sacrifices of large amounts of consumable goods were desirable, whereas for the Greeks such large sacrifices would often have meant spoilage. In the ancient Near East there was little impetus to exchange consumables for durable wealth, whereas in Greece there was a solid motive for this exchange.

So Homeric literature shows a tension that exists amongst two forms of redistribution. On the one hand there is a peacefully decentralized and religious group in which wealth is regularly redistributed through ritual. And on the other hand is a group wherein the leader controls the distribution of plunder according to personal will at irregular times and in irregular ways. We might call these communal and tyrannical. There is a contrast, then, of the stability of the group that is present in a homogenizing religious ritual, and the honor of the heroic individual that is competitive and demands personal differentiation in terms of value expressed in booty. This is a contrast of two systems of just distribution, redistribution through sacrifice and meritorious plunder.

12. Ibid., 44.
13. Ibid., 46.

Moving beyond Homer to early classical Greece, we see the merging of individual merit and communal redistribution as the giving of durable wealth to temples eventually comes to take a higher priority than the giving of animals. Animals are, especially in large numbers, not durable and very costly to maintain. The Greek temple system, as distinct from the Mesopotamian systems, did not place a strong emphasis on large temple complexes and priests, and so edible gifts were less desirable. Instead of gifts of animals, then, symbols often began to be offered in durable wealth, for example, bronze animals representing real ones. But these gifts also likely served to commemorate an event rather than just function as a substitution for a real animal. Their durability commemorates an event, just as a tomb or trophy[14] would commemorate an individual in Heroic society. And so, Seaford explains that these durable temple gifts combined the durability of the Homeric heirloom gift with the visibility and communality of the Homeric sacrifice.[15] In this way they provided a way beyond the crises of reciprocity that were present in the Homeric epics.[16] But what about the distributive element of Greek sacrifice? How would the problems that redistribution through sacrifice solved now be solved? Enter the state. With the development of the Greek *polis*, temples became storehouses of wealth that could then serve the common good of the city in times of feasting or in times of crisis.[17]

One of the objects that people used to represent sacrifice was the iron spit, which was mass produced. This means that it became homogenous and symbolic. Instead of being associated with a single historical act or person, as an heirloom would, they embodied something general. Iron spits were also of small enough value but manageable size that they could begin to function in a manner closer to currency. The value they represented was fairly obvious based on their weight, and in an exchange one would not need to carefully weigh them each out, one's hand could tell the difference. Small deviations were of little to no importance, unlike what could be said of small amounts of precious metals. And again, this is what begins to set

---

14. The Greeks erected trophies, or standing monuments, to commemorate a victory in battle.

15. Seaford, *Money and the Early Greek Mind*, 66.

16. And so we see here, as I will have occasion to point out, that Girardian understandings of human society are far too narrow because they do not take into account economics as a major force in averting the problems inherent in what he calls "acquisitive mimesis."

17. The gold plating on the statue of Athena was open to the city to use in case of need for war expenses, through it was a last resort, as Pericles says at the start of the Peloponnesian War. See Herodotus.

the Greeks off from other societies that used precious metals for exchange, like the ancient Near East.

But how does one get from iron spits to coins? Although there is no unquestionable archeological proof that shows the transition from iron spits to coins, there is some evidence that can be interpreted thus. Furthermore, the etymologies of the earliest Greek coins do suggest a strong connection. The *obelos* was a spit, which became a low-value coin, the *obol*. Likewise, a *drachma* once meant a handful of six spits, later coming to mean a higher-value coin. Plutarch makes this etymological connection in speaking of the corruption that the new gold and silver Athenian coinage brought to Sparta.[18] There are many further evidences that need not be discussed here,[19] but they suggest that these spits began to be used in exchange at temples. Also, certain mystery cults would distribute token memorials of a sacrifice, an object that signified one's participation in the ceremony would thus be invested with communal value. The spit, and sometimes other objects, like bones, were convenient and powerful reminders of one's participation, and thus these standardized objects, are invested with value beyond their use. They have symbolic value, but this is not the same value that an heirloom would have formerly had, because an heirloom gets its value by differentiation. Money, or these sacrificial remembrances, attain their value through unity and lack of differentiation. And so, whereas heirlooms would reinforce social ties through gift giving, the state or large social institution is able to create social value and connection through communal action.

The increasing supply of more precious metals perhaps led to the move away from direct objects of sacrificial value, like spits, tripods, and cauldrons. Precious metals had long played some money functions in the ancient Near East and in Greece. As electrum, a naturally occurring alloy of silver and gold, was found in Lydia in abundance, it is likely that people began to merge the function that sacrificial spits had played with the convenience of precious metals. Seaford thinks that it is the meeting of the ancient Near East and the peculiar Greek religious practices that gave rise to coinage. The ancient Near East long had the technology to develop coinage, but nevertheless did not widely use coins, even after coins had spread from Greece to Persia. Although the Lydians seem to be the first to produce coins, the Greeks are the first to make widespread and common use of them. But Seaford is very forthcoming about the impossibility of knowing for certain the actual motives that brought about the formation of money. Though the

---

18. Plutarch, *Lysander*, 17.3.
19. See Seaford, *Money and the Early Greek Mind*, 102–15.

motives may be irrecoverable, our inability to construct a valid and complete genealogy of money does not negate the impact it had on thought.[20]

The function of a stamped image on a piece of metal references the more ancient practice of seal making. Seals had existed before coins and operated as an extension of the ruler himself. The seal is a means of substitution, and so a seal is a symbol. But a seal is a symbol with a single highly personalized referent. Coins, on the other hand, symbolize something universal but impersonal: reified power itself. In this way we can begin to see the metaphysical nature of coins come into play, since they must refer to something actual but impersonal, something universal and imperceptible, something hidden but the focus of communal belief and respect.

To summarize the genealogy of money: heroic society was a gift-based society that both gave wealth in the distribution of booty according to honor, and redistributed wealth equally through sacrifice. Earlier Greek religion did not often utilize temples and so most gifts were of cattle, which provided a *measure of value* and a way to *meet social obligation*. The gift was directly given by the wealthy patron and directly redistributed to the participants. But this was a somewhat contradictory system that led to crises of reciprocity or justice. The wealthy and powerful actually controlled distribution, giving up only what was necessary in sacrifice to keep those with less honor content. As gifts became more durable and temples more important in the growing *polis*, this crisis of individual tyranny was solved by the state. A depersonalized state, represented by the patron god or goddess, became responsible for the storage and distribution of wealth. Temples became storehouses of durable wealth instead of directly redistributing what it was given. A temple currency developed in the form of ritual iron spits that commemorated the sacrifice and could be traded for temple services and became *generally accepted*. These were mass produced and attained their value by being *homogenous*. Iron spits and other sacrificial commemorations provide a transition from heirloom to money. Because seals were already available, the imprinting of a symbol on a coin could become a token of participation in a sacrifice, much like the machines that smash pennies to commemorate visiting a tourist attraction today. The homogenous token of sacrifice able to be used to meet social obligations thus takes on the quality of *fiduciarity*. The increasing availability of precious metals at that time also helped transform the iron spit into the coin. The *polis* then was able to take advantage of this, stamping a coin with an image representing the city's deity or sacred symbol like the Athenian owl.

---

20. Ibid., 134.

Mass produced coinage really began in Miletus, a town on the western coast of modern Turkey. Miletus was geographically near to Lydia, and it is significant that at nearly the same time as the first coins were being produced, the city of Miletus became the birthplace of philosophy with the three major figures of Thales, Anaximander, and Anaximenes. The coincidence is not by chance. And as we shall now turn to discuss, and as Seaford argues, coinage was one major, and perhaps the most important, of many factors that governed the founding of the metaphysical inquiries of this group of people.

Money and Metaphysics

But could money really have played such a major role in the foundation of metaphysical inquiry? Let us first look at what these first philosophers were actually studying and attempting to explain. We are accustomed to think of philosophy as a rather narrow field that thinks about thinking, the ideal, and generally concepts that have little to do with normal life. For the ancient Greeks, however, philosophy was a very broad field that encompassed physics, biology, language and literature, political philosophy, ethics, metaphysics, astronomy, mathematics, and even at times music. Thinkers were willing and able to transcend the boundaries of these fields, sometimes with impressive ability in most of these areas, like Aristotle.

But the Milesians were primarily concerned with physics and metaphysics. The Greek word *metaphysics* is a compound of the preposition *meta*, which here means "above," and *phusis*, or "nature." Metaphysics was an extrapolation of physics. It was thinking about what makes up that which lies beyond the realm of the perceptible. Now the Milesians had some rather peculiar ideas that make it difficult to follow their train of thought. In looking at a world with so many different things, the Milesians and many of their other pre-Socratic followers were all concerned with identifying the one unified thing that lay behind all of reality. For Thales (ca. 624–ca. 546 BC) it was water.

Anaximander (ca. 610–ca. 546 BC), his student, thought that everything was made up of *apeiron*—the indefinite or unlimited. All things do battle against their opposite, and thus owe each other justice. There must be something undefined behind what we see with the capability of becoming anything else to "give penalty and retribution to each for their injustice according to the disposition/assessment of time."[21] Anaximander views the

---

21. This comes from the *Fragment of Anaximander*, which is preserved through Theophrastus (a disciple of Plato ca. 371–287 BC) in Simplicius (A Neoplatonic

cosmos as at war, each thing with each other, eventually coming to justice by the *payment of a penalty*. Now retribution or reciprocity are features of all societies and their conceptions of justice. But what is unique here is the depersonalized nature of this reciprocity, all things must refer back to their source in the *apeiron*. In societies without a strong state or government, retribution or vengeance is the normal means of justice. Judicial procedure significantly reduces violent vengeance by meting out punishment by the state. But it is with the development of money that justice truly becomes a third thing, that murder can be transformed into money, just as rape or theft can. Monetary fines can be imposed and in this way one can become financially indebted to society or the state by criminal conviction. The transformation of an idea like bloodguilt into financial debt benefits the state and, insofar as it is acceptable by the people involved, eliminates violence from the process of justice. Anaximander's *apeiron* seems likely to be a projection of this new kind of justice, a justice in which transgressions of all kinds are resolvable by recourse to the unlimited, which as we saw was one of the major features of money.

That all things can spring from and return to the *apeiron* is a concept that is hard to fathom without recourse to money. For although justice and politics existed before money, they were personal and limited. Before the invention of money there was no object or concept that could have led to the idea of the *apeiron*. Philosophical ideas do not arise *ex nihilo*. They are the product of intelligent people reflecting on the world in which they live. The development of ideas is a dialectical process where ideas are formed by a wide variety of experiences, and experience is formed by a system of ideas.

The three Milesians: Thales, Anaximander, and Anaximenes, were all monists, believing that all things are ultimately made up of one thing. Anaximenes (ca. 585–528 BC) disagreed with his teacher and said air was the basis of all things. Monism must be distinguished from monotheism, which sees God as distinct from the rest of reality, as monism can take the form of pantheism. They disagreed about what that thing was, but these three and many who followed, notably also the atomists, concentrated a notion of a material One.

Monism is a strange idea because it goes against nearly all experience. What would posses a man like Thales, who in other respects was deemed a very wise man, to claim that all things were essentially made of water? Earth, fire, air, people, all of these may have water in them, but it's also true that earth, fire, water, and people all have some air in them. Michael Stokes says:

---

philosopher ca. AD 490–560).

There has been suggested in print no good reason for so strange a beginning in Greek philosophy. Nor does common sense afford any suggestion to alleviate its strangeness; the world around us has nothing obviously suggesting a single material.[22]

Of course, Seaford then suggests that money is what must have caused this perspective to form. Other scholars have argued that myth, psychoanalysis, politics and the mystery cult have a role to play and Seaford agrees, though it is money that is the deciding factor among these causes. In Hesiod, monarchy is projected onto the cosmos and so order is brought out of chaos by a king. This is personal authority projected. Money is already a reification and so projecting it onto the universe is, on the one hand very easy to do. But on the other, money is essentially impersonal and so ill-suited to becoming a god and thus having personal sovereignty. Seaford says:

> Unlike monarchy, money is *impersonal*, and is exchanged into, and is the undifferentiated *equivalent* of, all things, each of which somehow embodies monetary value.... A factor in these radical departures from the Hesiodic model was ... the new model of money as a (controlling) universal, impersonal, and unlimited means of exchange and measure of value: all things may be transformed from and into money, but are (like things in Anaximenes) differentiated quantitatively—they embody (even in the same size) different sums.[23]

Money as a controlling universal begins to be projected onto the cosmos by seeing its properties behind all other things. So we can see that material monism has quite a powerful affinity to the nature of coined money. There is an essential oneness that lies beyond the world of seeming in which all individuals inhere. It is impersonal, unlimited, undifferentiated.

Though the Milesians were initially unique in holding a material One, later philosophers built upon their views to come to similar perspectives of an essential oneness that lies behind experience, and these perspectives also show profound influence from the nature of money. A very brief overview of the relation between metaphysics and money in some of these thinkers will be helpful for future discussion.

---

22. Stokes, *One and Many in Presocratic Philosophy*, 39.
23. Seaford, *Money and the Early Greek Mind*, 225. Italics original.

Xenophanes of Colophon

Xenophanes (ca. 570–ca. 475 BC) is a remarkable figure for being the first in known history to understand the human practice of projection in religion. It would take Europeans until Feuerbach and Marx to again rediscover this notion. But Xenophanes, like other thinkers, is not guiltless himself of projection, even if it is not the same old gods. Xenophanes seems to build on Anaximander's *apeiron*. Xenophanes believed in one god who was not like humans in body or thought. This god was self-sufficient, did not move because he did not need to, and was eternal. All of this god thinks, sees, and hears, and "shakes all things by the thought of his mind."[24] And it seems this god might also be identical to the universe. Xenophanes's god is inconsistent, however. It is impersonal, yet engages in personal action. If it is totally impersonal, how can it shake all other things with its thought of *its* mind. How can mind be universal and impersonal? Aristotle at least follows this through better by describing thought thinking itself.[25]

This inconsistency was also apparent in Anaximander's *apeiron*, even though the *apeiron* was fully impersonal. Again, money seems to be at the heart of this inconsistency. Seaford explains:

> For both Anaximander and Xenophanes there is a single divine thing that is impersonal and yet omnipotent, eternal, and in some sense the equivalent of all things. So too money is impersonal and yet omnipotent, must pre-exist and outlive all transactions, and is the equivalent of all things. Crucial here, for understanding the conceptual shift, is the startling historical novelty of power that is universal, social, and yet impersonal. In the premonetary age a king, backed up by his army and the gods, extracts (and redistributes) goods and services by power that is personal. The mystery of money is its universal *impersonal* power to extract goods and services.[26]

So the transition from the universal personal power of the king to the universal impersonal power of money leads these philosophers to struggle to express a consistent portrayal of the One.

---

24. Xenophanes, frag. B25.
25. Aristotle, *Metaphysics* 1072b.
26. Seaford, *Money and the Early Greek Mind*, 213.

Pythagoreanism

Though not a lot is known about the man Pythagoras (ca. 570–ca. 495 BC) himself, we are told a lot about him. The movement that bears his name was made up of a cultic society that had political influence and was based on an orally transmitted philosophy that said that number is all. This cultic society, Seaford hypothesizes, was a reaction to the newly monetized society. The social transformations that money brought about can hardly be overstated and it should not surprise us that a movement that combined an almost superhuman sage, Pythagoras, with a puritanical belief system (they famously abstained from many foods including beans), and political activism was a powerful way for people to cautiously integrate into the new system.[27]

Pythagoras was not an aristocrat, but the son of a gem-cutter. He is said to have introduced weights and measures to Greece, which is certainly false, but an important story point to show how this strong leader was wise in the ways of a newly mathematized society. Some scholars suggest he brought coinage to Italy.[28] In any case, he arrived at around the same time coinage did in Italy.

The notion that "all is number" is probably not a developed and mature perspective of mathematics and science, but the attempt of people to explain the primal power in a world in which mathematics through money has such overwhelming political and social power. Pythagoreanism, though hard to pin down exactly what it taught in much detail, seems to be a philosophy for the merchant. And, as we can see, it also teaches a monist perspective, even if it was not materialist. Numbers are immaterial, but everything is able to be quantified, at least so long as one can refer to a universal system of valuation like money.

Pythagoreanism was also interested in the mathematics of music, but it was not through music that they imposed number on all things. Many of their terms for proportionality in music are in fact derived from language of calculating interest on loans.[29] This suggests some projection of the features of money onto the cosmos. Everything humans produce, and much that they do not, are able to be valued by money. Seaford thinks that it is "inevitable" that the Greeks would project the universality of money onto the

---

27. Ibid., 266–75.
28. See ibid., 267 n9.
29. Ibid., 273.

cosmos, just as they had done for monarchy and reciprocity earlier in their history.[30] Pythagorean number monism is a major attempt at such a project.

Heraclitus

Heraclitus (ca. 535–ca. 475 BC) was a younger contemporary of Xenophanes and hailed from Ephesus, which was between Colophon and Miletus. He is most known for writing in aphorisms, such that even in his day he was known to be confusing and hard to understand. But this writing style was not accidental, it conformed with his philosophy wherein everything was in flux. Fire was the prime matter, though he did not take this as literally as the material monists. Fire operated more as a metaphor than as the actual single element of which all things consist. Fire is the image of something always changing. He compared this fire to money, which is universally exchangeable, blatantly using the metaphor of money to describe the cosmos.

Heraclitus is also well known for the idea of the *logos*, which is usually translated to "reason." Many modern philosophers miss that this word has a very old usage in financial accounts.[31] For Heraclitus, the *logos* was a measured proportionality in the flux of the universe, not unlike Anaximander's *apeiron*. The fiery flux of the universe is not chaotic for Heraclitus, it occurs in a balanced and measured cycle in accordance with the *logos*. Heraclitus's world is one in which exact transactions take place. I will discuss the relationship of money and justice elsewhere, but it is important to note here that this conception of all things being ruled by an exact reckoning of accounts producing balanced scales is an image that comes from economic transactions. In a monetary society money is not only the means to other ends, it becomes an end in itself, as Aristotle laments in his *Politics*. Because of this money actually drives the circulation of goods, because traders begin looking to make a profit. This seems to give money an active power, almost a will of its own, and yet this is a very precise will. Hence the *logos* not only informs how things ought to be, it actively imposes itself on all things.

But the *logos* is not just an accounting notion applied to the universe, it has connotations from Orphic mystery religion, by which Heraclitus was influenced. The *logos* was not just a myth told in the cult. The cult would read

---

30. Ibid., 273.

31. Evidence is attested from the fifth century BC, but earlier usage of λόγος as a numerical account cannot be discounted since earlier literature does not touch on everyday issues where this kind of accounting would come into play. LSJ places the numerical accounting as the primary usage of λόγος. See Seaford, *Money and the Early Greek Mind*, 231.

on a deeper level, finding cosmological code in older myths. And for this reason the Orphic declarations were aphoristic riddles. Orpheus's riddles were a "sacred *logos*."[32] In this way the older myths were reinterpreted by people who believed in a depersonalized cosmos by allegorical interpretation. In the Orphic religion, as we know from Plato, people have an ancient "Titanic nature," which means that they are lawless (the Titans were the lawless pre-Olympian gods that Zeus imprisoned beneath the earth). The soul is punished for its Titanic sin by imprisonment in the body. So the spirit is contained in earth just as the Titans were imprisoned under the earth. And the *logos* of the mysteries explains that the soul cannot escape by suicide.[33] This means that the soul is transferred through many bodies or prisons. The *logos* of myth, the Titanic nature, and the *logos* that governs the universe, the soul, are then one and the same. The immortal fire that makes up the universe is in the soul. So the universal and the particular are also one and the same. Seaford argues that the combination of this mysticism and money is the root of the Heraclitean cosmology:

> Just as in mystic doctrine the soul circulates through the cosmological elements, so for Heraclitus the fiery soul circulates through the cosmological elements, with the death of one element as the birth of another. Our two contradictions now inhere in the universal circulation of fire. The transition of the same contradictions from mystic genealogy to the universal cosmology of Heraclitus is effected by the influence of the universal circulation of money. Like Heraclitean fire and the mystic soul, monetary value is a single entity that in a sense persists (albeit transformed) through all exchanges. Just as the individual is mortal and yet contains in his soul the immortal fire that persists beyond the transformation we call his death, so money contains the permanent value that persists beyond its transformation into goods.[34]

Though at first this argument seems rather convenient, its cumulative effect with his arguments from other philosophers leads to a rather compelling case that money indeed lies as a major influence behind the development of metaphysics.

The Heraclitean *logos* will be profoundly influential on later thought, especially Christian theology. The influence of Orphic mystery religion and its idea of original sin leading to the imprisonment of the soul in a body will

32. See the Derveni Papyrus, column VII 6–7.
33. Seaford, *Money and the Early Greek Mind*, 234–35.
34. Ibid., 237.

also bear many similarities to common Christian interpretations of Genesis 3. This suggests, not that Christians were necessarily deeply influenced by mystery religion, but that money enabled the allegorical transformation of a mythic narrative into a cosmological account. Thus, money has had a significant role to play in the shaping of Christian theology as well.

Parmenides

Parmenides (ca. 515–ca. 460 BC) was born in Elea, in Italy. In him the distinction between perception and reality becomes total. Perceptible reality is illusory when it suggests that there are many things that change. In reality all is one and unchanging. Parmenides is the inventor of ontology as a topic of study in itself, which in many ways makes him the most important of the pre-Socratic thinkers in terms of lasting influence. His thinking is almost the opposite of Heraclitus and the two are often juxtaposed. Whereas Heraclitus emphasized the fiery and money-like changeability of all things, Parmenides insists on the unity of Being. Parmenides believed that all that can be thought truly exists, and all that exists exists fully. The universe for him was unlimited, unchangeable, immovable, indivisible, and homogeneous.[35] Parmenides could be seen as the one who dematerialized monism. Instead of thinking that there was one primary element of which all other things were composed, he taught that all elements inhered in something immaterial, Being (*ousia*). Now, *ousia* has similar linguistic problems as *logos* does. A modern student of Greek would translate *ousia* with "being" and *logos* with "word" or "reason." But both of these translations are anachronistic and probably reflect the long assumptions of philosophers after ontology became an established discipline. *Ousia* firstly meant one's substance, that is, what one owned.[36] Parmenides is thereby consciously hypostatizing wealth and making it to be the essence of the universe. This sense of *ousia* suggests, exactly as the English word *property*[37] does, the ideal of self-sufficiency that belongs to the aristocratic class, to the gods, and this is then projected onto the universe itself. Much can and should be said about how Parmenides's ontology is based in large part on the experience of money. Seaford does an admirable job constructing convincing arguments along these lines. See his work for much more detail on this.

---

35. Kenny, *New History*, 21.
36. See LSJ.
37. From Latin, *propreitas*: "one's own."

Protagoras

Protagoras (ca. 490–ca. 420 BC) is the author of the famous dictum, "Man is the measure of all things." This translation and its standard interpretation is challenged by Seaford. He argues a better translation would be "Of all things the measure (*metron*) is humankind, of the things that are that they are (*hōs estin*) and of the things that are not that they are not."[38] He thinks it curious that most interpreters do not notice the strangeness of the word *metron* in this circumstance. Plato seems to render *metron* as criterion (*kritērion*) or judge (*kritēs*), and this is followed by Aristotle and Sextus Empiricus. But this interpretation is awkward and polemical on Plato's part. Nowhere else, Seaford claims, does *metron* have this meaning. *Metron* has a much narrower meaning of quantitative measurement in terms of limits. Do the limits of things, of categories, belong to the human mind or to beings themselves? This is the ultimate question of metaphysics, and Protagoras comes down firmly on the human mind as the one that sets categorical limits and thus delimits the measure of all things. To make a long and complicated argument somewhat shorter and less complicated, Protagoras seems to be stating that *humanity* (not the individual, though the individual is implied in the whole) is the author of all ontological distinctions. But the language he uses to make this point has a distinct financial ring to it. The word translated "things" in Protagoras's statement is *chrēmata* for which the normal and most common translation is "goods" or "money." If Protagoras meant "all things" as we normally understand it, he would have said (*ta*) *panta*, instead he said *panta chrēmata*. So Seaford suggests,

> Protagoras' emphasis, I have noted, is on *humankind* (*anthrōpos*). It is the *combination*, in the monetary *metron*, of universality with manifest subjectivity that produces the idea that the universe of delimited, quantified things depends on delimiting quantification by humankind. This is not to say that Protagoras' statement is about monetary value: *metron* refers rather to any kind of quantifying delimitation. My suggestion is rather that it was merely the human projection (despite its fundamentality) of universal monetary measure that was, consciously or unconsciously, an important factor in the emergence of Protagoras' universal subjectivism.[39]

This combination refers back to the dual nature of coinage that Seaford called fiduciarity. There is clear subjectivity in money. Its value is relative to

---

38. Seaford, *Money and the Early Greek Mind*, 285.
39. Ibid., 290. Italics original.

people depending on their character and desires. But its value is also universal, hence the emphasis on humankind instead of the individual. For even though the individual will value money in an individual way, nevertheless the whole ontological category of value is something human. Protagoras's position is not just the kind of relativism evident in the lazy caricature of postmodernism: "it's true for you if it works for you, but it's not true for me." There is still a realist perspective of truth here that is being accessed. Protagoras is claiming something even more radical, "what you value is relative to you individually, but value is itself a projection of humankind." Aristotle will have a similar notion in relation to money, as we shall see.

Parmenides projected the abstract One from the reality of money. Protagoras deprojects this abstraction, returning money, and all of ontology, to human rational calculation. Each of these philosophers seem hard pressed to speak about ontology without recourse to monetary language. Seaford is right to note that this is not a claim to make money as the sole cause or language of metaphysical speculation, but it seems to be playing a very important part.

Plato

Plato (ca. 428–347 BC) thought that there were five things that could be said about a concept: (1) the name, (2) the definition, (3) the image, (4) knowledge of the thing, (5) the reality of the thing in itself.[40] Because Plato saw that a perfect circle could never be produced in reality, it followed that, if there was such a thing as a perfect circle it must exist, but not within reality, or even within the mind only; there had to be some further reality in which a perfect circle exists. His fifth distinction is the basis for his theory of the Forms in which he posited the reality of a form of all things with which each individual thing participates to some degree. Plato sees that a name is symbolic for something beyond, and so he attempts to find the beyond by going through the symbol to the reality. Reality, then is understood as something immaterial. This metaphysic is somewhat similar to that of Parmenides, and like Parmenides, Plato was himself an aristocrat, which suggests that his concentration on what lies beyond the symbol, in what is self-sufficient and divine, had something to do with his social perspective.

Plato's vision of the soul demonstrates this rather well. In the *Republic*, Plato's utopian political treatise, he says that the guardians would have no need of human money, which corrupts. Instead they are to have divine gold

---

40. Plato, *Seventh Letter to the Syracusans*, 342.

and silver in their souls.[41] This means that money is Plato's "model of invisible value."[42] Money and property corrupts, so the guardians are to live in a communal way, having only the basic necessities as private property. The incorruptible divine gold and silver of their souls will then be their benevolence that they can impart, like gods to mortals, to the less intelligent of the city. The divine gold is wisdom and direction rather than endless self-indulgent acquisitiveness. There is pollution in the material world because the individual is always between being some quality and not fully instantiating that quality. The material world is Heraclitean, and the world of the Forms is Parmenidean, with the latter being far more preferable and godlike.

This means that Plato did not devalue money in and of itself, but found that it had great value, so long as it was withdrawn from circulation. If money is withdrawn from the pollution of circulation it is the store of immense value because it "renders homogenous and commensurable the being (*ousia*) of things of whatever kind."[43] Withdrawn money is valuable because it tends toward the universal, the divine. So "In Plato, no less than in Parmenides, sublimated money is homogenous, permanent, self-sufficient, and invisible."[44] It has a deep and abiding value insofar as it resembles Being or God.

Aristotle

Aristotle (384–322 BC) follows Protagoras in the notion that humans measure or provide the definition to all things. That is, categorization is a human task, which leads him in his *Politics* to express this striking conception of the natural world and its economic relationship to people:

> So that clearly we must suppose that nature also provides for them [viviparous animals] in a similar way when grown up, and that plants exist for the sake of animals and the other animals for the good of man, the domestic species both for his service and for his food, and if not all at all events most of the wild ones for the sake of his food and of his supplies of other kinds, in order that they may furnish him both with clothing and with other kinds of appliances. If therefore nature makes nothing without purpose or in vain, it follows that nature has made all the animals for the sake of men. Hence even the art of war will

---

41. *Republic* 416e.
42. Seaford, *Money and the Early Greek Mind*, 259.
43. Plato, *Laws* 918a.
44. Seaford, *Money and the Early Greek Mind*, 259.

by nature be in a manner an art of acquisition (for the art of hunting is a part of it) that is properly employed both against wild animals and against such of mankind as though designed by nature for subjection to submit to it, inasmuch as this warfare is by nature just.[45]

Note the argument, "If therefore nature makes nothing without purpose or in vain, it follows that nature has made all the animals for the sake of men." By this reasoning humans create purpose for other animals and, by hierarchy, the rest of nature. So Aristotle views nature as an entity who delegates categorization to humans, even for wild animals. These must be tamed, just like a forest or a mountain must be tamed by their management through forestry and mining. Resources are given by nature, indeed, made for human beings by nature herself. It is, therefore, just to even war against the wild aspects of nature to bring them in as resources either for human livelihood or limitless capital accumulation. Aristotle realizes that the power of categorization is the power of creating purpose or meaning, and this meaning is entirely economic. Aristotle makes the exploitation of resources a natural law.

A further outcome of following Protagoras is a surprisingly modern view of coinage. Aristotle understood money as a having only conventional value, the value given to it by people. By the time of Aristotle money had permeated society to a high degree, to the point that he created a genealogy of the origin of money that bears many similarities to that of Adam Smith.[46] He also thought that money is an abstract means of quantifying demand. Aristotle argues for this etymologically: *nomisma* (money) derives from *nomos* (law), and it is thus in human power to change its value or render it useless, just as people can with laws.

His discussion of money is only part of his larger argument about the nature of justice and injustice. This is what is truly remarkable about Aristotle's account, for it reveals the depth to which money has penetrated his world. Money is, for him, one example of how proportionality is at the heart of justice and injustice. Since Aristotle argues for the golden mean, injustice is a disproportionality in exchange, a lack of reciprocity. Although Aristotle is generally a defender of natural law he does recognize that exchange value is based on local demand and supply conditions so that it is not unjust if the price of wine is lower at wholesale than it is at retail. But Aristotle brings this back to metaphysics. His ethic of reciprocity in exchange is based on the universal notion of proportionality in justice. Though the particulars are

---

45. *Politics* 1256b.
46. *Nicomachean Ethics* 1133a.

multiple and various, justice is one. This notion of proportionality is based in natural law, in the cosmos, even though value itself is conventional. Aristotle's notion of justice in proportionality is mathematical. This is a novel concept, for he does not describe justice on the basis of a narrative or myth or relationship, but on mathematical proportions in nature, thus pointing to the universal beyond the physical world. Money has conventional value, but it is one, whole, universal. It is a perfect portrait of his metaphysics.

Aristotle's ethics are unashamedly aristocratic, further showing how his philosophy is built in a cosmos constructed by money. Having a suitable amount of external goods is a prerequisite to *eudaimonia*, or happiness. The good must be something final and self-sufficient.[47] It is a godlike situation. So it becomes clear that the maimed, the poor, the slave, those who lack external goods, cannot truly be happy. For although one can be virtuous, virtue is not equivalent to happiness, though it is also a prerequisite. This vision of happiness is based in a thoroughly aristocratic perspective, and as such, the impact of external goods, especially of wealth, is of vital importance. Instead of a religious or monarchical perspective of happiness focused on duty and allegiance that one might expect in premonetary societies, Aristotle gives us one aspect of an ethic influenced by the rise of coinage.

Nevertheless, Aristotle is against the pursuit of wealth for its own sake, which is the purview of the merchant. This kind of wealth-getting, as he calls it, is a violation of natural law.[48] True wealth-getting is for the self-sufficiency of the household. This perspective again reveals the aristocrat's notion of value in the removal of wealth from circulation, as opposed to the merchant's notion of value through circulation. And so we see that money has come to play a very important role, not only in metaphysics, but also in ethics, and that the monetary society of classical Greece was able to give us two main perspectives that we could divide between the aristocrats and the merchants. On the one hand there is Plato, Aristotle, Heraclitus, Parmenides, and the Miletians. On the other hand are the merchants like Pythagoras, Epicurus, and the Atomists. Though these all had their unique metaphysical and ethical perspectives they nonetheless worked on the same metaphysical stage that divided the world of seeming from the true reality that lay beyond what is immediately perceived, so identifying the common ground and perspective they all shared, a perspective that has significant affinity to the fiduciarity of money.

Though there are many other figures in pre-Socratic philosophy that we could discuss, like Anaxagoras and the Atomists, the major points have

---

47. Ibid., I.7.
48. Aristotle, *Politics* 1257b.

been covered. That a coin has value beyond its constituent material, *fiduciarity*, is an essential way that money can be seen as a major foundation of metaphysical speculation. Metaphysics requires a distinction between seeming and truth. It rests on a division between what is experienced and what can be conceived. When a coin is stamped with a seal of the state, it is receiving value from its future acceptability. Although money does change in value by inflation or deflation, it is, amongst all commodities, extraordinarily stable. Its homogeneity leads to stability and the fact that other commodities are valued by money also gives it stability by its universal exchangeability. Something real and material whose meaning, purpose, and value are not determined by its constituent elements demands metaphysical speculation because it requires one to posit something that exists beyond that material that gives it that meaning, something not required for any other object. Though the ancient Greek philosophers disagreed on much, they all operated on the same and new metaphysical stage. They all saw a single kind of explanation for the structure of the cosmos—a reality perceivable to reason that looks through or beyond the senses. Thus many came to a monist view, whether materialist or not. Whatever their perspective, they nevertheless produced a fundamental dichotomy between visible multiplicity and invisible unity, an essential characteristic of money. The pre-Socratics thus all agreed on the fundamental premise that there was a division between the many and the one, that true knowledge consists in being able to see beyond common perception and common sense, to go beyond physics to metaphysics.

Platonic and Aristotelean philosophy attempted to give a more nuanced perspective than the extant work of their predecessors, explaining that some things were at rest and others were in motion. But Plato, as much as any of the earlier philosophers, was interested in metaphysics and the division between the many and the one, or for him, the real and the ideal. For Plato, the ideal was more real than reality, as his famous parable of the cave wonderfully describes. This parable of the cave is very telling, because of the way in which Plato tells it. Living by means of what everyone can normally perceive is slavery. It is a lamentable state. It demands liberation by means of education or enlightenment. Being enslaved in the cave of normal perception is a lower form of existence. It is problematic. This parable tells a very monetary gospel, which is described below.

Literature

Classical philosophy was not the only place in which money created new metaphysical speculation. In wider literary forms we can see the influence of money as well. Metaphysics functioned as a new method of cosmology. Instead of narrating a story or myth in which gods warred and reproduced with each other, they were attempting to explain change and stasis, energy, movement, and unity all in a new form of literature and study. Whereas ancient Near Eastern and Homeric literature is often very repetitious and full of lists, these new philosophers began to write in dialectic, in dialogue, and in dichotomies. Instead of a mythical cosmology that was sloppy, with many different variations of similar themes and different aspects or identities for different gods in different places, philosophical cosmology provided a more coherent and careful analysis that could be debated with others. The form of discussion changed from story telling to dialogue, dichotomies, paradoxes, and systematic inquiry.

Homeric and ancient Near Eastern literature is characterized as paratactic; it was full of lists stuck together without an organizing principle. There was the plot, but the lists one finds in the *Iliad* or the genealogies of the Pentateuch are rarely essential to the plot and could be eliminated without much loss of meaning to modern minds. Why did they expend such precious writing material on these, then? This literature probably demonstrates the way in which people thought. Their worlds may have had a cosmogony, but there were no *logos* to govern the world and link the cosmogony to all aspects of life. There was no unifying principle and no distinction between seeming and reality. Philosophic and tragic literature from classical Greece present a new vision.

Tragedy itself is the fruit of a universe in which there lies an essential problem, often from which there is no escape. If humans are composite and inherently sinful, as the Orphic texts suggest, there is naught but fate, and human lives are the fulfillment of oracles. Tragedy is radically different from epic heroes and its style fits those differences. Instead of a single bard reciting an epic, there are actors and a chorus. The one bard telling a story fits the heroic world. He is one man retelling heroic deeds that have been passed on to him. He is, in many ways, a debtor to previous generations and, though he controls the narrative, he is faithful in its preservation. The tragic theatre, on the other hand, is no longer narrating a story but performing it. People take on roles, living out the conflict. But the tragedy is an example of a guiding principle, whether of fate or hubris. The play now has an author who reinterprets traditional stories into forms that fit a new environment. In many ways the same allegorical interpretation that happened in the mystery cults happened in the theatre, which is unsurprising if the theatre's origin is in the mysteries. Indeed, Seaford argues that tragedy grew out of the animal sacrifices in Dionysian mysteries.[49] A play was no longer a way to honor ancestors, it was a way of using tradition to explain a guiding principle of the universe or a timeless truth about the human condition. Tragedy was an important way of expressing the difference between seeming and truth. The truth was expressed through the symbolic actions of the actors.

The chorus is yet another aspect of this new world in that it incited the audience to participate in the dialogue. Instead of only hearers or observers of an epic recitation, they relived the story and its emotions, instantiating the principle of the story in themselves and, in a way, mystically participating in the universal truth beyond the mere appearance. The communal participation of animal sacrifice is reproduced in the theatre, with a similarly cleansing catharsis.

Philosophy was also a new kind of literature. Heraclitus is perhaps the most radical with his aphorisms and oxymora. His belief in an essential unity expressed in movement and change is best expressed in antithetical expressions. Only the initiated and intelligent will go through the contradictions to perceive the *logos* that unites all diversity in a measured way. Plato's dialogues accomplish something very similar in the Socratic method. Through the process of dialogue one is able to ascertain truth and unifying principles of the world. Like the theatre, the Socratic method enables novices to be initiated and not just observe or hear a story, but participate in such a way that new knowledge is gained. What was before undifferentiated can now be categorized. One has participated in the world of the Forms and has become more enlightened through dialogue.

The Gospel of Metaphysics and Monetary Society

Now that we have summarized classical Greek literature and related how the metaphysics of its philosophers was related to the new reality of money, let us attempt to tell a single narrative that holds these thinkers together, a gospel replete with an essential problem and a solution available to those who will take it. We of course risk massive oversimplification of the variety of thoughts of the Greek metaphysicians if we try to say one thing about all of them together. But, if Seaford is right, and his evidence is very compelling, then we ought to see the characteristics of money at the heart of all of these metaphysicians, though each emphasizing different points.

---

49. Seaford, *Money and the Early Greek Mind*, 308.

Let's begin at the beginning where Hesiod speaks of the Five Ages (Gold, Silver, Bronze, Heroic, Iron). Note that it is quite important that he classifies human devolution by an association with metals. Gold, long before it was valued as currency, was believed to be divine and representative of divinity for its immortality or resistance to oxidization.[50] So in the Golden Age, people lived with the gods and lived for quite a long time, never really growing old. Each subsequent age sees a reduced humanity (except the Heroic, as he had to account for all the great preexisting myths). Now, Hesiod, one against whom the philosophers strove, nevertheless sets out a narrative framework for successors to follow, whether consciously or not. There is first a Golden Age from which people have fallen. There was once an ideal situation and now there is not. This fundamental problem is inherent in the various narratives I will trace in each of the three ages we discuss in this chapter. Of course Hesiod is not the first to narrate a "fall," but the kind of story he tells informs the Greek philosophers, even if only in their attempts to oppose figures like Hesiod.

The problem for the philosophers is not that people are impious, but that they are composite. We saw the allegorical interpretation of the Orphic cult to take Titanic impiety and transform it into the metaphysical problem of the soul's imprisonment in the body. By the creation of universals and the notion of the symbol it becomes possible to imagine a world beyond appearance that is not peopled with superhumans but with universals themselves, hence Plato's world of the Forms. What people took away from Greek philosophy was this composite nature of humanity and the necessary result that, because we all participate in the universal "human" we are all imperfect instantiations of it. Instantiated humans are, by definition, imperfect. The body becomes the prison of the soul in Orphic religion and is popularized by later Neoplatonism. It is taken up by many Christians and later philosophers, notably Descartes. The dualist conception of humanity, though not taught by each of the Greek philosophers, nevertheless was the view that most appealed to later generations, even with the reintroduction of Aristotle in the days of Albertus Magnus and Thomas Aquinas. This dualism, for Plato and the Neoplatonists, was able to be overcome by going through the symbolic to the real behind the symbol. Thus, the Neoplatonists become rather mystical and participation in the Ideal became possible by thought. What was the essential problem with humanity for all of these? The ignorance of one's composite and contradictory nature.

Greek thinking reveals an intrinsic dichotomy of seeming and reality, though it was narrated in many different terms. This dichotomy gave rise

---

50. Ibid., 31.

to the core problem of humans: ignorance. The unenlightened person lives a lower form of life because metaphysical philosophy had radical ethical implications. Certainly many of the Greek philosophers were aristocratic and had an appropriately aristocratic view of commoners, namely Plato,[51] Aristotle,[52] Heraclitus, and Parmenides.[53] When it comes to considering what it means to be human, and thereafter what should be done about it (ethics), we begin to see a cosmology form, though not often told in story form, of an idea consonant with a traditional idea of original sin. Humans are an admixture of the real and the ideal.

This problem of the ancient Greek mind I am calling a "gap." In every story there is a conflict, and so in every metaphysic or cosmology there must be a gap between the real and the ideal, between what seems to be the case and what really is the case. Indeed, the existence of any philosophy, besides one that parrots commonsensical ideas, assumes that there must be a gap between the ignorant and the learned, otherwise no one would practice it, for it would have no benefit. But for many of the Greeks this gap of ignorance takes on a metaphysical tint so that the gap also becomes a problem with human nature. Humans are composite, seemingly immortal and yet sufferingly mortal.

Now, the solution to the gap of mortality and immortality, between seeming and reality, between ignorance and enlightenment is knowledge of symbol. People who are ignorant of the way a symbol operates, by using something to point to another, are lost and need saving, like those in Plato's cave. Those who think that they are able to equate a subject and an object without reference to a third thing are ignorant. Those are actually projected shadows on a cave wall. Outside is the true reality of the forms and, by enlightenment, one can exit the cave.

Humans are composite of something particular and universal, like money, and this is the problem. Money and symbol introduce a strict division in the person that places them in a metaphysical dichotomy. Achieving enlightenment takes one through the symbol to its referent, so abandoning the body to liberate the soul. To escape the prison of the body is the final end for many philosophers, nearly all of whom taught that death was not to be feared as an evil, but a necessary path for the soul to take. One must go through the reality of the coin (the body) to its referent in order to have true wealth (the One).

---

51. Evidenced not only in his parable of the cave, but also in his notion of philosopher kings in the *Republic*.

52. See his notion of *megalopsuchia* or magnanimity in *Nicomachean Ethics* IV.3.

53. Parmenides speaks of "ignorant mortals" and "undiscriminating hordes" in frag. 6.

We have seen how certain thinkers were aristocratic, and others were more of the people, and we saw how their theories tended to support their class. The aristocratic thinkers sought to achieve godlikeness through self-sufficiency or aseity by either acquiring real gold (Aristotle) or spiritual gold (Plato). Parmenides exemplifies this aseity with his notion of Being or the One: what is one and indivisible, immortal, and eternal must not depend on anything else. In order to solve the problem inherent in being human, they needed to transcend the limitations of humanity. By pursuing thought, personal discipline, or virtue, these thinkers attained communion with the One by contemplation. This kind of practice would gain popularity in asceticism, continuing through Neoplatonism and into Christianity, and continues to this day, though more derived from Far Eastern practices.

Now those who were of and for the people tended to be more materialist in perspective and democratic in sentiment. They were less interested in the aristocratic, self-sufficient estate management initially called economics (*oikos* + *nomos* is Greek for house-law, that is, the practice of household management). Instead they had vested interests in trade and profit making business endeavors. These philosophers prioritized volatility over stability. So the solution for these thinkers was in the opposite movement, a denial of any ideal and the pursuit of moderate pleasures, since there is nothing beyond the moment. Epicurus represents this perspective well, following on the atomists like Democritus.

The narrative has moved from golden age to a transgression or gap, and from there to a solution, or a "bridge" that involves at least some level of enlightenment. For many philosophers this bridge is the escape of the soul from the body, or the perception of reality through the symbol, eventually leaving the symbol behind. Metaphysical transcendence is the solution.

But here we first see the problem we will see again in premonetary society and modern postmonetary society, that the gap and the bridge are actually one and the same. For the monetary Greeks it seems that fiduciarity enables people to perceive and begin to understand the notion of the symbol. This leads them to describe their experience of the world and explain the hidden structure of reality in symbolic language, quite often using money itself as that symbol that describes reality. But if symbol introduces the problem of a metaphysical dichotomy that eventually is applied to the human body and soul, it is symbol that also paves the way to salvation, whether through philosophy or Orphic mystery religion.

The problem is symbolic and the solution is symbolic. In a way, then, we can describe the problem and solution as an economic relationship. As Greeks mediate their relationships with others through money, money begins to be a major part in how they symbolically construct their world. If the problem is economic, the solution is inevitably economic. The divine self-sufficiency observed by the aristocratic-minded philosophers is largely equivalent to the idea of the soul transcending the particularities of common life to commune with the ideal. But the notion of economic self-sufficiency is self-deceptive because economic value depends on corporate valuation. So it is with ideas of the soul transcending the body to commune with the divine or the ideal. The dichotomy begins in the human mind, introduced in large part by interaction with money. This dichotomy is then projected onto the cosmos, making the cosmos in the image of money. This projection is unconscious and so unrecognized. Then philosophers begin to study the world (already constructed in the image of money) and they find that it is dichotomous. What is happening is little more than partial self-discovery, but this comes at the steep cost of forming the world in the image of money, which will have an incalculable number of consequences for future life, the first of which is that human relationships become mediated through money, which is now, thanks to the philosophical systems, justified metaphysically. And so money transforms premonetary societies from a more tribal and family orientation to the *polis* and national society. The institution really comes to life by means of money and taxation, and this in turn changes notions of self-identity and identity of others or foreigners. So it is that the monetary world narrates its problems and solutions, its narrative of meaning, in metaphysical terms, terms that are projections of the nature of money onto the cosmos. But money has not always existed and has not continued in its dominance since its introduction. Many societies in the ancient world, in medieval Europe, and until relatively recently, did not construct their societies and their *cosmoi* based in money, but through personal debt and credit relationships, which we investigate next.

PREMONETARY THOUGHT: DEBT AND CREDIT RELATIONSHIPS

The first thing that must be said about premonetary society is that most modern economists have an incorrect perspective of it, derived from Aristotle and later Adam Smith. Philosophers of money tend to construct the history of money in terms that could only come presupposing the existence of money. For example, most modern economists speak first of capital and from there narrate a story as to how money came into existence to aid in the production of capital. But ancient societies were not barter based. No anthropological evidence for a primarily barter-based society has ever been found, and anthropologists have long been critical of the Neoclassical economic myth of barter evolving into monetary exchange marketplaces. Rather, premonetary societies were based on debt and credit relationships where each person was indebted to one another in a wide variety of ways, but none of which were monetary.[54]

Marcel Mauss wrote his famous short book on *The Gift* in which he describes "gift-exchange societies."[55] His work sparked the interest of anthropologists to study social relations in such societies. The idea of the gift does not do sufficient justice to these older societies, but it is a start. Instead of imagining that there are people with a surplus of a good that they produce going to a marketplace to attempt to barter their goods in trade for necessities and luxuries, these societies worked on the basis of debt and credit, like gift giving. If you or a neighbor lacked for anything, the need would be made known and your tribe would provide for you.

The myth of barter, as Graeber calls it, is built upon the "double coincidence of wants." One economics textbook describes it this way:

> A barter system requires a double coincidence of wants for a trade to take place. That is, to effect a trade, I need not only have to find someone who has what I want, but that person must also want what I have.[56]

It is simply not true that a double coincidence of wants is required for a transaction. This is an anachronism from the monetary age where transactions must largely be completed immediately by strangers or basic acquaintances. In premonetary societies, however, transactions could take place over a long period of time by using the concept of debt.

Money did not come about by the inconvenience of trade by barter, but by the complex social, religious, and philosophical factors we discussed above. Societies prior to ancient Greece, China, and India, and those existing throughout the world until recent times, had a rather different social arrangement and thus had a very different economic relationship upon which their societies were built. And this is an important point, for we cannot turn to ancient tribal societies as though they are noble savages, living in a time before the "fall" of the introduction of money. That is not the narrative we are telling here. Instead, interpersonal relationships were mediated just as much by economic considerations, though this was not monetary. So let us turn to describing relationships based on debt.

---

54. Graeber, *Debt*, 21–41.
55. Mauss, *The Gift*.
56. Case, *Principles of Economics*, 564, in Graeber, *Debt*, 22–23.

Debt

Everyone is familiar with notions of debt, but our modern systems of corporate debt, student debt, mortgages, and national debt are not the best starting place to understand ancient debt, or notions of debt we might find in the Bible. Graeber defines debt in this way:

> Debt is a very specific thing, and it arises from very specific situations. It first requires a relationship between two people who do not consider each other fundamentally different sorts of being, who are at least potential equals, who *are* equals in those ways that are really important, and who are not currently in a state of equality—but for whom there is some way to set matters straight.[57]

This definition highlights the importance of relationships in debt, though it is open to question. What does he mean by "equal"? In a society in which there is no universal means of valuation, like money, this is not a quantitative equivalence. This equivalence has the sense of equilibrium, harmony, or peace. For debt cannot be confined to just a notion of material things or money, it also applies to morality. In fact, as Nietzsche pointed out, and is true in many languages, terms for moral guilt and obligation derive from terms for debt. German *Schuld* (guilt) is similar to *Schulden* (debts). English has similar etymologies related to *should* and *ought*, both of which have origins in material debt: Old English *sceal/sculan* (should) meant "to owe" and Old English *āhte/āgan* (ought) also meant "to owe." In the end, how ever one conceives of this equality, the presence of a debt requires a notion of inequality and thus the right of treatment in accordance with a difference in valuation of the person. That is, debt necessitates hierarchy. This is a very important point that will again appear in modern times.

Debt, then, is actually somewhat difficult to pin down. What is it that is owed? In a premonetary society there is no recourse to a single universally commensurable currency by which debts can be calculated and canceled. This means that the debt either needs to be repaid and valued in kind, namely, a pig for a pig, or it must be transferred to something else due to the impossibility of repayment. Few people would repay a debt in kind, for otherwise there would be little exchange happening. A pig farmer would not want a pig in repayment. Before money the debt would thus be repaid out of kind. But because many objects were not really commensurable, or of equivalent value, debts would have to accumulate a moral, that is, a social aspect to them. In this way hierarchy could be solidified. Achilles in Homer's

---

57. Graeber, *Debt*, 120. Italics original.

Iliad would not accept any wealth in trade of honor, even though he is dishonored by an unfair distribution of booty. Honor was incommensurable, and Agamemnon was in debt to Achilles for honor. This debt would turn into the wrath of Achilles, a social and moral stance against Agamemnon.

Long-standing debt could lead to the establishment of rights and honors due to a creditor, and the debt of honor or loyalty would not be repayable in any way that would conceivably make a peasant into a king. Nothing could make the king and peasant commensurable, because the peasant had no honor to confer on the king. In this way, long-standing economic debt can be transformed into a moral debt and into stratified social relations. This does not mean that economic considerations are the *only* source of social stratification, but they do play a part. Let us look at some of the characteristics of relationships defined by debt.

Debt Strengthens Relations

The first consequence of debt is that it strengthens relational ties, even though these ties are based on hierarchy. Debt relationships are built on trust. Without trust one will not allow someone to leave with a product and no payment. One has to know that the debtor is "good for it." If this relationship isn't present, debt becomes impossible and trade begins to take on a violent and sometimes sexual quality. It is in this way that barter has been observed in premonetary societies, namely, between strangers and potential enemies. This is because a group of people are always aware that the other may try to get something more valuable for less. For some groups, like the Nambikwara of Brazil, there is a real possibility of violence when one group trades with another. The women and children are hidden until the terms of the deal are sealed and peaceful dealings are ensured. And for the Gunwinggu of Australia there is a sexual exchange between the trading groups, along with music, dancing, and symbolic violence. For these people there is no distinction between economic life and other behavior.[58] Indeed, Adam Smith's terms, "truck and barter," were quite pejorative terms all across Europe a few centuries before Smith. They generally meant "trick," "lie," "deceive."[59] So barter occurred, but it was not the normal exchange relationship that people would have. It occurred amongst enemies, or at least people with whom there were no lasting ties and no great desire to establish lasting ties. For normal and closer relations, exchange occurred through debt and credit arrangements without recourse to money in the sense defined above.

58. Ibid., 29–33.
59. Servet, "Troc primitif," 20.

Debt and credit relations strengthen social bonds rather than weakening them. Though the kind of relationship is not necessarily the most positive one can imagine, being in debt to someone usually results in that person taking an interest in your life and wellbeing, and you in theirs. Graeber describes this mutual indebtedness in this way:

> If we insist on defining all human interactions as matters of people giving one thing for another, then any ongoing human relations can only take the form of debts. Without them no one would owe anything to anybody. A world without debt would revert to primordial chaos, a war of all against all; no one would feel the slightest responsibility for one another; the simple fact of being human would have no significance; we would all become isolated planets who couldn't even be counted on to maintain our proper orbits.[60]

Graeber, of course, desires that all human interactions not be based on exchange. But so long as people imagine they are, debt will be necessary to solidify human relations and structure society.

To owe no one anything is a statement of having no responsibility, and such a person is a danger to society. Debt alone does not hold society together, but its role can hardly be overestimated. And this is where René Girard's theory of the scapegoat shows its limit.[61] The violence that begets a society in a sacrifice is quickly turned into an economic transaction. Indeed, the whole notion of a scapegoat requires a notion of communicable debt so that one may die for many. This death is a down payment, one might say, of the future sacrifices that would continue to reaffirm the group's bond. Most sacrificial rites had no small element of wealth redistribution, which shows the economic concepts lying at the heart of religious expression. Christian theology became heavily influenced by both a notion of a scapegoat as well as the payment of infinite debt by one, with the continued redistributive element of the sacrament of Communion. This sacrament is discussed in more detail in chapter 6.

Debt Creates Hierarchy

Once two equals enter into a debtor-creditor relationship they are no longer equals. In a monetary society loans have set collateral; in a premonetary society the debt may not be strictly contractual and the collateral may be

---

60. Graeber, *Debt*, 126.
61. Girard, *Scapegoat*.

somewhat nebulous. When a person puts themselves up for collateral, as often happened, indentured servitude resulted. The hierarchy that is created can transcend the boundaries of economic life, and frequently does. Now, as hierarchy develops over time by the nonpayment of debts on a generational scale, people become unequal in identity and can no longer enter into relationships of reciprocity. A noble, king, lord, chief, cannot receive a gift from a peasant, it must be tribute. Whereas gifts are designed to create a debt that will then be repaid and thus build a relationship with that person, gifts to a king cannot be reciprocated without undermining the hierarchy of kingship. It is (or was) a custom in middle-class America to give a new neighbor a non-disposable dish full of baked goods. That neighbor would have to return the dish, and it was expected that the dish be full of baked goods again. This little act of gift giving and debt creation created a relationship of mutuality. If the plate returned empty it was a sign of minor offense. But this cannot happen with a king (or celebrity). Instead the king would receive gifts and redistribute them through largesse. Giving a gift to a king does not get you "one up" on the king, instead it becomes tribute, a symbol of submission like an offering to a god. And often it becomes part of established custom so that a one-time gift could be demanded on a yearly basis.[62] The establishment of customary tribute further reinforces social stratification. Taken to a larger level, Graeber argues, this can lead to a caste structure forming. And the formation of this caste leads to the creation of essential identities:

> This last point can't be overemphasized because it brings home another truth regularly overlooked: that the logic of identity is, always and everywhere, entangled in the logic of hierarchy. It is only when certain people are placed above others, or where everyone is being ranked in relation to the king, or the high priest, or Founding Fathers, that one begins to speak of people bound by their essential nature: about fundamentally different kinds of human beings.[63]

Long-standing debt relations are transformed into identity relations and economic hierarchy becomes social and moral hierarchy with fundamentally different kinds of behavior assigned to each group. A structured hierarchy eliminates competition by subordinating one to another. This subordination is based on a paternalistic idea that strengthens relations by familiarizing people rather than depersonalizing them as money does. So, without recourse to money or violence, a hierarchy requires generations to

---

62. Graeber, *Debt*, 110.
63. Ibid., 111.

change because it involves core identities. With money and violence, however, hierarchy can be transcended by reference to a universally desired object, and political power is able to be acquired by money. Seaford shows that in ancient Greece there was an awareness that money and tyranny continually go together, and that democracy could be regained by money as well.[64]

Debt is Historical

Debt, by its very nature, requires time. Whereas cash transactions begin and end in a very short period of time, such that the temporal aspect is negated, debt relations are spread over time. For people this is essential to produce what is necessary for the repayment of the debt, but it also transforms the identity of the debtor for the season in which they are in debt. For objects that circulate in a premonetary society, the greater the circulation, the greater the value. An heirloom has value because it has exchanged hands between storied people. An heirloom becomes something greater than the possessor who knows that his possession is only temporary and that he serves the object at least as much as the object serves him.

Whereas money acquires value by being homogenous, objects and people in a premonetary society are storied and therefore unique. Genealogy is of the utmost importance for establishing one's personal identity. Respect for one's ancestors is a moral necessity because to destroy one's connection to one's past is to destroy one's own value. It is not accidental that the parts of ancient literature so dull to modern readers are the endless lists of ancestry. The book of Genesis, for example, has many such genealogies that are of vital importance for the flow of the narrative by bridging long spans of time though not vital to the plot. But they are more than just a literary technique, they establish the identity of characters. Cain's descendants have the character that Cain did, and Seth's descendants are contrasted to this.

People have history and names have meaning because particular relations to certain people confer material benefits or lead to shame, ostracism, and material disadvantages. Consider the ancient Near Eastern practice of a personal name combined with a patronymic, for example, Joshua son of Nun. The connection of a person with his or her parentage summarized the most important details of what one needed to know about that person.

Those who become aristocrats are those who have the most illustrious family history. This usually had to do with wealth. Those who could maintain large herds, a large household, and many servants or slaves would

---

64. Seaford, "Tragic Tyranny." See also Herodotus 5.63, 66, Thucydides 6.53, and Isocrates, *Antidosis* 232.

themselves be freed from labor. They were of a different kind of people than the commoner: self-sufficient and with free time to think and engage in the finer aspects of life. As we saw, many of the Greek philosophers came from aristocratic lineage, and this is not accidental. But the aristocracy must continue to favor ancient systems of personal debt, for money wipes out the history of the aristocrat. The aristocracy must be rooted in tradition, culture, and subtlety that personal relationships of trust rest upon. Money destroys these things by its homogeneity and immediacy.

Aristocracies can be formed because debt is not removed with the death of the debtor. Instead generations of people may be indebted. This is part of the importance of the biblical Jubilee,[65] to break a cycle that can lead to a dramatic social imbalance by vesting too much wealth in a few creditors. Because debt carried on from generation to generation the imbalance of private debt became very great. It was a Babylonian and earlier Sumerian tradition for the king to forgive all private debts.[66] The need for this arose because private debts would lead to debt crises that threatened the social order of a kingdom or empire. In years of bad harvests people would mortgage their land or pledge a family member so as to feed the rest of their family. Unable to pay back, they would lose all they had to the wealthy who only got richer. The idea of debt forgiveness is not unique to the biblical Jubilee, it was a somewhat common ancient Near Eastern Bronze Age policy and used in lesser ways by others like Solon, or Julius Caesar.

On the one hand, debt forgiveness liberated all people from historic debts that could drive generations into poverty or indentured servitude. But on the other hand, it was simply a transferal of debt. Now all debtors owed the king a major moral debt for being their liberator and giving them a gift they could never repay. Debt was transformed from private relations to state relations. And instead of it being a material debt able (in theory) to be repaid, the people now had a debt that was incommensurable with anything they could produce or own. They owed a debt of honor or loyalty that fundamentally changed their identity. By the liberation of debt, the system of hierarchy was actually strengthened.

The transferal of debt to the king is one reason why the aristocracy are traditional enemies of the crown. The crown subverts their system of hierarchy by transferring all debt to itself, thus devaluing the aristocracy by the creation of a super-history. We can see this exact phenomenon in the transformation of Russia in the nineteenth and twentieth centuries from

---

65. See chapter 5 for more on Jubilee.

66. Hudson, "Restructuring the Origins of Interest-Bearing Debt and the Logic of Clean Slates."

the liberation of serfs in 1861 to the Soviet Revolution. The liberation of the serfs might be seen as the beginning of the end of the Czarist tradition, for it abandoned systems of personal caste identity that it required to legitimize its power. The Soviets gave the liberated serfs a new history through which they could have a new identity. But ultimately it was not a liberation to radical freedom, but the transferal of identity and fealty from an older aristocratic system to a new and even more centralized state that freely encouraged the use of violence and terrorism to achieve the never realized dictatorship of the proletariat.[67]

Projected Economic Relationship

The structure of debt favors a certain kind of social order and identity. And as such it is not surprising that this structure is projected onto the cosmos. When one tries to make sense of something incomprehensible, one can only access what one already knows, and thus what is known is superimposed, or projected, onto what one does not know. Human relations are thus projected onto the cosmos to make sense of what otherwise feels like chaos. Projections of debt are apparent in various cultures and religions.

Human existence itself was understood to be a form of debt in the Brahmanas (expository commentaries on the Vedas). Human life was owed to death, and only when one sacrifices himself to death is he redeemed. This means that human life is on loan from death and no one would really want to pay it off. Instead, sacrifices are understood to be a kind of interest payment on the loan of life. This notion spread to other areas as well. If sacrifices are done correctly, one could break out of the human condition and achieve eternity—paying one's debts without going through death. This could happen in a number of ways, since one was not only indebted to death, but also to the Sages who created the Vedic learning, to ancestors, and to all humanity. In this way one was under continual moral obligation to many parties, obligation to study, to have children and become an ancestor, and to give hospitality to strangers.[68]

Although Graeber identifies some significant issues with taking this one example too far and making an anthropological principle out of it, as though debt is necessarily projected, it is telling that these very ancient texts

---

67. So Trotsky argued for the continual use and justification of terrorism to achieve the communist ends by reference to the new Soviet identity, Trotsky, *Terrorism and Communism*.

68. See Graeber, *Debt*, 56–68. Graeber here is summarizing the arguments of primordial debt theorists like Michel Aglietta and Andre Orléans.

do cosmically project debt. It is entirely possible and logical that people who emphasize debt end up creating an economic relationship with the cosmos. Whether necessary or not, the phenomenon becomes far more common as time progresses.

There are counterexamples, however, but these examples tend to show that, if debt is not projected, economic relationships are. Whether one begins with the inequality and hierarchy of debt that leads to the formation of a caste system, or the equality of hunting cultures that lead to an identification of human anthropology with sharing,[69] one ends up in the same place: economic relationships as a primary mode of making sense of the cosmos. Graeber does raise the interesting point that notions of sharing in the Eskimo culture require some notion of gift exchange and debt, given the way in which debt is despised. Thus, we come to a classic division in human society: hierarchy or equality. These notions depend upon economic distribution, even though they are not limited to economics. These relationships of hierarchy and equality, with deep connections to economics, end up being projected onto the cosmos itself.

Economic Relationship Transformed into Morality

Once an economic relationship is projected onto the cosmos, it is necessary that it become the language of morality, whether this is through religious or natural law. All manner of human relations begin to be conceived in terms of debts. Sin is debt. Life is debt. Love is debt. Justice is debt. Or, equality and sharing is a moral imperative, which is a reaction to notions of debt.

Some interesting examples of economic debts transferred into moral debts come from Chinese Buddhism and notions of infinite debt. Karmic debt is a notion of cosmic debt, a ledger of sins and good works that may take many lifetimes to balance out. The acquisition of material debts created spiritual debts due to the suffering that would inevitably be created in other beings. In this way medieval Chinese Buddhists identified what has now become quite a popular idea, that acquisition involves exploitation and creates moral or spiritual debt, hence the notion of so-called fairly traded goods. Chinese villagers constantly had debts they could never repay and so such a notion of karmic debt would match their worldly experience quite closely. As one solution, Hindu and Buddhist monasteries created the idea of an Inexhaustible Treasury, which seems to be one of the first examples of an organization operating off of interest payments alone: a perpetual endowment. The monasteries would receive donations and would provide loans.

---

69. As in Freuchen, *Book of the Eskimos*, 154.

The interest on the loan would provide for specific needs of the monastery and the principle would not be touched. In this way the one-time donation would have everlasting good effects, thus canceling out much karmic debt.

Another interesting example of an infinite moral debt arising from an economic relationship is another Buddhist notion of the milk debt.[70] This idea was that one's mother was a pure, selfless saint, exemplified by the act of breastfeeding, which transformed her flesh and blood into milk. This kind of debt could never be repaid in the slightest, because it was incommensurable with anything else. Nevertheless, giving to an Inexhaustible Treasury could help alleviate this debt to one's mother.[71]

Friedrich Nietzsche in *Genealogy of Morals* made one of the first attempts to show how morality was based in economic relations. And though his account is historically very inaccurate, he does sense a deep connection between debt and morality. There is no real evidence for the kind of brutality he describes.[72] Nevertheless, if one imagines that exchange relationships or debtor-creditor relationships are essential to human nature and that we imagine all other things through this lens, it follows that morality will be formed in just such a way. He points to strong etymological evidence to support this. Etymologies do not prove necessary connections but suggest a development of thought that begins with economics and ends up with morality.

Nietzsche would surely have been aware of the existence of *Wergild*, a kind of token repayment to the victim of a murdered kinsman, that was in existence in medieval Europe. Perhaps his fantasy of barbaric mutilations is an extrapolation of this, or of Shakespeare's *Merchant of Venice*. The *Wergild* is yet another example of how economic and moral debts were transformed into one another. *Wergild* set rates of financial repayment for the murder of someone based on their social value. Its existence enabled cycles of vengeance to cease by transforming moral debts into economic ones. A similar concept occurred in ancient Greece, and continues to this day, though with murder it is not usually monetary compensation, but "paying one's debt to society" by prison time.

Graeber's *Debt* is an attempt to show that debt is not the only way to conceive of human morality, and when we transform all of human morality into the language of debt cruelty and violence are the inevitable result. And though I am sympathetic to his attempt, I'm not sure it can be ultimately

---

70. A similar idea existed in Turkey as well: White, *Money Makes Us Relatives*, 75–76 in Graeber, *Debt*, 434 n38.

71. Ibid., 263–64.

72. Nietzsche, *Genealogy of Morals*, 2.8.

successful. Graeber speaks of different human moralities related to hierarchy and equality. One encourages customs and qualities, the other needs and production abilities.[73] But the problem is that, while customs and quality may not in and of themselves be based in debt, they are nonetheless thoroughly economic, as are needs and abilities understood by what he calls "baseline communism." So long as human life is imagined primarily as economic or material, ethics and society will be shaped by economic considerations. Nearly all of life as we know it consists in what we do with and to others and their things. Exchange, sharing, trade, theft, buying, selling—all of these are economic activities—and so it is hardly surprising that so many have imagined the world in economic terms. It is nearly impossible to do otherwise. This means that the economic relationships that are projected onto the cosmos and transformed into morality, while not an anthropological fact, are nonetheless a historic regularity that suggests something about human relations. It is possible to conceive of relations without direct reference to debt, but it does not seem possible to describe morality in non-economic terms.

The key is this: are economic relationships essential to our conception of morality? Do we require notions of material exchange in order to imagine language, justice, and social cohesion? Theologically, must we refer to debt in order to understand any human relationship with God? And if not, is the solution to much of humanity's problem of violence and brutality the greater separation of morality from debt ideas? Modern morality as a concept must be seen as the fruit of economics, being based in rational calculation. Consequentialism, to be sure, is thoroughly economic. Though its moral dilemmas are not often framed in terms of debt, they are clearly solved by an economizing of the outcome in some term of goodness. This notion of goodness, due to its universality and homogeneity, looks suspiciously like the characteristics of money. Deontological ideas follow a more ancient debt-based line of reasoning. Duty requires hierarchy by a prioritization of categories. Humanity, for example, is a higher category than the individual, so the individual has a duty to humanity. While this does not require a reference to economics in itself, we have seen how metaphysical hierarchy is constructed and shaped by money.

Ethics, as a distinct field of philosophical inquiry has its Western roots in Greek philosophy. Ethics are the fruit of applying metaphysics to questions of behavior. Plato's construction of an ideal society in his *Republic* is one example. Aristotle's ethics are unashamedly economic and aristocratic. Nietzsche's ranting against the herd looks very similar to the rants of

---

73. Graeber, *Debt*, 121.

Heraclitus. The herd are those who are distinguished by their lack of intelligence and virtue. Ability or performance must be rewarded to be valued, and value is expressed economically.

The problem with a purely anthropological account like Graeber's is that it cannot escape the material realm due to its methods. So long as questions of behavior are posed as material questions, morality will be inescapably economic.

The Gospel of Premonetary Society

If we were to describe a generic and vastly oversimplified, though useful, narrative of the premonetary society, it would run as follows. In the beginning there was a situation of equality or equilibrium. Everybody had a fair share and no one experienced want. There was once a wholeness, an undivided and peaceful cosmos. But jealousy and envy arose, whether of honor, status, or possessions. There was a fall from this peace so that some became powerful and others weak. Some exploited the weaknesses of others. First there was envy, then there was theft, and finally there became violence. As time wore on the rich became richer and the poor became slaves. The equilibrium was upset and there would be no way to repay the accrued debts of generations as they are transformed from economic debts to moral debts. Debt becomes infinite. Sin is a qualitatively infinite debt because it is incommensurable—no amount of economic wealth can purchase redemption. Death is the only way to finally repay this debt, for some, but for others this debt is perpetual through many lifetimes. But there is hope. New religious ideas develop a fusion of economic and moral debt that enables commensurability. Whether it is through the offering up of one's wealth in sacrifice to the gods, a sacrifice that will then be redistributed to the community, or it is a donation to an Inexhaustible Treasury, these acts can alleviate one's cosmic debt. And there are other ways of obtaining release from these debts. One can be redeemed by another. The merit of a saint may be claimed for oneself. A kinsman may redeem another. A king can forgive all private debts, redirecting them to himself.

The good news of the premonetary society is debt forgiveness or alleviation by reorientation. But this idea of redemption or forgiveness is inherently problematic for it only reinforces the legitimacy of the debt relationship that existed in the first place. The solution presupposes and reinforces the problem, because it is narrated in the same terms as the problem, just as we saw in a monetary culture. A communistic sharing is another solution to the problem of debt that only serves to reinforce the primacy of the economic relationship by placing each person in each other's debt. It is simply a horizontal form of universal indebtedness.

Premonetary societies do not express their ideas of the cosmos in the metaphysical way that the ancient Greek philosophers did. Their primary concern was with interpersonal relations and thus with ideas of morality or sin. The gap that exists between wholeness or equilibrium is a moral gap expressed in terms of debt. The bridge over this gap is not the reconciliation of body and soul, or the liberation of the soul from the body, but the redemption or forgiveness of the debtor and the return of equilibrium, which is the utopian vision of many ancient peoples. The promised land is a land flowing with milk and honey, a land in which there is such an abundance of wealth that ideas of distribution become irrelevant because of the ubiquity of luxurious sustenance. A significant proportion of ancient debts were contracted because of farming hardship and the inability to care for one's family. Thus it makes sense that the final solution to the problem of debt would be a land where debts would never need to be contracted because one would simply eat one's fill without any difficulty.

I will discuss Christianity's appropriation of these various concepts later and how it is that God might speak through these systems without thereby legitimizing them. But here we can see vast carryover into Christian notions of sin and redemption, and the spiritualizing of a promised land in traditional versions of heaven.

MODERN POSTMONETARY SOCIETY: UNIVERSAL HUMANITY

Ancient Greece, as an exemplary and early monetary society, showed us how money transformed society, the mind, and literature into an image of money itself. Its story of redemption was one that could only be told in light of money and money was its driving force. Premonetary societies formed their worlds in terms of debtor-creditor relations. These relations created value through trust and history. Monetary societies, on the other hand, created value by masking history and individual identity in favor of universals. Modern postmonetary society, as we shall see, is a curious synthesis of these two perspectives.

Modernity is a very slippery concept. It can mean almost anything one wants it to, and it is often used to categorize one's opponents as premodern and therefore not worthy discussion partners. At this point as well it is important to address postmodernity. Postmodernity generally states that a modernity characterized by the rule of metanarratives is over, and hence the dominance of a single narrative for a group of people is no longer accepted.[74] I think this concept of modernity and postmodernity is not a very apt appraisal of the contemporary situation because it is simply not the case that metanarratives are rejected—instead, they have become remythologized. That is, metanarratives have become hidden. This is observable by the moral agreement of the much of the Western world on specific issues. One would expect that a lack of a controlling narrative would lead to a situation of moral chaos. Instead what is observable is not moral chaos, but a moral realignment. Egalitarianism of some kind, for example, is nearly universally accepted without question. There are absolute values that determine the shape of a society's morality, and these values generally come from adaptations to the environment in which a group lives.

What follows is not intended to be a full description of modernity, but a characterization of how modern postmonetary economics has helped form and inform contemporary minds. There is no modernity as such, just as there is no ancient world as such. There are different perspectives and much diversity, with some similarity. And though I am drawing on similarities, that should not lead one to think that there are not exceptions, or that this is an exhaustive description.

We begin by looking at the corporation, which is the major entity upon which modern postmonetary economics is built. The corporation is a strange fusion of the personality and historicity of premonetary societies and the impersonal universality of monetary society. We then look at the notion of self-interest and its curious genealogy, again synthesizing premonetary and monetary ideas. Through Adam Smith many of the disparate forces of the emerging modernity coalesce into a coherent account of modern economics. Smith writes at the same time as the political theory of the social contract is being put into practice. This theory builds society on the basis of the economic concept of self-interest. These ideas help us discern the synthetic metaphysical perspective that characterizes modern economics and politics. Finally, we see that the gospel of modern economics is the fruit of this metaphysic: the creation of the fully human being by participation in a global market.

The Corporation

One of the great creations that has shaped modernity is the corporation. Without the corporation the modern world would be impossible. But the

---

74. See, for example Lyotard, *Postmodern Condition*.

corporation can be seen, broadly, as the fusion of the premonetary world built on relationships with the monetary world and its metaphysics.

The prehistory for the corporation has often been attributed to Pope Innocent IV in AD 1250 by his introduction of the concept of *persona ficta* into canon law.[75] And it is not surprising that it has many similarities with other metaphysical speculation that was occurring at the time, namely consideration of angels.[76] An angel is a messenger, one who communicates the divine will to humans. Angels highlight the ontological difference and distance between heaven and earth, but they also emphasize that the two ought to be in communication. Now, communication requires common ground, and communication is furthered as common ground increases. An angel is the means by which the ideal is communicated to the real and thus the real can conform more and more to the ideal, to put it in purely metaphysical terms. Angels have an in-between existence predicated upon that of God and that of humanity simultaneously.

Now, corporations are similar to angels insofar as they have an in-between existence. They are not purely ideal, nor are they real. They are *persona ficta* or "fictive persons." A corporation engages in all manner of activities like a real person from the legal perspective: birth, marriage/merger, divorce/spinoff, property ownership, death. But a corporation also transcends personality in that it is potentially immortal, it functions independently of the will of any one person, and its task is to divest individuals of legal responsibility for the corporation's proceedings. In a sense it is (potentially) eternal, immutable, and above human morality. Yet it is also like an angel in that it performs a messenger function, allowing the ideal to be communicated to the real. The corporation is able to achieve superhuman feats due to its massive infrastructure and resources. The corporation is the major means by which visions and ideas are actualized in our modern world, and so they establish a common ground between an ideal or utopia and the individual consumer and producer.

Corporations are thus dependent on holding a particular metaphysical perspective that merges premonetary debt relations with monetary impersonality. The concept of the corporation exists for the primary purpose of taking on debt while divesting the individual of responsibility for that debt. Instead of creating personal relationships of debt, the corporation creates systematic and impersonal debt. Metaphysically this requires one to assume a realist standpoint that accepts that there is some actual reality to the

---

75. Graeber, *Debt*, 304.

76. An idea suggested by the German Medievalist Ernst Kantorowicz, *The King's Two Bodies*, 282–83.

corporation, that it becomes a thing-in-itself. And yet it does not resemble the metaphysical cosmologies of the pre-Socratic thinkers. Instead of being taken to the final degree of monism, the corporation has a dependent existence. No one, to my knowledge, thinks that all things are made up of corporations or the Corporation.

The corporation involves the metaphysics of money modified by debt relations. In order for a corporation to contract a debt or become a creditor it must have a relationship of some relative metaphysical equality. That is, the corporation cannot be too ontologically different from its customers or stockholders, otherwise it would only produce moral debts. This mediate existence becomes a rule for many other institutions, like the nation-state. Instead of a divinely legitimated kingship whose borders were equivalent with that of a god, the nation-state becomes a depersonalized reification to which one can swear allegiance, and for which one may die. Nation-states exist, after the pattern of the corporation, as fictive persons. This metaphysical perspective is all important. This is what characterizes modern thought, a strange in-between place that actively or *de facto* denies the reality of the personalized gods, and yet does not go so far as a thoroughgoing material monism that would undermine the essential entities of the corporation and nation. Modern economics is, in many ways, the study of this synthesis of premonetary debt and depersonalized money relations.

Self-Interest

One of the primary concepts that created modern economics is now common sense: that people are governed by self-interest. This concept is a product of the Enlightenment and the turn to the self we see so profoundly in Descartes. If one begins with the self and predicates the existence of all else in terms of the being of the self, as in the *cogito ergo sum*,[77] then appetite and desire become world-forming faculties. The good-for-the-self is then good-for-all-else, because our understanding of the being of all else is dependent on the self. Self-interest then becomes a logical necessity of Enlightenment epistemology and views of human ontology. Graeber points out, however, that the origin of self-interest as a term is not based in any rational research of human beings: it is based in theology. St. Augustine, in *The City of God* draws a division between the city of God and the city of man. The city of God is characterized by the love of God. The city of man by self-love.[78] This self-love is the fruit of original sin. Were it not for government and the rule

---

77. Latin: "I think, therefore I am."
78. *City of God*, chapter 28.

of law, there would be nothing but competition and war. Augustine's view of self-love is taken up by Italian historian Francesco Guicciardini, a friend of Machiavelli, in 1510. Guicciardini, attempting to get beyond language of passion, decided upon the Roman legal term *interesse* as a suitable replacement for love. So self-love becomes self-interest. This, as Graeber points out, sounds mathematical and scientific. Instead of humans being ruled by selfish passions, they are instead ruled by a calculated and quantifiable desire. But, as interest payments continue to grow, so does self-interest or self-love.[79]

The foundational idea of modern economics, that individuals are rationally self-interested beings and that a science of economics can be made of this, was never based on historical research, but in a reinterpretation of Augustine's view of sin. This is a theological idea repurposed to explain a feature of human ontology, and this concept will remain, being taken up by economists time and again as modernity arises. Self-interest then is a secularized theological anthropology, a distortion of an idea rooted in biblical narrative.

Adam Smith

Economically speaking, modernity is usually said to begin with Adam Smith's *Wealth of Nations* in 1776. In Smith we see modern economics have its first full expression. Smith challenged the notion that economics should be subservient to political interests, instead proposing that politics should serve economic ends. Smith thus submitted personal relations to financial matters. He showed that mercantilism was an economically disastrous policy and it was having equally bad political ramifications, not least in the form of the dissent of the American colonists. By the separation of economics as an independent field of study from politics Smith became a spokesman for a modified conception of human ontology, *homo economicus*. For Smith humans are distinguished from other animals by the fact that they "truck and barter."[80] We saw earlier that this was a convenient genealogy Smith told that has no historical merit.[81]

---

79. See Graeber, *Debt*, 332–33.
80. Smith, *Wealth of Nations*, 22.
81. "No example of a barter economy, pure and simple, has ever been described, let alone the emergence from it of money; all available ethnography suggests that there never has been such a thing." Humphrey, "Barter and Economic Disintegration," 48. She later explains that barter requires a specific set of preconditions, one of which is the knowledge of money and the inability to afford to keep it.

Humans are characterized by rational and calculating self-interest and the task of politics is to provide and protect opportunities for this self-interest to lead to the commonwealth. Augustine believed that self-love would lead to limitless competition and war. By transforming this notion of self-love into self-interest, from the uncontrolled passions to the controlled rationality of the mind, the theological orthodoxy of Augustine is transformed into a secular Pelagianism. It would be precisely through harnessing the rational self-interest embedded in human nature that would secure the commonwealth, and the whole process could be observed and predicted because it rested upon a rational view of human nature, designed after the fashion of Newtonian physical laws.

Smith added to Guicciardini by the application of later Enlightenment concepts of the primacy of the individual to economics. He described an ideal of perfect liberty in politics and economics. On this view humans are primarily thought of as independent units brought together for the purpose of facilitating material exchanges. Smith followed the Enlightenment idea that the individual is primary and society is a construct, rather than the individual as a member of a social group. Government existed to ensure liberty and liberty is expressed in free and equal transactions of goods, services, and labor. Each individual would rule himself, joining in society of his own free will when it suited him on terms that were fair to all parties.

Smith's own utopian vision of impersonal markets is understandable when long-standing debts ruined families for generations and led to the creation of hierarchical social structures that limited one's role to the station into which one was born. At a time when monarchy and class privilege were being thoroughly criticized, Smith provided an economic perspective to complement these challenges. The thoroughgoing egalitarianism that Smith imagined was that of an equality of opportunity that would reward the bold innovator and so encourage progress. Those who stockpile and save should only do so for the sake of making a large investment. But those who think to become established by the accumulation of wealth by removing it from circulation, the aristocrats, are economically foolish. Smith has many examples of how the landed wealthy make poor investments as they are too concerned with their objects and the appearance of their estates. What Smith is ultimately pointing at is a notion of the common good or commonwealth that hierarchy tends to ruin. Smith redirected the idea of self-sufficiency away from the aristocrat to the investor and the bourgeoisie. He democratized self-sufficiency and this has had powerful metaphysical and political repercussions.

Social Contract

If humans by nature engage in economic transactions and human nature is rationally self-interested, it follows that social groups become artificial constructions that arise through the notion of a social contract, as Rousseau and Locke set forth. Now, not only is human nature understood to be economic, society itself is made up of contractual relationships. People give to their social group only as much as is necessary for the preservation of individual liberties, the preservation of their lives and property from evils too powerful for them to combat themselves.

The political consequences of such a perspective should be fairly apparent. Either there is a need for the rule of a despot to control the excesses of self-interest, as in Hobbes, or the people should form a social contract with each other in a representative or democratic mold. The latter has prevailed in our times, though not without notable exceptions. The social contract, as an economic idea, creates a more or less harmonious group of people who all work together to create a rational society in which all are able to thrive. This is the dream. And it is important to understand it as a dream. The first nation that formed itself primarily on this concept and not on an antecedent identity is the United States of America, as William F. May points out. He says,

> The phrase *e pluribus unum*, emphasizes America as a project, a construction out of materials hitherto and perhaps continuingly multiple. Unity (the indispensable condition of identity) results from the construction. National unity issues from a choice.[82]

This constructed unity is ongoing. In a sense it is never achieved, never solidified, and always future oriented. It is also accompanied by an ever-present anxiety, as the future always is, as May argues. Like debt, the social contract creates relationships, but these are never very positive relationships. The social contract ostensibly creates an egalitarian relationship whereas debt obviously produces hierarchical relationships. But this egalitarianism must rest not on an actual situation, but on a certain view of human nature as somehow equal in a way nearly impossible to define in reality. This equivalency is usually transformed into rights language. But rights only exist where there is a right giver. In a social contract relationship, the right giver is the other person or party, the one with whom you're making a contract. It is not in nature, but in the contractual agreement. This right giving can and has been projected onto a deity as in the *Declaration of*

---

82. May, *Testing the National Covenant*, 82.

Independence. The "creator" has endowed all with equal rights, presenting a notion of rights foreign and anachronistic to the Bible.

And so we see the beginnings of the radically contradictory perspective of modern economy and politics. On the one hand we believe and are continually indoctrinated with an ever expanding list of individual human rights, and on the other this secular vision claims that power comes through consent, so that rights cannot be imposed, but can only be agreed upon in a contract form. The language of *individual human* rights should clue us in to this paradox immediately, but because it is the language of common sense now, the paradox is imperceptible. How can a species identity *human* contain *individual* rights? How can a universal category confer something distinct to each individual of that universal? Blueness conveys only blueness. It is an incoherent argument to refer to nature or ontology to confer rights. It is incoherent, but rhetorically very powerful. If it is part of our species identity, then it must be respected.

And this brings us back to the myth of barter. The reason why Adam Smith narrated the myth of barter was that it made sense of a people who were primarily self-interested individuals approaching other totally self-interested individuals. But as anthropologists have found, barter existed only amongst people who were strangers or potential enemies, people over whom one could work to get an advantage without further relational repercussions. And many of these actual barter relationships were accompanied with ritualized or possibly real violence. The social contract is a barter relationship, and this makes rights the fruit of barter, with parties trying to get one up on one another. Unsurprisingly societies based on the social contract have strong political animosity and political parties can themselves be strong factors in conveying personal identity, as it is through the political party that one encounters those with whom the social contract is always being negotiated. This also makes the resultant government a very dangerous force, always a potential enemy if it transgresses the social contract. Government is a necessary evil on this view, as it is always a compromise given with some grudging. The only obligation one has to another is the obligation that has been bartered for. One must contract a social debt. And in this sense, the social contract is quite the reverse of hierarchical belief systems like Confucianism, which has a strong sense of noncontractual social debt.

In sum, the notion of the social contract has deep roots in economic thinking. It is politics mediated through the concept of self-interested individuals encountering one another in a political barter. And this gives rise to a particular kind of contradictory metaphysics.

Postmonetary Economic Metaphysics

Postmonetary economics is grounded in an economic human ontology instead of in the field of religion, morality, or cosmology. That is, human nature is understood as primarily material and therefore economic. Economics thereby becomes separated from nonmaterial fields of human enquiry, which ultimately means that those fields of enquiry, where in conflict with economics, inevitably submit to economics. So, economic necessity produces a certain kind of morality that renders religious moral objections of small merit in the public square.

What is truly unique about the postmonetary situation as opposed to the similar ancient Greek situation is that we have returned to a primarily debt-based system, and yet this system of debt has been fundamentally transformed by monetization and the rise of the dominance of technical thinking. Modernity, from a larger perspective, might be understood as a synthesis of premonetary notions of debt and the kind of society that money produces. Debt is no longer a personal matter that builds relationships and is dependent on relationships of trust. Rather, debt is institutionalized and depersonalized. In the postmonetary age people and fictive persons of all kinds are in debt to other fictive persons. Credit cards, mortgages, payday loans, investment banking, national debt, all are kinds of debt relationships that purposefully do not involve personal relationships.

Depersonalized debt has its benefits and drawbacks. On the one hand, it frees people from situations of being indebted to a certain family that then demands moral debts or other services in token repayment of the debt. Thus personal hierarchies are avoided. On the other hand, depersonalized debt has led to a particular moral situation in which all feel obliged to repay their debts, when in fact the largest creditors who also are often the largest debtors simply do not repay their debts. Indeed, the non-repayment of debt is precisely what enables the modern economy to function. To understand that point we must go back to 1694 when the Bank of England began by buying royal war debt. Goodchild summarizes its inception:

> The Bank of England, formed by an act of Parliament at the instigation of William Paterson, provided a permanent loan of 1.2 million pounds at 8 percent interest to King William II for his religious wars. At the same time, the Bank also provided a note issue, in units of 20 pounds, of the same amount, guaranteed by the security of the government's promise to pay through taxation.[83]

---

83. Goodchild, *Theology of Money*, 7.

In this way money was no longer owed to the king and borrowed from his treasury, but was in fact money owed by the king borrowed from an imaginary public treasury by taxation. It was, as Graeber describes, "a mirror image of older forms of money."[84] From thenceforth the way money has operated is on the promise of future repayment of some unspecified kind at some unspecified time. A dollar is money owed by the government, not money owed to the government. In earlier times this was justified by tying a currency to a precious metal at a set rate. Since the total disconnect between a precious metal and money, this dollar no longer symbolizes any specific or particular value. Money has become itself debt. Instead of signifying present value it signifies future value dependent upon the corporation or institution that guarantees its value. Deficit spending is borrowing from future generations, but payback does not occur.

And this is the major drawback of depersonalized debt: there is almost no recourse to repayment. Indeed, if William II had repaid his loan to the Bank of England, it would have ruined the value of the paper money. All the paper would have to have been called in and exchanged for gold, and the Bank would itself be out of a function. Instead of repaying the loan, like the Buddhist Inexhaustible Treasuries, the interest accumulated on the loans could be the only real repayment. What this ultimately means, however, is that everyone must pay off their debts, except those with power. The largest debtors are the ones on whom the value of a currency depends, and this means that there is little reason for them to repay their debts. Major corporations have been declared "too big to fail" and the only governments that are required to repay their debts are those with lesser military power. The foreign debt of the United States dwarfs that of all third world nations combined, and yet the US does not repay these debts, though the third world nations must.[85]

This means that violence, whether actual or potential, lies at the heart of debt money. This is not bare violence, but violence mediated through a system of rules that produce a semblance of justice. Violence has long been the method of debt-collectors, and yet on the corporate and international scene this violence is thoroughly masked behind systems of impersonality and therefore seeming impartiality. Thus Graeber rightly raises the question as to whether the practice of selling national debt to other nations, specifically nations that already have a US military presence within them, should really be understood as a loan or as tribute demanded by a powerful empire. That America refuses to consider itself an empire is essential

---

84. Graeber, *Debt*, 339.
85. Ibid., 5–6.

because to do so would unmask the power relations that go under the guise of justice. There is an essential myth to international politics that is based on the metaphysical commitments of people who buy into the global system of economics.

To put this myth another way, hierarchy seems to be eliminated by the removal of long-standing personal debts that could be transformed into moral debts. But it is not eliminated. In fact, hierarchy is strengthened by the myth of equality that pervades the political rhetoric. This means that the positive aspects of hierarchy—taste, culture, education, a concentration on quality—are eliminated in reality but retained by the myth of equality. All must receive the same range of products made in a few Chinese factories. All must listen to similar kinds of music, wear similar kinds of globalized clothes, all at a price that must be in market equilibrium. Instead of a concentration on the education of a ruling elite, all must receive the same quality of education by right. And all this would seem just, were it not a pretense. Instead of our egalitarian culture and education leading to a situation of economic equality, our own era is witness to the largest wealth inequality yet known in human history.

How could it happen that such radical economic inequality arose at the same time as political rhetoric finds ever new ways to improve the equality of individual human rights?

This is not a great conspiracy against the public by a team of evil corporations. Instead, it is a systematic necessity of modern economics. More recent modernity has been described by Jacques Ellul as a technical age, defined mainly by an obsession with means, such that means become their own ends.[86] This obsession with means is most evident in technology and the rise of gadgets, though it is also equally prevalent in the sciences and social sciences, especially economics. Now, as technology becomes ever more complicated and integrated into our narratives of meaning,[87] it becomes increasingly more costly and difficult to advance. Whereas a single man like Thomas Edison could create numerous inventions in fairly different fields, contemporary R&D departments and corporations have immense

---

86. Ellul, *Technological Society*, 133–41.

87. For example, one of our major narratives is that the world is on the brink of disaster by climate change, and the solution is inevitably in better, more efficient, and more advanced technology. I am unaware of any serious suggestion that people simply stop exploiting resources that lead to greenhouse gas emissions. This shows that technology is an integral part of the structure of meaning and future alternatives are largely built upon it. Science fiction is another great example. The genre does not usually explore fictions of science, like imagining a universe with no law of inertia, but fictions that imagine where our technology will take us in the future. More properly the genre should be called technofiction.

teams working on relatively smaller problems. Contemporary life is lived in a veritable environment of technology.[88] And because the narrative of technology is dependent upon interminable progress, as is that of capitalism, progress is a moral necessity. This progress comes at an ever increasing cost and this means that larger and larger corporations must take on the mantle of progress. A small start-up corporation can raise some capital for the creation of something new, no doubt, but it is inevitable that this small corporation will be bought out by a larger conglomerate or become quite large (in terms of capital, not necessarily workforce) itself. This tendency toward large corporations with large amounts of resources, the trust of stockholders, and some stability leads also toward the larger payment of those who distinguish themselves as able to lead such large corporations. At the same time, those who invent something really new and influential, say Mark Zuckerberg of Facebook fame, are able to rise to such meteoric heights because of the progress that larger corporations have made and the products that they sell that enables social media to exist at all. Facebook can have such wide distribution that it is able to make billions of dollars per year due to its increasingly widespread hardware applications.

That is to say, the increasingly unequal distribution of wealth in our world is integral to the narrative of progress in technology and economics. It is simply an economy of scale. One could argue, of course, that such a distribution of wealth is morally wrong, but there is no common ground on which one can base this argument. It is not a violation of individual human rights to be successful. There is a moral common ground, however, and it is based in a metaphysical common ground: the combination of pre-monetary debt relations transformed by the impersonal nature of money. Coinage, as we saw with the ancient Greeks, led to the establishment of a particular kind of metaphysical perspective. Fiduciarity, that a coin can be worth more than its intrinsic metal value, led to a depersonalized universal concept. Quite often this was a material monism, but in nearly every case it led to a depersonalized view of the cosmos. With this came the separation of the body and the soul. There was material stuff, which is primary, and something else that gives that matter identity and value. Though some like the Atomists believed the soul to be material, others like Plato held that it was immortal and immaterial. The discussion between the philosophers had immense common ground, and many of the particularities were due to considerations of social class.

When recombined with a debt-based economic system, this metaphysic is modified and attenuated. It is no longer as radical as before. The

---

88. Ellul, *Technological System*, 35.

modern metaphysics of the marketplace must take into account the pseudo-reality of fictive persons like corporations or nation-states. Corporations are said to exist, to be more than the sum of their parts, to have a culture, a brand image, a public image. Corporations have departments to manage human relations, thus subordinating actual relations to economic concerns. These corporations are at the heart of the global economy, replacing individual people in actual marketplaces with fictive persons in an analogical marketplace. The same can be said in the political sphere of nation-states. So the forces that govern much of the material lives of people are not, as in premonetary societies, divine beings, nor impersonal ideas like the *logos* or *apeiron*, but are these strange, in-between beings called corporations.

A god is beyond matter, giving it value, a story, importance. A god does this for a people as well. A god is a being with whom one can have some kind of relationship, usually mediated through hierarchical structures of priesthood or kingship. A god is responsible for the economic concerns of the people, whether the harvest will succeed or fail, whether a trade will be fruitful or not, whether new lives born into the group will be healthy and well integrated. All of the above can easily be said of corporations in the modern world. They are beyond matter; they exist legally and in the minds of others. Corporations or nation-states give value to objects, people, and places. Formerly the notion of the Fatherland or Motherland was fairly exclusive in this role, but increasingly individuals take on the symbols, the logos, of corporations to construct their identities. One can have a relationship with a corporation, as an investor, customer, employee, competitor, fanatic, or devotee. These relationships are mediated through hierarchical structures strictly limiting the appropriate kinds of activities one can perform in each of these relationships. Corporations are responsible for the economic wellbeing of a people. No longer are the gods responsible for health and wellbeing, but supermarkets, health care networks, insurance companies, governments, and a myriad of other organizations take care of the aspects that once were left to the gods.

Metaphysically, it is absurd to believe that the individual stands alone as the one responsible for the construction of meaning in his or her own life, given the kinds of economic relationships that pervade every minute of modern life. Brand names that stand for corporations and the billions of people that are involved in a global economic system pervade nearly every space in modern life. Everything we use is branded, and so bears the symbol of ownership or provision by a higher power, like money. And yet, modernity and modern economics are built upon a nearly opposite narrative. Individual human rights are said to be primary, and it is through our human cooperation that we can all join together as one species, living in peace and harmony with all. What do we all have in common? Our DNA. So it is our basic material, almost monistic, metaphysic that unites us in this narrative, but this is so imprecise and so hard to apply to daily life that another narrative, that of self-determination and individual rights, exists simultaneously. This is a strange metaphysic because it has replaced the gods with corporations, all while living under a myth that we all are or can be self-sufficient.

And so we return once again to the divide between equality and hierarchy. On the one hand our lives are engaged in massive and global structures of hierarchy. Our lives are governed by fictive persons of corporations and nation-states. On the other hand, we believe that we are all born free, with total individual liberty to determine where to go and what to do in life. We are told daily that all people are born equal and remain equal. Everything must be "equal opportunity." In the United States where the economic hierarchy of slavery was legally overturned over 150 years ago, and we annually celebrate the life and work of Martin Luther King Jr., the myth of equal opportunity has continually grated against a reality of injustice that often explodes into violence. We live in a deeply hierarchical world, but we are continually told and tell ourselves that we live in a radically free and equal society.

This contradictory perspective is deeply pernicious and yet it is essential to our economic system. It is a self-perpetuating contradiction with the practical result that relative poverty has never been greater in human history. The concept of an absolute level of poverty that is given by many governments and accepted by charities who want to end poverty forever masks that the solution to absolute poverty is greater relative poverty. It is by integrating people into a global economic system in which the fewest of the few can hold real power, that the poverty of substandard (for the twenty-first-century West) living conditions can be overcome. The idea that one need only receive a small loan, start a business, get on the internet, and participate in the global economy in order to be liberated is a curious concept. Undoubtedly the formerly third world individual will feel part of something greater, a universal humanity, but this comes at the cost of actual human relationships.

Our modern metaphysic requires that individual human relations are mediated through economics. One acquires personal worth and value economically, and this means that personal relationships are mediated economically. This has a disastrous effect on communities and has led to the need for the creation of things like insurance companies and welfare organizations. Charity has had to be outsourced. Individuals are no longer really capable of making a difference without joining in a corporation or NGO that will do charity on a systematic scale.

This all leads to a notion of a universal humanity. Because our relationships are increasingly mediated through reifications, through corporations, it is inevitable that this will be taken to its logical, singular conclusion. We must remember that the ancient Greek philosophers were nearly all against the traditional portrayal of the gods, and many were monotheistic, like Parmenides and Aristotle. Their gods were the first principle, the natural end of their metaphysical speculation. And so it has become for us. The final universal concept to which we can all appeal is the first principle of our metaphysical system: the individual human being turned into a universal. Humanity is the beginning and end of our pursuit. But what is humanity? It is that which we value. As Protagoras said, humanity is the measure of all things, that is, we are what we value and what we value is determined by us. We are self-constructed by a projection of what we value onto a metaphysical universal. Humanity today is defined by the ability to participate in what we value, for only then are we self-determining beings. The corporation is the means by which the individual can participate in the universal humanity by self-interest.

We now witness the subordination of distinct cultures to a more monolithic conception of humanity as those who participate in the technological and global economic system. The good, which is to be pursued, is economic participation. It is a human right to earn one's living, regardless of what a previous culture thought about gender roles, skin color, sexuality, or religion. And this brings us to the gospel of modern economics.

The Gospel of Modern Economics

The advent of the European Union is an informative example for the modern economic perspective. The EU has always been a political vision of cooperation instead of the violent competition expressed in two World Wars. While the League of Nations was an earlier attempt to achieve a similar end on a much larger scale, it, like the later United Nations, has not had nearly the success politically as has the EU. And this may have something to do with how the EU came about. The first step in the creation of the EU was the formation of the European Coal and Steel Community (1950), an obviously economic cooperation designed to bring heavy industries associated with the production of war material under common management. In 1957 with the Treaty of Rome, the European Economic Community (EEC) was formed, also known as the "common market." Its hope was to allow for the free movement of people, goods, and services across borders, not realized until 1993. In 1962 a common agricultural policy was formed. In

1968 customs duties were removed on trade between partner states. The first plan for a common currency was developed in 1970, though the Euro was not introduced as the single currency of the EU for another thirty years. And so the story continues.[89] Each new political development of the EU is pioneered by an economic cooperation. Human rights are expanded and improved through economics. Its history is enlightening, especially when compared with previous revolutions and large-scale changes in the political makeup of Europe. Rather than achieving political ends with primarily political means, through war, or through violent revolution, a large and new state institution is created. The ideas of the Enlightenment led to a series of disasters for France in its revolution and imperial periods because these Enlightenment ideas were advanced through violence. The EU, on the other hand, holding much the same Enlightenment perspective, could advance in the wake of brutal war to reconciliation through economics. This should not be surprising, since we've seen already how debt creates and strengthens social relations.

Economics proves to be the hero of this story. It is through economic cooperation that broader human communities may be formed that can overcome former and very long-standing animosities. But once again this leads us to the same problem we saw with the previous two gospels. The problem and the solution are the same thing, and this creates a self-perpetuating cycle of injustice and cries for justice.

What is the gospel of modern economics? We shall be speaking mainly of mainstream economic perspectives, but the alternatives, like Marxism, share some fundamental similarities. The first unique aspect of the modern economic gospel is that it does not begin with an ideal situation from which people have fallen. Because it requires the idea of interminable progress and narrates history largely through that lens, there cannot be an ideal that is to be recovered because that would limit growth to some static utopian situation. So the "fall" here is not so much a fall from grace as much as it is a simple progression from savagery to an ever more enlightened state, of which the present is the culmination of history,[90] and yet also just the beginning.

The story Neoclassical economists tell usually runs in some variation of the following: in the beginning humans were savages engaged in very rudimentary relationships. As they developed *technologically* they found

---

89. "The History of the European Union," accessed July 25, 2015, http://europa.eu/about-eu/eu-history/index_en.htm.

90. This notion set forth firstly by the Hegelian Alexandre Kojève and more recently and famously by Francis Fukuyama. Yar, "Alexandre Kojève"; Fukuyama, *End of History*.

that they could develop a division of labor and so produce different products that could then be traded, and that the quality of each product thereby improved. Eventually marketplaces developed where barter happened, each person taking the fruits of his or her labor to the market to exchange for other goods based on some bartered exchange rate. As this was cumbersome and inefficient, people eventually started to use money in many forms as a third thing to exchange for goods and services. Though there were some high points in Greece and Rome, the Middle Ages saw a "reversion to barter" and primitive economic conditions. In modern times with technology and the proper thinking that accompanies all who are modern, economics has become a scientific pursuit, which has ensured the liberty of those formerly enslaved to hierarchical relations. Now complex economic models are possible wherein we hope to one day predict the market with such success that endless affluence is possible for all. All ships rise with the tide. The affluence of some trickles down to others. The invisible hand will ensure that enlightened self-interest in competition will actually lead to the greatest commonwealth. Everyone gets a bigger slice of pie by enlarging the pie.

Now, Neoclassical economics is not the only major narrative, and as we saw in the development of the EU, it can be utilized for political ends. The modern gospel is much larger than economics, but as I will attempt to show, economic relations are at the core of this gospel. The major problems that people observe in the world today are some version of a list like this: climate change, third world poverty, lack of access to education (ignorance), lack of access to appropriate health care, extremist Islam, terrorism, and war. This list is not, of course, exclusive. In narrating the problems and injustices of our world we can begin to see a picture of an ideal come through by imagining the opposite of the injustices. We want sustainability, equality of economic opportunity for all people regardless of nationality, education for all to have equal access to become influential in the global marketplace, appropriate healthcare for any who are in need, safety, religious toleration, security, and peace. To this list we can oppose the other two values of the economic gospels we explored: enlightenment or truth, and, honor and moral relationships.

Modernity has little need for truth if it is not pragmatic. What works is what is true, and what works is what leads to one being able to participate in the global economy, and grows the economy. Truth is not determined by speculation on the nature of things, but by what is able to advance the means of humanity to interact with each other and the world. So truth is very technical. If an idea is not pragmatic it belongs to the realm of personal opinion. Whether God exists or not makes no difference for the economic wellbeing of an individual or their ability to contribute to the economy as they might. All it can do is lead to decreased productivity due to moral qualms that are out of touch with economic and technical morality. Enlightenment is not what people seek as an end in itself, instead it is a means to supplement the personal wellbeing of the individual, which is why what is true for one person may not be for another. Religion, we could say, is part of the economy of means, not an end in itself.

Modernity is also fairly unconcerned with moral relationships on the personal level. Modern morality is expressed corporately in both senses of the term. It is primarily expressed through corporations and large-scale groups. The large moral problem of injustices we mentioned above are not personal problems. After all, so long as the individual is personally involved in contributing to the economy by working, making purchases, and paying taxes, the whole thing ought to operate like clockwork. And as we see the faces of starving children, hear about villages without clean water because they insist on living in primitive conditions, then our solution is to send modern secular missionaries to alleviate those problems. To put it another way, charity is outsourced. It is given to businesses who take a percentage of the profit and donate it to a charity. Of course the businesses are not reducing a bottom line to help charity, such a thing would harm their stockholders. Rather, the consumer is giving charity by being a consumer. The business is acting as the conscience of the consumer. So long as each person has a modicum of personal responsibility, the system will work, and we just need to supply those poor souls who can't afford to purchase products with the economic means they need to advance to our level.

Our reference to the language of debt shows this corporate morality clearly. When people give to charity they speak of "giving back." One cannot simply give; one must be in a reciprocal relationship. Instead of using a gift to create a personal relationship as in older debt societies, modern charity is precisely designed to attempt to integrate those who are outside the Economy into it.

And this reveals one of the major points we have been discussing about modernity: egalitarianism. For this is the good news and the utopian vision of modern economics: that all can become equal (whether in opportunity or in satisfaction of needs) by having sociopolitical equality through economic means. Homeric Greece was, like so many debt societies, based on notions of honor and personal relations. Because of this it was thoroughly hierarchical. The strong are praised, their feats are heroic. The weak are justifiably ruled by the strong. It was by human and divine nature that the stronger rule.[91] Modern rhetoric is strongly opposed to this. We

---

91. Thucydides's *Peloponnesian War* contains an interesting speech of the Athenians

have or desire "liberty and justice for all." This egalitarianism has proven highly mythical, especially for Native Americans. Nevertheless, because modern economics holds ineluctable progress as a given, this egalitarianism always remains in the future. The sin of modernity is economic injustice and the solution to this sin is economic justice. And yet this is never achieved, not least because a state of equilibrium would negate growth and the future orientation of fiscal credit.

The problems of the modern world are mostly all caused and solved by the combination of technology and economics. The two go hand in hand as we already saw in the enormous economy of scale that never ending technical progress requires. Climate change and other ecological crises are problems caused by economics and technology. Technology provides the means of creating the problem by addressing a previous problem. Economics provides the impetus to the rapid and often careless expansion and advancement of technology. For example, at the turn of the twentieth century New York City was a cesspit due to the number of horses on its streets. A new technical innovation on the horizon, the horseless carriage, provided a much cleaner, more reliable, more economic, and quicker mode of transportation. It also helped that it introduced a large number of new industries that would lead to job creation. But the automobile transformed the fabric of society. The automobile itself became a major source of pollution, now no longer confined to major urban centers, but pollution of the whole world. It also transformed the economic system. The need for rapid and cheap production to maximize the car-buying audience led to Henry Ford's famous assembly lines. This created a wealth of new jobs in new industries, but also helped transform industries reliant on craftsmanship—like that of the cartwright, wheelwright, the horse breeder, the saddle maker, and the farrier—into lower paid, lower skilled, and lower satisfaction assembly line jobs. Though new jobs were created, others were destroyed, and in the process wealth was redistributed to the wealthy entrepreneur and manager who could economize production, like Henry Ford.

And yet, when it comes to narrating the solution to our environmental problems, the solutions are inevitably the same as before: new technologies to make production and consumption more efficient. Jacques Ellul points

---

to the inhabitants of Melos in which the Athenians justify their largely unprovoked and wholly one-sided conflict with Melos as the natural result of the powerful over the weak, and that, if they were the strong and the Athenians were weak, the Melians would have done the same. "Of the gods, we believe, and of men we know, that by a necessary law of their nature they rule wherever they can. And it is not as if we were the first to make this law, or to act upon it when made: we found it existing before us, and shall leave it to exist for ever after us; all we do is to make use of it, knowing that you and everybody else, having the same power as we have, would do the same as we do" (5.105).

out that time and again this formula leads to nothing but increased consumption. Bandwidth creates demand rather than lessening congestion. Attempting to overcome scarcity by increasing resources and quantity of goods only increases scarcity.[92] And this should be no surprise, because as a thing tends toward the unlimited, as we saw with the advent of coinage, people increase consumption, giving rise for the need of notions like moderation, which summarizes the "green" movement. Consumption in the postmonetary world is not governed by rationality or morality, but by bandwidth, quantity of potentiality, or supply of resources.

What we narrate as an environmental problem quickly becomes a technical-economic problem whose solution must be future oriented. This is because the metaphysics of modernity, based as they are in the primacy of the individual, must always be future oriented. This is the case because for an individual to construct himself, he must arrive at identity in the future. To look into the past and to established social identities that are imposed on the individual is the same hierarchical evil that the Enlightenment rid us of. So the individual is always undergoing construction, or is searching for their "true" self. The individual is always becoming what one is. The individual cannot rest in a constant identity because this identity is not formed by an individual *ex nihilo* as Descartes might have imagined. Rather the individual is continually responding and adapting to the cosmos in which she lives. As the cosmos changes, and it does at an increasing rate in modernity, identity must also change. If the identity of the individual is future oriented, then that of society, which is a contractual relationship of individuals, is put even further into the future. When one adds to this the milieu that technology itself has become for modern people, solutions based in the present, in the past, or in alternatives that undermine the foundations of technology and technical economics itself are systematically inconceivable. And therefore, if we are going to narrate a solution to our problem it is going to be a futuristic, technological, and economic solution.

Poverty is an ever more clear example of the gospel of modern economics. Poverty is a very slippery term, itself being a reification of a relative concept. Someone is poor in relation to someone who is rich, and so poverty is this state of affairs in general. But just as there can be a reified Economy or Market, so too there is a reified inverse of this, Poverty. Poverty can be quantified and many nations do so to determine who will receive financial assistance. Let us call this *absolute poverty*, because it is defined by relation to an absolute like an income level or quality of life index. In this case poverty is the state in which one is unable to pay for oneself and

---

92. Ellul, *Technological Bluff*, 298–99.

one's dependents' livelihood with one's financial earnings. This understanding of poverty is based in a notion of self-sufficiency. We saw in the ancient world how self-sufficiency was the purview of the aristocrat, and the gods, so that the modern egalitarian world assumes all have the right to a somewhat similar kind of identity. We saw that this was always a myth, there is no such thing as self-sufficiency. But whereas ancient people had recourse to large social bodies for mutual dependence, modern people have few alternatives but to turn to the government, corporations, or charities for aid. This is usually a necessarily impersonal situation. The person is treated as their income, and the quantity of that income and their ability to reach that income by taking on further jobs is all that really counts. The self-sufficiency of the aristocracy has always been a mythical and self-deceptive belief, it is equally so today.

One difference between many of the ancients and ourselves, however, is that we subscribe to the idea of egalitarianism. This means that we live with a double myth: that the normal and ideal economic situation is one of self-sufficiency, that all are entitled to this, and that the majority of people in fact do live like this. What is truly pernicious about this modern story is that people are in fact increasingly dependent because of the division of labor and specialization of skills that technology continues to develop. Those who are most well integrated into the economy, those who feel themselves to be largely self-sufficient, are often those who are the least skilled in a variety of basic survival skills that would be necessary for the more true self-sufficiency of older tribal peoples. But whereas older tribal cultures would readily acknowledge their mutual dependence on each other, the gods, and the earth, modern people believe themselves to be independent. And again, this goes back to the metaphysical perspective of modern economics. The individual must come first, and because of this, to be a full individual is to be able to define oneself with as little reference to the labor of others as possible.

Getting back to poverty, then, we can see that the definition of poverty requires that its solution be that individuals and people groups alike become full participants and contributors to the Economy, in order that one be able to pay for one's own bills. For true freedom is self-sufficiency, a godlike aseity, and that means working to make money to pay for what one owes. Absolute poverty is therefore the creation of the modern metaphysical ideal of an egalitarian though aristocratic self-sufficiency. To alleviate this kind of poverty requires a fundamental change in perspective for people in third world countries who may currently believe in the value of mutual dependence. This makes charities that try to alleviate this kind of poverty into secular economic missionaries little different to the imperialistic missionaries that went before them. This kind of poverty can be eliminated, at least in utopian dreams and rhetoric, by the inclusion of people in the Economy and by global evangelization in the gospel of the modern metaphysics of money.

But there is another kind of poverty, *relative poverty*, which is not dependent on an absolute index of poverty, but on the distribution of wealth and power. Our current time is the most unequal in all of human history. The majority of wealth has never been in the hands of such a small percentage of people. This is the natural result of the increase of wealth itself, given that wealth is given value by scarcity. This kind of poverty cannot be wholly eliminated, except in communist utopian visions. But again, we see that the gospel of modern economics is itself the problem and the solution. It has become one of, if not the main, voice in moral and political discussion.

The Marxist narrative is quite different, but has some key similarities: There have always been classes, always systems of hierarchy that oppress people. Technology and the elimination of religions of projection (a kind of enlightenment) liberate the working classes. Once the working classes are suitably enlightened they will rise up, throw off the chains of their oppressors, and eventually create a classless society where the maxim is, "From each according to ability, to each according to need." This is a utopia where everyone has what is needed for livelihood.

These simplified narratives are similar in their progressive mentality, the reliance on technology and enlightenment, liberation, and the end result of a commonwealth where all are enriched. The gospel of modern economics begins, not with a fall from grace, but an initial problematic state. This is essential because these are technical gospels wholly dependent on the notion of progress. In the beginning humans were idiots, barely evolved apes, who engaged in only rudimentary exchange relationships. They were dispersed, unable to work on common projects because of a lack of division of labor, and generally suffered in a miserable "state of nature." Eventually classes developed and things, in a way, got worse. Slavery was a hallmark of empires, and so the rich got richer and the poor were enslaved. So ignorance and hierarchy are seen as the twin forces of evil that lead to a bad state where people are unable to flourish.

There are still deep sins that exist today. Hierarchy is not undone. People still don't have clean drinking water, or access to some normal standard of living. Many people in third world countries and in first world ones as well live in economic ignorance. They don't know financial strategies for how to use debt to one's advantage, instead they become dependent on welfare systems and usurers like credit card companies and payday loan agents.

The Marxist and Neoclassical gospels are nearly equivalent in terms of the problem and the desired result, where they differ is in the means to that end. The Marxist gospel tends to see a large nation-state redistribute wealth so that people are more free and equal. It focuses on language of equality of outcome. The Neoclassical gospel desires that corporations redistribute wealth through free competition in the consumer and job marketplace, so it focuses on language of equal opportunity.

In each case to be fully human is to be an equal participant in economic livelihood. Those who are forbidden access to an ostensibly self-sufficient livelihood are not yet fully human and it is the task of those who do have this access to bring them into full humanity by communion in the Marketplace. Justice, it seems, requires that each person have equal access to the Marketplace. Those who are denied justice are denied the ability to live a thriving and fully human life. But this fully human life is, of course, one specific narrative of human ontology. By empowering the poor of the poorest nations they can be liberated. What do they need liberation from? Poverty.

In the modern discourse of justice, economic concerns, especially poverty, hold the first place. And this should not be surprising, because the dominant metaphysical perspective we have explored above is materialist enough to only be able to conceive of justice in terms of economics and reciprocity.

So then, the ideal situation to which the modern economic gospel leads is to the achievement of full individual rights and justice for all through the universal cooperation and thus construction of a commonwealth of universal humanity. This is a universal humanity constructed economically, however. And it is a universal humanity that exists by isolating people by integrating them into a constructed universal. Ancient aristocracies could remove wealth from circulation, create large estates and households, even govern small city-states of their own, but they became self-sufficient only by self-deception, as the individual was increasingly dependent upon the labor of others. And the same is true for our modern gospel. We desire that all have some true liberty, true individuation, and yet this comes only by joining in with a globally depersonalized and technological economy that thrives on the division of labor and not on self-sufficiency. It is a future oriented identity that never becomes what one is, but must continually work to become. Thus the vast majority of time is devoted to labor, to the creation of wealth as stored value, so that one can eventually exchange that wealth for selfhood, a selfhood that is impossible to achieve due to the impossibility of recognizing mutual dependence.

THE ECONOMIC RELATIONSHIP

There are a few important similarities in the above three societies that create what we might call the economic relationship. This is a relationship on all levels mediated by economic concerns. Indeed, the way in which the notion of "world" is formed for each of these societies pertains to their particular economic structure. And this world, in turn, forms and informs the kinds of relationships people have with each other and all other things. The economic relationship is primarily about mediation through material objects. In the premonetary society heirlooms have the ability to create a person's identity and social status. A crown, scepter, or throne is often used metonymically to refer to the king. These objects have more than symbolic meaning. In some cases, the king cannot exercise authority apart from these objects. The objects make the king as much as the king creates the meaning of these objects. In the monetary society the material is the gateway to the transcendent and one must make the choice to either pursue material wealth, or attempt to go through it as a symbol to a higher reality. But in both cases the understanding of people and things is mediated by money. In the postmonetary society the material becomes the transcendent. Symbol loses its power as the sign and the signified are merged into one. Economics and money become the fabric of reality instead of a pointer to something beyond. Thus there is a close connection between money and technology, technology being the means of wealth creation by enabling the continual growth of capital. In each of these three societies the material world provides the primary mediation, which is what leads to the construction of many other things in its image.

This can be seen in social relationships. In the premonetary society debt forms the glue of a society, gifts providing an important means of establishing hierarchy and meaning. Right relationships, or justice, is established and reestablished by reference to debt. The *lex talionis*[93] is one example of a notion of justice built upon exact compensation for a loss. The idea of a balanced scale, which must always be primarily a marketplace symbol, fits this kind of justice perfectly, especially if we imagine one tooth balancing out another. In monetary societies money transformed and deeply disrupted traditional forms of social relations by submitting them to the fictive person of the state. Justice was now owed, not to the gods or the victims, but to the state, and could often be paid in money. Right relations, then, had

---

93. Latin: "the law of the tooth." This refers to the biblical rule of retribution found variously in Exod 21, Lev 24, and Deut 19. But this is not a code unique to the Bible, the Code of Hammurabi, which is likely the earlier (ca. 1754 BC), is largely built upon this as well.

much to do with money. In the postmonetary society justice is primarily understood in economic terms so that in some situations the word justice itself is a stand-in for proper distribution of material goods. Even the state must submit to economics, as we saw with the development of the European Union. Now economics forms the state in its image.

The form of religion is also part of the economic relationship. The structure of religion pertains to the economic relationship of its situation. In the premonetary society religion is debt based. Sacrifices are often one of the primary expressions of religious devotion as a means of reestablishing right relations between the gods and people. It is through giving the gods material goods that the gods are made happy, just as gifts and tribute establish and confirm human hierarchies. In the monetary society sacrifices continue, but take on a new and more transactional basis. Roman religion was very transactional and contractual, sometimes understood in the phrase *do ut des*,[94] which Durkheim rightly understood as essential to the nature of sacrifice in itself.[95] What is unique about a monetary society like Rome, however, was the monetized economy of the sacrifice. That a human could bargain with a god, vowing to give an exact quantity of a sacrifice in hope or expectation that such a quantity would be attractive to an immaterial being, is what caused the philosophers to do away with such piety altogether, instead holding that the gods were far removed from the marketplace and entirely self-sufficient. In the postmonetary society religion in its traditional forms, like all systems of symbolization, is thought to be transcended by the complete merging of sign and signified. God is dead because God is no longer a useful concept. And because the Christian God was once dominant in the West and is now discredited in many quarters, those who feel trapped in a barren wasteland without symbols turn to modern reinterpretations of a variety of ancient beliefs and practices such as magic and neopaganism, other equally useless concepts. So religion has become submitted to "the Economy" and to "Humanity." It has become an individual human right to believe and practice whatever religion one chooses, so long as it is not overly harmful to others. That religion is a personal choice must be seen as the result of the metaphysic that modern economics exemplifies. Because religion is no longer socially profitable in providing the common narrative for ethics, politics, or group identity, religion can only exist as recreation.[96] Recreation can be taken quite seriously and is a very profitable industry segment, indeed, some of the highest paid individuals are performers. But

---

94. Latin: "I give that you might give."
95. Durkheim, *Elementary Forms*, 257.
96. I argue this in some greater detail. See Wagenfuhr, "Religion comme jeu."

play usually takes on forms that reinforce and integrate people into the more serious segments of life, and religion is similar. Teachings on justice in the Christian world, for example, tend to follow the basic divide between capitalism and socialism, offering no overarching critique to this false dichotomy of options, but happily joining the debate on one or another side with reference to sacred documents written thousands of years before the advent of such concepts. God may be dead, but he can live on in the hearts of believers, so long as this God reinforces the economic relationships of our world.

Finally, the economic relationship determines relationships with the nonhuman world. In the premonetary society all things were the creations of the gods and inhabited by gods or demigods. There was nothing that could not, potentially, be personalized. Because of this the nonhuman world was treated with great respect, fear, love, and gratitude. Useful plants and animals were gifts. Animals would not be killed for eating without a religious ceremony recognizing that a life was being taken to feed another life. In the monetary society, as we've discussed at length, universal concepts came to the fore in philosophy. Aristotle speaks of the earth and animals as given meaning only by humans. They are commoditized. Animals are worthless until given worth by use or exchange. The world begins to be exploited for trade and profit. In the postmonetary society there is, once again, a curious duality to our approach to other creatures and the Environment. It is given great respect and we deeply desire to "save" it from ourselves. But it is also entirely commoditized, ruled over, managed. It is no longer personalized on an individual level as it was for the ancients, nor is it blatantly commoditized as the monetary society made it to be, but it is universally personal and universally commoditized. The earth is once again our Mother, and it's a mother that we command. It's an "environment," as though we could potentially exist independently of it. It's an ecosystem, a machine. This duality again expresses our unification of symbol and reality. The symbol, Mother Earth, is one side of a coin, the Environment is the other. The contemporary word "sustainability" belies the entirely economic relationship the postmonetary world has with the nonhuman world.

The economic relationship, then, is a mediation of our important relationships through economics. The kind of economy changes and that in turn changes the way people have related to other things. But what remains unchanged throughout is this mediation. It is not the only mediation, nor always the primary mediation. I certainly do not want to reaffirm some notion of *homo economicus*, that humans are defined as being economic beings. But this is one important aspect of history and world-formation.

CONCLUSION

Dividing human economic history into three parts is somewhat convenient and oversimplified. There is a large diversity of economic expressions in human history, and this tripartite scheme simply enables us to consider how human society and economic relationships have changed over time. As is always the case with such divisions, they must not be pressed into creating firm boundaries. Their imprecision is as important as their precision. It is clear that the introduction of money transformed human societies, literature, and thought patterns. Through the rise of money ancient Greece was able to develop its philosophy based on a division between seeming and reality, a notion that seems based in the fiduciarity of money. Money transformed earlier debtor-creditor relationships by depersonalizing them and increasing the power of the state. Premonetary societies were incapable of speaking metaphysically, for they lacked the distinction between seeming and reality. In modern times there has been a synthesis of personal debt relations with the impersonal and metaphysical relations that money creates.

In all of these types of society we have seen that there is a different story that is told about what the fundamental problem of the world is and what its solution is. I have called these "gospels" and they are, indeed, very similar structures to that of sin and redemption found in many religions. This pattern of thinking is not unique to religion, but is common to anyone who has a concept of justice and injustice. Though the premonetary societies did not reflect on a distinction between seeming and reality, this distinction was there in personalized form of gods, heroes, and all manner of things in between. Justice existed, but was personal, and so it belonged primarily to the gods. But justice only exists as a concept because it doesn't exist in reality, so in order to describe a situation of injustice we must appeal to an ideal situation in which that injustice is eliminated, and a means to accomplish that. This is a gospel, and throughout human history it has taken on economic tones, given that the distribution of necessary goods understandably consumes much of our time and energy.

The question that lies before us now is what we do with Christianity in light of all of this. Is Christianity just another religion that narrates a problem and gives the problem as its solution? Is there anything unique about biblical revelation that offers a counter to these gospels? And if there is, how have Christians blurred this distinction and thus enslaved themselves to the gospels of economic relations? And finally, what can Christians do about it now?

3

The Creator-Creature Relationship

"'Show me a denarius. Whose likeness and inscription does it have?' They said, 'Caesar's.' He said to them, 'Then render to Caesar the things that are Caesar's, and to God the things that are God's.'"[1]

Jesus is a crafty person who always seems to manage to outfox those who attempt to trap him. But his wit is not empty rhetoric; Jesus questions those who question him, rejecting their narrative, and thus teaching an important lesson. There is something profoundly true about giving Caesar his own picture back: payment of tax is not an illegitimate demand if it is the government that creates and backs the value of all money.

"In God We Trust." This is, of course, the statement inscribed on all money of the United States. It is not an ethical or religious demand for faith, it is a statement of fact. "God" is the trust of the United States. Because trust is the basis of economic relationships it is not accidental that "God" is used to back American money. Though it alludes to the Christian tradition, the God of America is not the God of Scripture. This God is a metaphysical construct for the purpose of legitimizing the economic system of the nation. The most trustworthy entity conceivable, an immutable God, the being higher than which none can be conceived, serves as the ground of the economic system. American money is not only backed by the government, but by God

---

1. Luke 20:24–25.

himself who stands behind the whole system, guaranteeing economic value vicariously through the American government, God's treasurer.

In a crafty response to Jesus's wit, Americans have subtly and piously enabled their taxes to be simultaneously paid to God and to Caesar. America, as its *Pledge of Allegiance* says, is "one nation under God." As such, this unique nation has undercut the official division of those who have the power of the sword and those who hold the keys. God and state are deeply united in American minds. God, for them, has placed his *imprimatur* on the economic system and life of the country. God, whomever or whatever that/he is, is somehow over, inside, among, and behind America, not the government, but the fictive person called America. In this way the economy of America is sanctified, transformed from something profane and despised by the faithful, to something loved by the faithful. In this way the so-called separation of church and state in America is a subtle use of religion to legitimize the state. This mechanism is destructive to faithful Christian life and yet it is masochistically supported by many American Christians. For this dichotomization of material and spiritual life leads to a subversion of Christian faith, empowering the state to transform an explicitly transnational faith into a national-statist faith. The fact that money is the most obvious demonstration of this is not accidental. The value of money is based upon trust, upon good faith, and it is the government that serves as the foundation of this faith. Access to livelihood occurs through money. Life is, in many ways, mediated through money. A Christian might pray to God for daily bread, and this prayer is answered by American dollars. To have money is to be blessed, favored, fortunate, and with this money comes social responsibility—stewardship. God has given money to those that deserve it so that those who are incapable of proper financial management may be blessed by those God has blessed, making the philanthropist or steward into a priest in God the Economist's household.

America is but a convenient example of this type of economic subversion of Christian faith. All other nations are likewise guilty, but not with the same blatancy. The British Monarchy still rules "By the grace of God" and this phrase, abbreviated in Latin (Elizabeth II D.G. Reg.), is found on British money. These nations, as with so many other nations, believe that godly or pious relationships can be expressed economically. From those ancients who believed that the king bore the image of God to the people, to the Imperial Cult of Caesar in biblical times, to divine right monarchies, to modern democracies in which the voice of the people is true and powerful, all socioeconomic groups have believed that God, the gods, or whatever super-universal concept is in favor, were implicitly behind just dominion. By this belief it naturally follows that relationships of economy, when properly exercised, represented the divine will for the flourishing of the commonwealth. God, in many ways, is viewed as the divine economist. He is the guarantor and teacher of the almighty "common good," which is synonymous with the commonwealth.

Can we consider God the basis of our economic life? Is God rightly understood as an economist himself?[2] In creation, does God establish an economy, which is then later perverted by sin?[3] An affirmative answer to these questions, though not always made conscious, is a necessary consensus among Christians who believe that proper Christian relations can be expressed economically, whether through just systems or transformation of the system. This chapter shows that God is not properly understood as the basis of economic life, neither in himself, in relation to the creation, or in relation to the human creature. Rather, God's relationship with himself, the creation, and people, is seen to be intimately personal. This relationship that God has with each and every creature is a very similar kind of relationship that humans, in Eden, have with the creation and with God. All of these relationships are considered under the heading of the Creator-creature relationship. This relationship defines what it means to be made in the image of God. But this relationship is not eternal and is lost. This means that creation and Eden cannot form the basis of a Christian ethic, and certainly not of a Christian ethic of economy. Creation and Eden, however, begin a story. It is the beginning of a genealogical story that culminates in Jesus Christ who transforms the image of God into a new kind of relationship: that of a Father to an adopted child who is also an heir to God's kingdom, ruling with him after his character in reconciled relationships.

THE CREATOR

In speaking of creation we must begin, as revelation itself begins, with God. "In the beginning, God made the heavens and the earth." Even though we are respecting the order of the biblical narrative, it is not possible or desirable to be entirely diachronic. We have the full revelation of God in Jesus Christ and this must inform our reading of the entirety of the Bible. Thus, when we speak of God as the Creator we cannot just speak from Genesis 1–2. Nevertheless, it is important to understand that God has revealed himself differently at different points in the narrative.

---

2. So argues Meeks, *God the Economist*.

3. Such a view would follow Walter Wink's perspective on the powers as created by God as good. They then fell, but are redeemable.

Trinity

It is almost trite to begin speaking of God as Trinity in theology today. Often the reason for speaking of God as triune is to underwrite a specific kind of metaphysical cosmology in which plurality and unity are held together without contradiction, thus bringing relationality into the fabric of being. This is not my purpose here. I begin with the Trinity because it is vital to understand the character of this creator God if we are to understand the relational drama in which God is intimately involved. For as we shall see, the events of this relational drama are the very foundation of any and every type of possible economy. Though the Trinity is not revealed in the initial accounts of creation, we know from John and Paul that the Son, the second person of the Trinity, is actively involved in creation. Likewise, by traditional Christian interpretation, the Spirit is present in Genesis 1:2. It is important for the Christian to understand that the triune God is the Creator, not the Father alone: *opera trinitatis ad extra sunt indivisa*.[4] God is not divided against himself in creation. God is not seeking personal expression through material means in order to alleviate a felt lack of self-satisfaction.

The creation does not bear an imprint of God in himself precisely because this relationship is complete, lacking nothing. There are no *vestigia trinitatis*,[5] if for no other reason than the Creator is not ontologically related to his creation, even analogically. This is an important point because the relationship that God does have with the creation is one of choice, not one of necessity. It is a relationship of freedom for God—an expression of character not nature. Likewise, it means that the Creator-creature relationship is not self-love, but a love of nearly innumerable others. In loving his creation, God is not loving himself or a projection of himself, as humans are wont to do. The creation is not brought into the self-relationship of God, nor does the creation transform the self-relationship of God. God's self-love is complete, lacking nothing. Instead the creation, which is to say all individual creatures, exists in unique relationships with God the Creator, not only with the Father, but also with the Son and the Spirit together. This unique relationship is the Creator-creature relationship.

That God is satisfied in his own relationship would seem to mean that his relationship with the creation is magnanimous. Magnanimity is not the grounds for a close personal relationship. It is an aristocratic perspective that fits well an understanding of God as aloof but philanthropic. In himself

---

4. Latin: "the works of the Trinity outside himself are indivisible."

5. Latin: "vestiges of the Trinity." This means that we cannot know anything about God by reference to the creation, especially knowledge of the Trinity. There are no echoes of the divine, or fingerprints of God.

there is no necessary reason for him to continue in relation with his creation. Given the reasonableness of deism, it is conceivable that such a magnanimous and self-satisfied God could create natural laws and economic laws that govern his creation without any need for God to interact beyond the creation event itself. Nevertheless, God chooses to care for each sparrow, to call each person by name, thus showing the interested loving relationship of God for his creatures. It is this relationship that precludes the possibility of an economic relation between God and his creation. Rationally, we ought to expect an economy of relations between God and his creation, both in the sense of a house rule, and in the sense of an efficiency of effort expressed by the creation of natural laws. But this expectation is not met in the pages of Scripture because, as we will see, the purpose of Scripture is not to portray a rational metaphysical being but the relationship God has with his people.

Personal and Known in Relationship

God is personal. That is, God is not to be understood metaphysically, but personally. Instead of listing universal ideas that can be attributed to God, it is far better to speak of the manner in which God has related to his people. Instead of speaking about God *having* ontological *attributes*, it is more accurate to talk about a consistent *character*. This character may be described analogically by appeal to human qualities, but it is important to begin with the consistent person. We must not, however, confuse character and ontology as the Social Trinitarians do. A "relational ontology" is not actually all that distinct from a "substance ontology" insofar as both attempt to identify specific attributes of the being that is God. The relational ontologists propose that the primary ontological quality of God is relationality. This is problematic because relationality is itself a universal rather than a particular. God is not a universal, he does not inhere in any universal, nor is he the fount of all universals. God is fully particular. He is himself and there is none like him.[6] God is not a composite of universal properties in a unique individual, but is a person whose characteristics might be named by evidence in historic interaction. So the Bible does not really discuss immutability, but highlights

---

6. The cry found often in the Old Testament, "Who is like you, O God?" is usually answered by reciting his historic deeds rather than his divine attributes. See Exod 15:11; Deut 33; Pss 35; 71; 113; Isa 44; Mic 7:18. The traditional Jewish song, *Ein Keloheinu* (there is none like our God) similarly sings about God, not for his divine attributes, but as he is related to Israel, as King and Savior: "Ein keloheinu, ein kadoneinu, ein kemalkeinu, ein kemoshieinu" (There is none like our God, there is none like our LORD, there is none like our King, there is none like our Savior). Significantly, this is often sung during the Passover, during which the story of the exodus is recited.

faithfulness to covenantal agreement. What is important about God is not that he is the kind of being who engages in relationships, but that he is a personal God who is in particular relationships with particular people. Relational ontologists are subject to the same problem as substance ontologists—they identify the being of God in order to ground an ethical agenda in onto-theological terms, generally through the concept of the *imago dei*.[7]

Instead of an ontological approach to God, we have a historical approach that understands God, not through universals, but through particular people and relationships that are attested in Scripture. Knowledge of God in himself is not accessible to human minds. One cannot have a perspective God has not given, and one can only have God's perspective by being God. This is the structure of the idea of deification, that one could become ontologically like God and so gain his perspective.

It must be remembered that all ontology begins with us and is only understandable by analogy to ourselves. We simply cannot transcend ourselves to know any being in itself. We always know-as, not just as humans, or as people in a particular social milieu, but as individuals with life stories. God cannot be understood by working upwards from human ontology, for this assumes a deep ontological connection between God and humans that is not justified in Scripture.[8] Nor is human ontology objectively observable, for we are always colored in our perceptions by the cosmos in which we live, and our ontological definitions of humanity are unfailingly self-justificatory. Because of this, identification of divine ontology almost formulaically ends with a moral self-legitimation or condemnation of our evil *du jour*. Because Scripture does not portray God metaphysically and systematically, it follows that God must not be understood economically. He does not live in an economic relationship with himself, his creation, or his creatures. This is a manner of thinking alien and hostile to the Bible, the means by which God has revealed himself.

---

7. Latin: the "image of God."

8. This is especially true when we consider the creation narrative in comparison to other creation stories, especially stories about how humans have come about and what their purpose is. Rather than humans as children or servants of the gods, or as the undesirable offspring of a decomposing god, there is no connection between the body or being of God and that of the man and woman. Instead Genesis 1 makes clear it is by the word, and Genesis 2 by formation of the dust that humans come about, both statements seem to be purposefully avoiding an organic connection to the Creator.

Spirit

God is spirit.[9] That is, God is immaterial, (or invisible to use the New Testament's preferred term), and personal. God is not the universal referent of many particulars, as the analogy from the fiduciarity of money would have us understand. God *reveals* himself, and by this we know that God is not evident. He cannot be found because he is not perceptible to the eye.[10] Because God is spirit, the relationship God has within himself cannot be quantified or turned into a *tertium quid*.[11] That is, in order to quantify something there must be a material referent. But God could not be understood as triune without the incarnation. Without God taking on human flesh there would be no knowledge or the Trinity, for, as we have already affirmed, *opera trinitatis ad extra sunt indivisa*.[12] So when God does reveal himself quantitatively he does so personally, not mediated through objects.

God's self-relationship is noneconomic, either in the sense of being ordered like a household, or in the sense of having a market of exchange. The ordering of the life in the Trinity is not governed by anything external to God himself, by law or by marketplace. The ordering of the Trinity is simply God's own life, self-governed without reference to anything else. Moreover, God's self-relationship is not characterized by any kind of third thing by which exchange is possible, in the fashion of money. Though many have said that the Holy Spirit is the love of God and the relationship between the Father and Son, such a view cannot be entertained here because the Holy Spirit does not represent a market of exchange. Such an analogy of the Spirit as the divine marketplace wherein the Father and Son exchange value is troublesome as it implies self-incompletion, unsatisfied desire, and a divided self, not to mention the depersonalization of the Spirit.

God does not posses value in one person that is lacking in another that might be exchanged for something else. God has no lack, no need, no want, and therefore no exchange. God is triune and is therefore unified in will. Thus, there can be no difference in value between Father and Son and Spirit. Where there is no difference there can be no exchange. Though ontological links between God and humanity are the fodder of all kinds of religion that conveniently base ethics in the imitation of a celestial self-projection, it cannot be said even by those who desire to maintain an *analogia entis*[13]

---

9. John 4:24.
10. John 1:18.
11. Latin: "third thing."
12. Latin: "the works of the Trinity outside himself are indivisible."
13. Latin: "analogy of being."

that human economy is based in the life of God himself; it must be mediated through natural law and is thus created. Spirit does not desire, acquire, trade, buy, or sell material things.

God's external relationships are not economic either. The "economic Trinity" is an infelicitous term used to describe the relationship of God to his creation. For God is neither the household manager of creation, nor is he an objective participant in a market, as is explored in the section below on the creation as not a household. Furthermore, God is not objective, in the sense of relating to other things as a subject to an object. God's perspective of creation and its creatures is not from some distant point from which their essential nature is rendered obvious. If God is personal, he has interested relationships with his creation and creatures. He does not treat his creation and creatures as matters of fact, as a collection of essential and accidental attributes, but as individuals in relationship with him. This type of personal relationship further undermines any notion of God as an economist. For that which is personal has immaterial value: "man looks on the outward appearance, but the LORD looks on the heart."[14] The value of a person to God cannot be created by reference to material concerns, like a person's appearance. God is not a disinterested observer, but an active participant. In consequence of this creation cannot be understood as a resource, as we shall see in the next section on the creation.

Aseity, or Self-Sufficiency

Because God created space and time simultaneously,[15] he is himself outside of both;[16] though he has chosen to act within time and space, as all external relations require space and time. God is *a se*, that is, self-satisfied. He has no external need. This need not be understood as a property of substance, but a description of God's unity of personality. God has no need of projecting himself onto something external by which he can augment himself. As we shall see this is precisely the mechanism that underlies the notion of property. God, because he is self-satisfied, has no property and needs no property. Thus, the aseity of God also means that God is noneconomic. For

---

14. 1 Sam 16:7.

15. "In the beginning, God created the heavens and the earth" and "In the beginning was the Word . . . . All things were made through him." Gen 1:1 and John 1:1–3 both attest this simultaneous beginning of time and matter.

16. Of course space and time have been shown by Einstein to be part of the same system such that space and time are malleable by mass and speed. This only confirms that God must be external to time if he is external to space and vice versa.

without a notion of property, whether private or public, there can be no economy, for there can be no right of exchange without ownership.

The aristocratic notion of self-sufficiency values the perception that one is not a dependent or subordinate and does not suffer want. This occurs by the accumulation of honor, often through wealth, landowning, and patronage. But this self-sufficiency is delusional, built as it is on relationships with others who pay rent and honor. The aseity of God does not come from the honor he has or the apparent wealth of his person. Rather it comes from his existence outside the creation and outside of space and time.

The biblical God is unique in this characteristic among other gods. Other creation narratives portray the gods as desirous of something: of human servants, of sexual relations, of violence. The gods thus impose themselves upon the world, the world often coming from their seed, or the body of a murdered god, or even the emanation of divine mind as in Neoplatonism. Christian perspectives that understand God as the fount of all universals are thereby seen to follow after the Neoplatonic conception of the world, making the world itself a part of divinity, which participates in divinity ontologically. Such understandings of the gods are highly amenable to an economic god, for these are gods who have significant psychological self-dissatisfaction. The creation narrative of Genesis 1–2 gives us no reason for the creation. Genesis 1–2 is profound by what it does not say in contrast to the creation myths of its neighboring cultures, namely, that God does not seek anything or have a motive, an end, or a purpose in creation. The reason for telling the story of creation is entirely different in Genesis than in other myths, for it explains nothing really about contemporary reality. The creation and humanity are not given a God-oriented purpose in creation because God does not need or desire such.

Thus, because God is self-satisfied or complete, he has no resources and no need of resources. When God creates the heavens and the earth he does so *ex nihilo*.[17] Creation has no cost. The resourceless creation means that God is in need of no exchange or purchase. This may all seem rather obvious, but it has not been obvious throughout human history. Other ancient Near Eastern creation myths, and others throughout the world in premonetary societies, cannot conceive of a creation that does not come from some kind of resource, whether it be chaos for the Greeks, or the oceans for the Babylonians. The primordial resource or *chaos,* in its original Greek sense, requires gods who can order this *chaos.* We might, then, speak of the gods as consumer-creators, for they must modify this primordial chaos in order

---

17. Though this point is hotly debated in Gen 1, it is confirmed beyond doubt in the New Testament by Paul in Rom 4:17, and Col 1:15–16, and the author of Hebrews in 11:3.

to create a sensible and livable world. In this sense, the gods are economic beings not unlike their human counterparts. If we move beyond creation to many other myths it quickly becomes evident that the gods lack many things that they desire and that they therefore must barter, purchase, or steal. The triune God of the Bible is one, or unified, and therefore does not enter into these kinds of agreements or undertake secret missions of theft or rape. The biblical God in the creation narrative bears a few similarities to the other gods of premonetary societies but with important differences. He is personal but does not engage in a debtor-creditor relationship with the creation. We shall discuss the covenants of God with people when we discuss reconciliation. As the Creator, however, God does not covenant with his creation, he contracts no obligations.

Work in Creation

Labor or work is the bedrock of economy, for labor is the temporal component of economics that all share. No matter what work one does, it all takes time, and time is what all humans have in common. But labor is not, by necessity, related to economy. Economy transforms work by creating a necessary relationship between access to livelihood and work. Work integrates a person into an economic society by giving them a calling or vocation, a purpose for which the individual is to live and benefit the common good. In this way, work tends to create a functional identity for people. Evidence for this abounds, perhaps nowhere more obvious than in the variety of function- or industry-related surnames, for example: Fletcher, Smith, Cooper, Shepherd, Wagenfuhr.

In creation, God does work. In Genesis 1, the creation of all things is a temporal process, taking place over six days.[18] Each day God creates and organizes his creation in time. But God's labor is not economic activity, nor does his act of creation define *who* God is. Rather, his act of creation reveals that God creates through a kind of work. But this work occupies one week only. It is not ongoing. Creation is finished on the sixth day. Creation is not the regular activity of God, but it is a singular event. In human economies, humans are defined by their work. Work continues endlessly because work defines a person and defines a social group. Time spent that contributes to the Economy is meaningful and valuable time. God does not work for anyone or for the commonwealth. His labor is different from human labor because his work is not instrumental. It is not necessary for livelihood, for

18. Let us bypass all debate on what the six days mean "literally" or "in reality," such debates only detract from constructive theological reflection.

wealth creation, or for self-identity. His work in creation is gracious and gratuitous, as God is not its beneficiary. Creation is not a philanthropic work designed to bring God glory, honor, and praise from creatures made specifically for this purpose. Genesis 1–2 is highly significant in its silence on any religious matter whatever. It contains no notion of prayer, worship, sacrifice, priesthood, temple,[19] or ceremony. God did not create a creation to satisfy a narcissism that needs praise. So, although God is known by his work, he is not his work. God is known by his creatures as the Creator, but his whole character is not comprehended in this action.

Restful after Creation

God's labor is not eternal. On the seventh day God rested. We have already said how God does not need to create and thus the title Creator does not identify him in totality. God's rest confirms this. By finishing his work as Creator, God in history is no longer actively creating. God interacts with creation thereafter in a different capacity: as Judge, as Reconciler, and as New Creator. This is not a different God who performs these different roles in history, but it is the same God, revealed in different ways to different historical circumstances.

The rest of God is not an admission that creation was hard work for God. This is not the rest of a tired laborer, but the rest of one who enjoys the fruit of his labor. The rest of God confirms his freedom from the creation at the same time it confirms his commitment to his creation. In this way, God at rest is God in relationship to the creation without a function. That is, God at rest is God in himself. But God in himself is, after creation, God in relation to the creation. Karl Barth explains this point well:

> When is He God more truly, or more perfectly Himself in the whole course of creation, than in this rest on the seventh day? Here it is revealed unequivocally that His work cannot have any

---

19. This point is contested. John Walton argues that Genesis 1–2 describes a "cosmic temple." But this is a highly problematic reading, not just for textual reasons, but also for theological reasons. My reasons for disagreeing on this point are far too numerous to elucidate here. (See my blog for a fuller attempted refutation of the idea: http://gpwagenfuhr.com/blog/2016/1/7/the-problem-of-the-cosmic-temple.) Suffice it to say that a temple is sacred space, but the sacred as a concept necessarily implies mediation of uncleanness, whether this be moral or, as Walton must mean, ontological. But for God and his unspoilt creation to require mediation means that creation is not actually good, but is an admixture of good and evil that requires ordering through religious structures. Eden is not a cosmic temple, but a royal garden, which is what the Greek term "Paradise" meant in its original Persian sense. See Walton, *Lost World of Genesis One*.

claim on Him or violate Him; that as the Creator He is always His own Lord, the One who is free and the One who loves, and in both cases God; that precisely as the Creator He has confirmed and revealed Himself as His own Lord, as the One who is free and the One who loves, as God.[20]

If God is most truly himself in his rest, this speaks volumes about God's noneconomic relationship to himself and to his creation. People in economic relationships are transformed into use value, or even in more extreme cases, like slavery or contracted athletes, transformed into exchange value. The concept of being who one is at rest prevents this kind of economic conception of a person.

Furthermore, God himself does not view his creation economically, because he is content to rest. Creation does not need continual refinement or improvement. It is not a product that needs ever new iterations to retain a competitive advantage. Nor is the creation like a cultivated field, which has work in season and rest out of season, and which needs continual maintenance and improvement. Creation is finished: "And on the seventh day God finished his work that he had done."[21] Many theologians miss this concept of a finished creation. M. Douglas Meeks is one example, following the common mythical tradition of viewing chaos as a force against which God/the gods and humans must continually strive. Meeks says,

> Creation is no easy victory. Those who see God's work against death in purely effortless terms are already submitting the biblical narrative to ideological use. . . . Nothing in creation is yet completely safe from death, the last and greatest enemy of God's household. God's work of creation continues every moment in God's liberating struggle against the power of death.[22]

This perspective, at once naïve that there is no neutral or pre-ideological reading of Scripture, also slavishly follows the ancient Near Eastern mythological tradition rather than closely reading about the dramatic differences between the Genesis narrative and its Near Eastern cousins. The biblical God is not fighting Mot, a rival god of death. On the common mythical view, God is in engaged in *Chaoskampf*[23] and the victor is as yet uncertain. *Chaoskampf*, like concepts of total war, allows for no rest until total victory is secure. Neither nothingness, *nihil*, nor chaos is the antagonist of God.

20. Barth, *CD*, III.1, 215.
21. Gen 2:2.
22. Meeks, *God the Economist*, 148–49.
23. German: "chaos war."

Such notions are metaphysical rather than relational. Human estrangement is God's antagonist in the story of reconciliation. In Genesis 1–2 there is no antagonist. There is no evil. Indeed, as we shall see, evil is a human creation. It does not preexist humans. God can rest from his finished work of creation because his act of creation is not a battle against nothingness or chaos. It is no battle at all.

Thus, once again we see that God is not properly understood as an economist or household manager because his act of creation is not an ordering of chaos, nor an overcoming of an antagonist. God's creation is, as we have said, free. It costs no resource and destroys nothing. God is not creating wealth, use value, or exchange value. The completion of creation thus signifies a change in God's relationship with the creation. He remains its Creator, but by the ever forward motion of history, this increasingly becomes a past event with no reenactment through religious ceremony or festival.[24]

THE CREATOR AND THE CREATION

We have seen how God in his self-relation and his work is not economic. We turn now to examine how God's relationship with his creation is not economic. The work of God in creation is one free action of God, not a function of his essence. An economic understanding of God instrumentalizes God, making God himself a means of production. If "Creator" were the whole of God's character, we would be right in thinking that God, for us, exists only for the purpose of being a first cause and nothing further. The economic or instrumental God is a God *pro nobis*, but this for-us-ness is limited to the establishment and maintenance of an order in which profane and mundane human economic life can occur.

Creation is Not a Household/Economy and God is Not Its Father/Economist

There is little more self-justificatory than an instrumental God who exists for us as the basis of our economic life. This structure of justification permits no critique of economic life. If in his being or in his relationship with the creation God is economic then it would follow that human economy, as economy, is like God's. Such a view is espoused by some Christian

---

24. Mircea Eliade and others have argued that many religious festivals represent the active participation in the creation of the universe. For the ancients, the cosmos is the year. Space and time are not distinct, and because time is cyclical, so too is the cosmos. See Eliade, *Sacred and the Profane*, and Caillois, *Man and the Sacred*.

supporters of capitalism in claiming that the Creator God left creation unperfected so that humans could exercise their creativity and entrepreneurial spirit in developing creation to a measure more in line with its potential.[25] The purpose of creation, on such a view, is to be the clay from which human potters make the creation into something useful and meaningful. God, on this view, makes materials and resources in their raw or rude state, waiting for humans to complete what he left in a state of potentiality. This capitalist divine economy recalls Aristotle's explanation of nature giving all things to humanity. Progress becomes an end in itself, production a means to further production. Wealth, on this view, is good. It is made in potentiality by God, and is justly wrought out of the creation. God is fully behind capitalism on such a view, indeed, capitalist development/exploitation is the created purpose of human beings.

But a similarly self-justificatory view is also espoused by Christian critics of capitalism who appeal to different attributes of God for the foundation of a proper economy. By understanding God as an economist through a kind of fatherhood over all creation, God's revealed work is thus an ordering of the created household. In this way economy is itself reconfirmed, though capitalism may thereby be rendered highly suspect.[26] That is, if God is the father of creation, he has ordained a certain just socioeconomic order of creation wherein the communist maxim, "To each according to his needs," is satisfied. But God cannot be understood as the father of creation, as the household manager or servant who properly orders the creation-cum-household.

Creation is not a household because it is not intrinsically related to God. This is why it was important to discuss the aseity of God above. The transcendent God does not lose his aseity by creation, and thus he cannot be understood as the *pater familias*, or head of household. The head of a household must be understood not only as head in terms of authority and responsibility, but also in terms of representation. God is not representative of his creation, for this would require that the creation be made genetically from God. Creation *ex nihilo* means that creation is not godlike. Creation is not passively related to God, rather God is *actively in relation* to his creation. This is an important distinction. God's relation to his creation is an act of choice, not one of nature, necessity, or obligation. The relationship exists on God's volitional terms. A head of household, on the other hand, is legally and morally bound for the provision of his dependents.

---

25. Novak, *Spirit of Democratic Capitalism*, 39.
26. This is a summary of the argument of Meeks, *God the Economist*.

God's fatherhood exists only within himself, as the Father is father of the Son. The Son is the only begotten of the Father. Creation is not begotten; it is made. God is Father of people, not through nature or creation, but through adoption by reconciliation in Christ. Adoption is a political or legal concept, not a generative concept. For God to be understood as the father, or head of household of creation is to resexualize the act of creation and thus make creation have an ontological connection to God. God once again becomes his work, and this work must become decidedly sexual.

Creation Is Not Property

Creation is not related to God as property to an owner. The act of creation is not owned labor. It is not work that belongs to another or done for the sake of another. God's relationship with the creation is not one of master-slave, or of householder-house. The master or householder in this analogy would be dependent upon the creation for his identity, and thus would not be a free self-satisfied and self-defined personal God, but a codependent alienated from himself to the creation. The householder is such because he owns and operates a household. That is, he owns "improved" property within which a family or group of people live out their lives. God is not who he is because of the creation. Property ownership changes both the owner and the property because each now attains a new identity dependent on the other. The future of each is bound up with the other. The owner plans for developing a property, thus tying in his personal financial future with the success or failure of this venture. The owner, just as in Hegel's master-slave dialectic, is also owned in the act of owning. God, however, remains formally independent of his creation. As a changeless person[27] God is not subjected to the changes that his creation undergoes. Unlike an owner or householder who is devastated by a natural disaster, God does not undergo a transformation by the devastation of his creation by his human creatures. Rather, as the creation undergoes the transformation into cosmos, God reveals himself in a different light, as the Reconciler, which I will discuss in detail later. In all this we

---

27. Heb 13:8. Though this text, and others like it, are generally assumed to be an ontological statement of God's eternality or atemporality, it seems more likely that they refer to the steadfastness of God's covenant commitments to his people. Nevertheless, these are not totally dissimilar. As a steadfast person with an unchangeable will God is a reliable covenant keeper. His unchanging will or personality means he is unswayed by the vicissitudes of time and space. So, even if these verses are not to be understood as giving a traditional theistic divine attribute, they do achieve a highly similar result. God's personality is changeless. He is the Alpha and Omega, and does not go on a journey of self-discovery there between.

can again see the dissimilarity of God and the economic relationship. God is not properly understood as an economist: either as a household manager, or as a wealth creator.

Creation Is Not a Resource

Creation cannot be understood as a resource or collection of resources. We have already discussed how the creation is not a resource to God in the act of creation, as chaos is to the Greek gods, but here we must consider that God has not created an impersonal world of things with use value. We saw that Aristotle claims in his *Politics* that the world is created by nature for humanity.[28] The purpose of animal life, domestic and wild, is for the benefit of human beings, thus transforming all of nature into use value. In regard to economy, at least, Aristotle is willing to speak of a thing's purpose as rooted in humanity's use of the thing, for it is only humans that are able to give meaning to a thing. The economic relationship cannot conceive that a thing does not either have use value or have exchange value, because all things must exist for humans to give them meaning.

In modern society this is readily apparent, though sometimes challenged by environmentalists. In the USA, its Forest Service is part of its Department of Agriculture. Those who manage the forests answer, at least financially, to those whose chief role is to guard the interests of land production for human, or at least American, consumption. Hence the Forest Service's motto for its forests is "The Land of Many Uses." By the *Wilderness Act of 1964* we might observe a movement against seeing natural land through the economic lens of use value. But even in this act we see the interest in preserving such areas is still understood through use value categories. The document states that "it is hereby declared to be the policy of the Congress to secure *for the American people* of present and future generations the benefits of an enduring *resource* of wilderness."[29] It is ironic that land set apart for apparently noneconomic use is itself only conceivable in economic terms. This speaks volumes about how fundamental the economic relation is in Aristotle and to modern people.

The creation is not given to humanity to be given meaning by human usage of it. The creation is given meaning by its relation to the Creator, not by its relation to the human creature. The meaning of creation is found in God, not because God imbues the creation with meaning, but because it is only in approaching creation mediated by God that one can know it as

28. *Politics* 1256b. See chapter 2 of this work on Aristotle.
29. Wilderness Act of 1964, Pub. L. No. 88–577, 78 Stat. 891 (1964). Italics mine.

creation rather than chaos or cosmos. That is, the very notion of creation implies Creator. Cosmos may be uncreated, it may exist in an eternal cycle, it may be the product of the big bang, but it does not necessarily imply a Creator.

But God is not the source of meaning in his being, as though he is a fount of meaning that imbues all things with meaning, which spring from his fecund waters. Rather, all true meaning comes through a living and active relationship with God. Things have no meaning in and of themselves, they have meaning in relation. Creation only has meaning by being in relation to the Creator. And this means that the things of creation are not things-in-themselves known objectively by the Creator, but are each personally related to the Creator who knows them personally. This is made evident by the teaching of Jesus: "Are not five sparrows sold for two coppers? Yet not one of them is forgotten before God."[30] God does not create species or universal categories, he creates individual creatures. Though the causality of such an arrangement is very difficult to understand, God chooses to be related to each individual. God, of course, creates processes of generation. In this way God does not treat his creation as an object or resource. Rather, everything is personal to God, for of all things that have been created, they have been created by God.[31] Because of this personal relationship with the creation, everything has personal value to God, not economic value.

If the creation is not resource for use or exchange value, this also means that it cannot properly be understood as material. *Material* or *matter* comes from the Latin for *timber* or *substance*.[32] Matter, as originally understood, is understood as use value. Something is matter if it is useful for production. A tree is not material until it becomes timber.[33] In our postmonetary technical age all things have become means to the end of further means, as Jacques Ellul argues.[34] For people who live in this technical cosmos, use value has its purpose not so much in livelihood, or even in exchange value, but in further use value. A thing is only meaningful insofar as it is useful for participation in the global, technical, social life, and it is useful only if it can be further used to make means of production (not necessarily industrial production).

---

30. Luke 12:6.

31. John 1:3.

32. *Materia* (timber for building) was distinguished from *lignum* (firewood), Wilson, "Raw Materials," 139.

33. Of course etymologies are not sure sources of meaning today, but they do indicate the development of ideas.

34. Ellul, *Technological Society*, 19.

A thing is meaningful, then, only when it provides a surplus of use value that can be reinvested to create further use value.[35]

We do not live in a totally capitalist world whose sole interest is exchange value. As Ellul explains, the Marxist notion of commodification is no longer entirely apt.[36] Use value has not been totally eclipsed by exchange value. Rather, our understanding of use value has been transformed by the creation of an ever increasing baseline of technological integration for participation in social life. In order to have access to full social life it is no longer a question merely of sufficient capital, or of owning the means of production, it is a question of having the capability of engaging with the technical world through technical know-how and access to technology. For example, it is not enough to have a large surplus of capital to be influential in society, one must also know how to manipulate public opinion through image crafting in mass and social media. The wealthiest people in the world are not only those who are solely in the wealth-creation business, but those who enable the global system of technological life to thrive and progress. All this to say, what gives meaning to a thing in our cosmos is its use value, a use value that is no longer limited to food, water, clothing, shelter, or means of production. To say that the creation cannot be understood as use value is to describe a radically different world than the one in which we live now and indeed, as we will see, we no longer live in God's creation.

The Abundant Creation

Many Christian theologians interested in economy rightly point out that God has not created a world of scarcity, but one of abundance.[37] Scarcity should not be understood as a quantity of resource, but as a kind of relationship qualified by competition, mimetic rivalry, and thus a psychological feeling of lack or want. Scarcity is not so much about limited supply as it is about unlimited demand, which we saw was the fruit of the development of money. By understanding scarcity to exist on the supply side we project our

---

35. As a side note here, the importance of recycling in the technical milieu is less about satisfying conscience, but about the addition of further value to a consumable good. Recycling has become something of a religious idea precisely because it transforms waste into means of production. Were waste and sustainability really the motivating force behind recycling, it would be far simpler to reduce consumption. But a reduction in consumption is inconceivable to most, and is economically deleterious to our present system.

36. Ellul, *Technological System*, 12.

37. Meeks, *God the Economist*, 170–77; Bell, *Economy of Desire*, 178–81.

inability to be satisfied onto the world itself, thereby removing any need for personal discipline or development and requiring technological progress.

The creation itself, then, is not the source of scarcity. Because creation, as creation, is not a resource, it cannot be understood in terms of scarcity. This is not to avoid problems of scarcity—poverty, starvation, lack of water—that exist in our contemporary world, which will be discussed later. We do not live in the same world that the ancients did, nor in God's creation. Here resource scarcity is a serious and highly complex problem that is bound up with far more than ethical issues. And here is where the division between creation and cosmos must be given in the strongest possible terms. The development of human civilization does not occur within God's abundant creation, not because the world itself has undergone massive alteration, but because the relationship of the Creator to his creation has been broken by humans. Humans, with unquenchable thirst for resources, reconceptualize the creation as a container of resources given to humans for human use and consumption. Scarcity is a result of sin—not so much because sin has caused an ontological change in the world—but because sin transforms the human relationship with the creation from one of grace to one of domination and exploitation.

Creation is abundant because its relationship with the Creator is living and active. Its abundance rests upon the grace of God who transformed that which was *tohu vabohu* or formless and void,[38] into a place full of life and fruit. It is not the creation itself that is characterized by abundance, but the relationship between the creation and the Creator. Creation is rich because it is creation, that is, it is personally involved with God. God blesses his creation[39] and it is this blessing that is the source of richness. This blessing that will be transformed in Genesis 3, but that is yet to come.

Conclusion

We have seen that the creation cannot be understood as economic, in either sense of the term we have been using. It is not the household of God

---

38. The Hebrew term here suggests not chaos like the Greeks and others understood, but wasteland. The scene is one of a desert or Middle Eastern wasteland and an ocean. It is a place without life, but not a place without God. The wilderness is not evil, not a chaos monster to be tamed and fashioned into cosmos, but a place over which the Spirit of God hovers. The wilderness is a place in which cosmos is most thin, most permeable, most transparent. Consequently, the wilderness is most often the place where God reveals himself, where his people must go for testing and refinement, where Jesus is tested.

39. Gen 1:22, 28.

who is its manager or steward. Nor is it a resource or marketplace that is conceivable in terms of either use value or exchange value. Creation does not exist in an economic relationship with God, with itself, or with humans. The meaning of creation comes by its relationship with the Creator who does not own the creation, nor treats it as a material resource. Thus, creation cannot be understood as a place of scarcity, but a place of abundance, not a place of abundant resources, but a place without a conception of resource. It remains for us to now consider human creatures and whether or not they exist in an economic relationship in creation.

THE CREATOR AND THE HUMAN CREATURE

The *imago dei* is perhaps one of the more diverse concepts in theological history. Many theological anthropologies are based on two verses: Genesis 1:26–27. It is rather telling that so much is made of these concise passages. There is a powerful human desire to be found to be like God or the gods, for in being like God there is implicit self-justification. Thus, it behooves us to look at any concept of the image of God with a critical eye, looking for the telltale signs of self or situational legitimation by the forging of a necessary link between God and man. Human nature or essence is never a justification in the sight of God, for justification comes by the alien righteousness of a relationship and thus cannot be delivered by an inherent quality.

The image of God ought to be understood as a relational, not an ontological concept. The image of God does not refer to one or another identifiable aspect of human nature that is analogical to the being of God. To read Genesis ontologically is anachronistic. Rather, the most immediate meaning of the image of God, found in Genesis 1:26–27, is the one unique command God gives to humans in Genesis 1, to rule over the creation. His command to be fruitful and multiply is held in common with the other animals and thus cannot be unique to the image of God. Dominion, then, is the image of God. As many scholars have noted, in ancient Near Eastern societies the king was the representative of the gods on earth.[40] This is actually not a feature unique to the ancient Near Eastern context, but is a fairly universal trait of monarchies,[41] even into the divine right monarchies of eighteenth century in Europe. But Genesis 1, as Genesis 1–11 does in nearly every detail, plays upon these commonly held beliefs and masterfully subverts them by slight modification. Whereas the monarch was the representative of the gods on earth, the Hebrew Scriptures universalize this to all people, thus

---

40. Caillois, *Man and the Sacred*, 91; Eliade, *History of Religious Ideas*, 61.
41. See Caillois, *Man and the Sacred*, 89.

effectively severing any hierarchical link between special people and God. Furthermore, whereas a king might be the representative of the gods in a genetic sense, such that birthright conveys this representation to the next generation, the image of God in Scripture is a relationship that exists by divine will, not by human species right.

The image of God is best understood as a royal charter. That is, the image of God is analogous to a political document legitimizing the vicegerency of people. A vice*gerent* is a person who has delegated authority from a sovereign, whereas the oft-confused vice-*regent* is a person who replaces the monarch due to absence or incapacity of rulership. The former is the more correct to use of human responsibility in Scripture. This charter has no necessary connection with the nature of humanity. Genesis 1:29–30 confirms this, as the provision of God is not given in respect of human *being* or human dignity, but as a divine gift, as grace, as a donation. As such, God is well within his rights and in no way violating human nature by the confiscation of his legitimation of human vicegerency.

The royal charter, then, is a political contract, a treaty, a writ of authority. It in no way reduces the responsibility of God but includes humans within his government of creation. This human participation in the divine government has important implications for the human relationship to the creation. Rather than being dominated by a fear of our contemporary zeitgeist in which the words "dominion," "authority," and "rule" cause embarrassment, Genesis 1:26–27 must be allowed to speak boldly of true authority because of the character of this authority. Dominion does not here mean a type of authority that exists through fear, coercion, or exploitation. Rather, the authority of the royal charter requires that each person act in keeping with the character of the Creator. The Creator is concerned for his creation at a deeply personal level. He cares for each individual creature, not treating them as species or as resources. Likewise, the image of God must have a similar, personal relationship with the creation. This means that human individuals would have ruled over only that with which they could possibly have had a personal relationship. This image of God would thereby be unable to systematically or objectively rule over a totality of creation. This is localized and personal influence, influence that is limited by the space and time in which an individual can move and have meaningfully personal relations.

The image of God in representing the person of God to the creation would not have treated the creation as a resource for personal gain or profit. As the Creator has a personal relationship with his creation on an individual level, the creation cannot be depersonalized. The notion of creation prevents its own commodification. The creation is not a collection of species, minerals, precious metals, and raw, untapped resources. Such a notion might lead to a critique of capitalism, but such a critique would be overly narrow, for it must be a critique of all depersonalized approaches to the world. Indeed, the very notion of "world" or "universe," of an all-encompassing impersonal universal category is foreign to the notion of a Creator and systematically militates against the creation by actively divorcing it from its Creator.

The image of God is a relationship of the human creature with the creation. It is a special and privileged position, but it is not thereby an independent rule, or even a rule focused on serving the gods. Rather, it is a political role of a personal sort. It is not an economic rule. The image of God is not well represented by the term *steward* because the creation is not in need of resource management. It does not need to be guided to its highest and best use through development. Rather, it is ruled over. It is dominated by humans with a domination that images the relationship the Creator has with the creation. The image of God, then, personalizes all things, not by pretending they are living beings with personalities, but by caring for them as the Creator cares for each sparrow. Economy, therefore, is antithetical to the image of God relationship, for economy possesses, universalizes, objectifies, and transforms what is personal into material value.

This is a somewhat different proposal to that of Martin Buber who conceives of all relations in terms of I-It or I-Thou.[42] For Buber, all things should be approached as in an I-Thou relationship. This personalizes all relationships, removing the possibility of turning things and people into objects, but understanding them as subjects. Inanimate objects, then, are treated as Thou by Buber and God is, of course, the eternal Thou. But Buber's laudable endeavor does not adequately consider the problem of mediation in relationships. To make all relationships I-Thou projects personality onto objects that have none with the possibility that the I creates the Thou. All relationships exist through mediation of various and many kinds. Language is one of the most essential mediators, but not the sole mediator. The character of mediation places an indelible mark on a relationship, forming and transforming the relationship entirely. Thus, money transforms personal relationships into economic relationships. But mediation, in our experience, tends to be self-concealing, so that relationships seem immediate. We do not normally reflect on how money or technology forms our relationships, these are more infrequent thoughts. For Adam and Eve, all relationships were personal, not because they inhere in a universal of personhood, nor because God is in them, but because the primary and immediate

---

42. Buber, *I and Thou*.

relationship is between the image of God and God himself. And it is this personal relationship with God that personalizes or individualizes each and every relationship.

Mediation and the Epistemology of the *Imago Dei*

The Creator-creature relationship is personal and immediate. That is, the Creator and creature live together without the intervention of angels, saviors, prayer, worship, sacrifice, ceremony, government, priesthood, or any other kind of intermediary. The immediacy of this relationship therefore mediates all other relationships, especially the relationship between the human and the other creatures. Indeed, sense perception of what would now be called material reality would have been mediated through the Creator-creature relationship in Eden. Beginning with the pre-Socratics, who referred to money to help form their distinction between seeming and reality, through Descartes, and culminating in Kant's transcendental turn, the challenge to the immediacy of sense perception has transformed epistemological reflection ever since. The linguistic turn of twentieth-century philosophy has continued in this tradition of further critically questioning the immediacy and construction of the perceptible world. What these philosophers have recognized is that our understanding of what we experience is not some kind of neutral reality. There is some kind of mediation between our perception of "reality" and some kind of reality in and of itself. Instead of identifying this as a problem that might be attributed to the traditional doctrine of the Fall wherein human reason has been touched or corrupted, it is far better to acknowledge that mediation between perception and understanding has always existed, even in Eden.

The immediacy of the Creator-creature relationship causes all other relationships to be mediate. This does not mean that Adam and Eve somehow had access to the exact thoughts of God, who would be considered the objective truth. God is not objective, as we have already discussed. What Adam and Eve had in the Creator-creature relationship was access to the creation as the image of God—benevolently ruling over it by a delegated authority. Epistemologically this means that there was a human-creation relationship moderately independent of active intervention of the Creator, but with constant and necessary dependence on the personal character of the Creator. There would be no knowledge of a "thing," but of a thing in relation to the Creator, over which the man and woman had dominion.

We might say that humans in the Creator-creature relationship interact with the material world spiritually.[43] God is spirit and the human relationship with God is therefore a spiritual relationship, even though it is also manifest in material reality. This is a spiritual epistemology, one that joyfully acknowledges a spiritual mediation of material reality without thereby populating the material reality with spirits. It is not a spiritualization of the material as paganism tends toward, nor a denigration of the material for the spiritual as in Platonism, nor is this an assumption of the spiritual into the material as in our postmonetary and technological cosmos. This is not a spiritualism, but mediation of the material through the primacy of a spiritual relationship with the Creator of all material reality. This primary spiritual relationship is not an ill-defined Schleiermacherian feeling of absolute dependence, nor the "creature-feeling" of Rudolf Otto. It is not Eliade's "hierophany." Whereas these have concentrated their attention on religious feeling and experience of a wholly other as punctuating mundane or profane reality, the Creator-creature relationship prevents any bifurcation of reality into sacred and profane. This relationship is primary and therefore is not a kind of theophany or hierophany, but the basis from which the phenomenal is understood. The material is inextricably linked to the spiritual as the material is entirely dependent upon the spiritual. The spiritual does not punctuate experience with miracles and wonders, it forms the basis of material experience. That is to say that the creation is dependent upon the Creator, and the structure of the human mind in the garden was founded upon this relationship.

The economic importance of epistemology cannot be underestimated. Economy is, we might say, a category of epistemology. It is a way of looking at the world, a means of transforming sense perception into a type of reality. Economy is based upon an epistemology that believes that sense perception is immediate and that all significance must thereby be expressed in terms of material quantity. Economy is founded upon the expression of spiritual value materially. The garden of Eden is a story that narrates a pre-economic situation and thus an alternative epistemology. To this narrative we turn, bringing the Creator, creation, and creature together into one place.

---

43. "Spiritual" is a difficult term to define and has a wide variety of meanings in different groups. What I mean by spiritual is that which pertains to God who is spirit, i.e., immaterial, pre-material, and pretemporal.

EDEN: THE CREATOR-CREATURE-CREATION "ECONOMY"

Genesis as Genealogy and Ethical Implications of the Genre

The garden of Eden is a story with powerful theological meaning, but we must understand its genre in order to understand its message. The book of Genesis is a genealogy. It not only contains many lists of descendants, but is itself structured in the form of a genealogy with the narrative compressed and expanded for various generations. The book of Genesis is divided by a specific phrase, "These are the generations of . . . ." This formula introduces stories of a patriarch and his descendants. This division occurs ten times[44] in Genesis and is meant to highlight an important patriarch amidst the whole catalogue of descendants. Such a format means that Genesis 1 is an introduction to a genealogy. Creation sets the stage for a family story to unfold. The first of these divisions begins in Genesis 2:4, which begins the second narrative of creation. This second creation account is intensely personal, rather than the transcendent perspective of Genesis 1. This creation account begins with God and one man, Adam, in a location suitable for their interaction. Eden ought not be understood as a cosmic temple,[45] but as a royal residence in which humans can suitably be the image of God. It is a place in which there is abundance, in which the creation freely submits to the dominion of the image of God.[46] It is not a paradise in the sense of a place in which all imaginable pleasures are satisfied: such is fairy tale. Rather, Eden is a milieu in which Creator-creature-creation relationships might be exercised.

Eden, then, serves as a place in which the proper state of affairs of *creation* exist. Whether or not it actually existed is irrelevant to our purposes. Rather, what the story says about economy is our task to investigate. Eden is an important story to understand in terms of economy because it is presented as both a real place and a real part of a genealogy with real people, and as an irretrievably lost place, actively hidden and guarded by God from the intrusion of people. It is a place one cannot approach.[47] It thus does not admit of imitation. We cannot recreate Eden. It is not a cosmological myth

---

44. The actual phrase אֵלֶּה תוֹלְדֹת (*eleh toledoth*) is used twelve or thirteen times, depending on whether one includes Gen 5:1. However, a few of these cases involve repetition or parallelism and thus should not be considered as separate instances.

45. Contra Walton, *Lost World of Genesis One*.

46. So, the animals parade before Adam in order to receive a name and be tested for suitable companionship. See Gen 2:19–20.

47. Gen 3:24.

reenacted by religious ceremony.[48] Eden explains the type of relationship and situation that is lost. But it is not thereby the foundation of any kind of Christian ethic. A true Christian ethic must be based in Christ and in eschatology, not in archaeology. This forward-looking conception of history is even present in Eden, as we shall see with the concept of the Sabbath.

The genre of genealogy fits quite well this unidirectional history. By following a family history through many generations we see the connection between father and son, especially in the vignettes of Lamech and Enoch in the seventh generation of Cain and Seth (Gen 4:19–26). Patterns of behavior are magnified and the inventions of the father are perfected by his sons. Cain fears vengeance for murder; Lamech takes vengeance and murders. Cain builds a city; his descendants perfect city and empire. Each individual is different, but is still heir to a tradition. Thus, what begins in Eden has repercussions throughout history. It is not a land beyond the mist-shrouded mountains, but a place wherein a family began; a place where what was became what could have been. Eden is a story of great potential and great loss, but time moves forward and so does the story.

The tradition that has arranged Scripture in this way has done wisely. For Genesis is the beginning of a family that, according to the New Testament, comes to its fullness and completion in Jesus Christ who is both an actual heir of the promises of God to the people of Israel, but is also the head of Israel, who forever changes its history by transforming genealogy. Matthew and Luke trace the genealogy of Jesus. Matthew returns to Abraham and David, emphasizing the family connection with the great patriarch and the great king. Luke traces Jesus to Adam himself, connecting Jesus with the first man and thus implicitly making a statement about Jesus as an Adamic figure, perhaps not so far from Paul's own concept of Jesus as the second Adam.[49] The importance of the genealogies is not really to legitimize Jesus, or even to connect him with this or that famous figure of the Hebrew Scriptures. Rather, these genealogies continue the family story of God's people by transforming genealogy entirely. Instead of flesh and blood, genealogy is made by reference to election and righteousness by covenantal faithfulness.[50] Jesus is God revealed as Reconciler. And as we shall see in due course, a Christian ethic of economy must be based in the current work of God the Reconciler, not the completed and effaced work of creation.

48. The Babylonian/Sumerian myths, which were likely known to the author of Genesis due to thematic similarities views the New Year as an annual re-creation of the cosmos from chaos in which the *akitu* festival brings in the people as participants in the cosmogony. See Eliade, *Sacred and the Profane*, 77.

49. 1 Cor 15.

50. Rom 9.

Eden is not a model of economy, but it is not thereby rendered meaningless. Eden is vitally important, for reconciliation is unintelligible without a broken relationship. The story of Adam and Eve is for the purpose of telling the story of reconciliation that leads to new creation. Eden is the prehistory, the introduction,to the story of reconciliation. Thus, Eden is a crucial situation when we consider economy, for it establishes a beginning and a direction. It establishes relationships that shed light on the problems of our own lives east of Eden.

Work and Reward

The story of Eden has usually been understood as a kind of golden age. In this way it fulfills a common economic escapist need through mythical structuring. The golden age, as Roger Caillois describes, is mythical time. It is a time apart from daily life, and thus it represents all that is different from and better than daily mundane reality:

> Man looks nostalgically toward a world in which all he has to do to pick luscious and ever-ripe fruits is merely to reach out his hand; a world in which obliging crops are stored in his barn without working, planting, or harvesting; a world that does not know the hard necessity of labor; in which desires are realized as soon as conceived.... Lastly, it seems like a time of idleness, abandon, and prodigality, for the return of which man vainly hopes while seeing himself condemned to work, penury, and frugality.[51]

Such a golden age is the imagining of a life is consumed by economic concerns. It is the paradise of a people alienated to their subsistence livelihood. Such a utopia is not quite the equivalent of folk utopias like the medieval Cockaigne/Lubberland or the hobo's Big Rock Candy Mountains, which are characterized by the smallness of their desires, that is, the satisfaction of any physical desire without work. The ancient golden age is intimately bound up with chaos and cosmogony, thus forming a mythically constructed reality that at least understands the fearful darkness of such limitless possibility. Cronus eats his children and the world is full of monsters. What folk utopias have in common with the ancient golden age is their disconnection of the link between work and survival or reward. The golden age and folk utopia are worlds in which rewards are given for no work, much

---

51. Caillois, *Man and the Sacred*, 105–6.

like the expression of desire revealed by the ancient phenomenon of magic and the modern dream of technology as the liberator of humans from work.

Is Eden just another wish projection that breaks the link between work and reward? No, a close reading of the Eden in Genesis is actually rather far removed from such a golden age. On the one hand, the ancient religious notion of the golden age is one wherein limitless possibilities lead not only to gloriously playful images, but also terrifying abominations existing in an ambiguous but strong relationship. The golden age is a time of disorder and possibilities of *all* kinds imaginable. Genesis 1–3, rather surprisingly, contains no monsters, no cosmic battle, and no evil gods, quite unlike its neighboring civilizations' cosmogonies. Eden is not a story of the removal of onerous mundane obligations and the satisfaction of pleasure without work. Eden is a place of abundance that is disconnected from work. But it is also a place of work. Eden is not a story in which we can fairly easily trace imaginative forays into all manner of possibilities when religious, social, physical, and economic rules are broken. During the golden age, "The entire universe was plastic, fluid, and inexhaustible."[52] The golden age tends to be conflated with formless chaos. Eden is not such a world. It is highly ordered and obedient to God and his image. Human wish projection tends to construct a positive world out of negations of the limitations or restrictions of the present world. Eden is a positive world, not a negation of contemporary restrictions. As an expression of desire, it might express a religious desire for communion with God. But this communion is not familial, nor is the *imago dei* self-justificatory. As a noneconomic world it is not understood as one full of luxury and resources, but one of subsistence. It is not a world of a magic that cuts through the boundaries of the work-reward relationship by means of incantation or ritual. Though much more could be said about this, it does seem quite evident that Eden, not the Eden of tradition, but the Eden of Genesis, lacks many or most of the expected signs of wish projection for the elimination of the work-reward relationship.

As we saw, God created a graceful abundance, not scarcity. Yet, even in this situation of grace the man is given work. The garden is not a bastion of order in the midst of rebellious chaos that must be tamed. It is not a defensive position in which the man and the woman serve in the watchtower. Thus, "to keep," "to have charge of," is a better image of the task here. Indeed, one might go so far as to compare this with a shepherd's work of "tending." Though the man is not keeping flocks, he is imposing his will upon the garden, working it into something it would not be without his intervention. This is simply the fulfillment of the divine mandate of Genesis 1:28 and it

---

52. Ibid., 104.

demonstrates the kind of dominion implied in that command, one of the benevolence of a shepherd.

The man is also tasked with working the soil. God has made the man into a gardener of the garden. This must not be understood as the sanctification of human work, as though work is itself blessed because God gave to the man this task. Such an interpretation misunderstands and likely mistranslates this verse. Typical translations go something like the NRSV: "The LORD God took the man and *put him* in the garden of Eden to till it and keep it." But an alternative translation could read: "And the LORD God took the man and he *brought him to rest* in the garden of Eden for the purpose of tilling it and keeping it." Here, the verb which most translations have simply as "put him," conveys an idea of giving a resting place, a dwelling, to the man. The garden is most assuredly not a workplace, but a living space in which his work is that of a hobby-gardener rather than a hired hand.[53] Does this mean we can return to the notion of economy as household management? Do Adam and Eve act here as stewards of creation in the garden of Eden? No, for again, such would imply that they are employed in the creation or acquisition of products for livelihood. Their food is provided for without labor. Their work, then, is not attached to any kind of reward, payment, or earning.

The man is given a rich dwelling place that he serves by tilling and watching over. His agriculture is not onerous, but is a blessing. There is no indication that his tilling is his means to subsistence. The trees are given for food, as Genesis 2:16 indicates. They preexist the man and this implies that they give food prior to and independent of any tending. Work and food have no necessary connection in the garden. This means that the man does not live in a work-reward economy. His service is carried out freely without regard to its merit or reward. His work is an end in itself, not a means to an end. It is thus ultimately fulfilling and enjoyable. This will be contrasted with the cursed ground of his exile in Genesis 3 where work is established as the precondition to survival. Again, this suggests a full life, where work is done for its own sake, much like God's own work in creation. Perhaps, then, we can consider the man here a flower gardener who grows flowers for pleasure, not for food. He enjoys the actual work of getting his hands dirty, of tending each plant. In the end he receives no life-sustaining benefit from the flowers, the work of gardening is the reward in itself. This is aesthetic or artistic work, not economic work.

---

53. The verb נוּחַ (*nuach*) conveys the idea of rest or coming to rest, of ceasing something rather than beginning something. In the hiphil, as it is here, it conveys the causative nature of the hiphil and thus often means 'to give rest' to someone. He is not simply "set down" in this place, God already placed him here in verse 8 (שִׂים, *sim*).

We might also call the man a tenant-farmer or a vassal. This rightly implies that there is no concept of human ownership here. The land worked by the man is not *his* land. By putting labor into the land he does not thereby attain it as property, cordoned off from others. His gardening is not claim-staking. Of course, there are, as yet, no other people mentioned. But the point remains, the man is a gardener or tenant-farmer, not the owner of the garden. Human ownership of land in the garden is not only not a divine right, it would be theft from God, or piracy. God is not its owner, of course, but its Creator. Ownership is an irrelevant term in a world without economy. But, if land ownership were established in the garden, it must necessarily be theft from God, for it can only be established by exclusion, by the segmentation of part of the creation away from the Creator. In the Creator-creation relationship, the concept of land ownership will always fail to recognize human relationship to the land as mediated through God's own relationship to the land. This has great implications for all possible economic systems, for all economic systems, by necessity, as depersonalized systems, exclude relationship with God from consideration.

The lack of a work-reward relationship is quite an important concept in the consideration of sin. Not only will this relationship be transformed by sin, it will characterize almost the entirety of human existence. Human life, in the garden, is not defined by work. Adam and Eve's identities are not bound up with being gardeners. They are the image of God and, as such, their identities are defined by their special relationships with the Creator. Indeed, they are individually addressed by God and have unique and personal relationships irrespective of each other. Therefore, they are not defined by a social or economic role, but by their individual relationship with the Creator. Without the necessary connection between work and reward, people are not to be defined purely functionally.

In the garden, a place where there is no psychological notion of lack or absence, there can also be no principle of scarcity upon which an economic system of exchange or use value can be established. Put another way, the man and the woman are satisfied, both psychologically and physically. Psychologically they do not feel the now ubiquitous sense of incompletion that must be ameliorated by the augmentation of the self through material possession. This means that they have no desire for profit, or even for trade. This must not be understood as a divine aseity, for they cannot be self-satisfied or self-completing. Indeed, "It is not good that the man should be alone."[54] The man is completed by his relationship with God and with the woman, his helper. It is in these living and active relationships that the man lacks

54. Gen 2:18.

nothing psychologically. And, because he exists in creation, which again is always and only conceivable in such a living and active relationship with the Creator, the man lacks nothing physically. If any one of these sources of satisfaction are lost, however, it is inevitable that need, want, and dissatisfaction result, leading to the creation of economy and therefore of envy and strife.

Rest

The Sabbath, or end of the week rest, is a pattern of life God enjoins to his people.[55] Though they are not to imitate God in creation, they do imitate the six days of labor and one day of rest. Here again we see how creation is itself setting the stage for reconciliation. As Jesus makes clear in Mark 2:27, "The Sabbath was made for man, not man for the Sabbath." The Sabbath is grace to the people of God, not a burden. It is not to be imitated because there is a magical quality to the alignment of the heavens and human activity, nor is it kept because God needs it. Rather, the Sabbath is a means of retaining identity in the midst of work through reference to the rest of God. Furthermore, as the author of Hebrews explains, the rest for the people of God is God himself in Jesus Christ.[56] Creation, in the very structure of God's work, points toward Christ as the end for which creation is made. The divine rest is an inbuilt eschatology in creation itself. Thus, each time the Sabbath is observed, one is participating proleptically in the eschaton: the divine rest. The whole of the Bible could be narrated in terms of preparing a people to enter God's kingly rest to rule with him. The Sabbath establishes a point of contact between God and his people in Creation. As I mentioned above, the creation is nonparticipatory. But God's people can and ought to participate in this one aspect of creation: the divine rest. This, then, gives the people of Israel a forward looking perspective on history, a waiting for the entry into the divine rest and a weekly reminder of this rest. It is a constant, weekly reminder that God himself rests and that he is calling his people to join him in that rest, now, and in a more full and complete manner in the eschaton. Time and history all point toward its completion in the rest of communion with God.

Furthermore, just as God's rest on the Sabbath confirms his identity, so also this rest confirms the man's identity in the garden. Like Descartes's famous *cogito ergo sum*, there is a continuity of action. "I think, therefore

---

55. See Exod 20:8–11. The Deuteronomy account of the Decalogue, however, bases the Sabbath in the exodus.

56. See Heb 4.

I am" really means, "While I am thinking, I exist." One of the problems with this formula is that periods of unconsciousness may mean that one stops existing, as with sleep.[57] As long as a definition of human existence has this durative property it is implied that the cessation of this property means that human existence has ceased. Not that anyone really considers human existence to cease in rest, but it is always an experience that is defined in light of work. Someone who ceases work is "retired," or "unemployed." This definition through social or economic function is a dangerous prospect, not only because cessation means starvation, but also because one can become little more than this function. A person can become a job or function, and thereby lose the richness of their character and relationships.

In the garden of Eden, however, work is itself restful. It is not strenuous and it is not, therefore, the sum of their essence. Restful work is work done as an end in itself. God's act of creation, linked as it is with reconciliation, is done for himself. God has no further end in creation than the expression of his lovingness for his creation and his reconciliation of his people. The work is restfully done because there is no deadline, no requirement, no necessity. This work is pure choice. It has no cause or influence external to God's own desire. The man's work in the garden is similar. His work, though part of God's will for him, is chosen. That work is an end in itself also means that it is not done for another purpose and can never thereby become compulsory. Edenic work is not wealth-creating because such fulfilling work is a kind of wealth in itself. Furthermore, there would be no need for storage of wealth.

As an inbuilt eschatology to creation, the Sabbath further provides people with a goal toward which they strive by their work. But it is not as though the weekly or final Sabbath rest arrives more rapidly by the acrimonious sweat of arduous labor. The Sabbath, like the eschaton, is not built with exertion. The kingdom of God is not founded or constructed by human work. It comes in due season according to the will of God. Thus, work is not the *telos* of human life, nor is it a foretaste of the eschaton. Work is, rather, to be enjoyed restfully, in light of humanity's restful *telos*.

Such an understanding of rest does not condone sloth. Idleness consumes a person. Total inactivity denies an understanding of the self as in relation to anyone or anything and thus is a kind of solipsism. The significance of the Sabbath lies not just in restfulness, but in the notion of a desired relationship. Entering the rest of God is the goal and purpose of God's

---

57. Though modern neurology states that the mind never is "off" as it were, what Descartes means is the self-awareness of conscious thought. The subconscious work of the mind in sleep is not always available to the consciousness, as in a dreamless sleep. Lack of self-awareness is generally the quality of restful sleep and it is this that poses a problem for Descartes.

reconciling activity. But this divine rest cannot be brought about by human willing, through human activity or inactivity. It must be actively waited upon, enjoying the foretastes of this rest as often as one considers the reconciliation achieved in Christ, whose burden is light. As the eschaton, the Sabbath rest is part of a new creation, a new action of God merging his roles of Creator and Reconciler. Thus, the Sabbath rest is proleptic and cannot be enjoyed in its fullness now.

Naked and Shameless

Nakedness is an important theme, not only in Eden, but also in economic considerations. Clothing is the first taste of material mediation of personal relationships. Nakedness should not be understood in terms of clothing only, though this is its surface meaning. Just as Paul can command the believer to "put on Christ,"[58] so also we may speak in various ways of clothing as representative of the self. The nudity of the garden of Eden means that the man and woman are unashamed of themselves as themselves. There is no division between a public and private image. Indeed, there is no image that can be projected whatever. Clothing signifies the desire to express oneself through material mediation. The need of clothing, then, expresses the need for mediation between people. It is both a self-concealment from oneself and the world, as well as a self-projection onto the material itself. The need of clothing demonstrates a self-lack, a desire for self-realization through the means of image construction. This is generally unconscious and is deeply deceptive, for our outer appearance can significantly affect our own self-image. The very existence of a self-image means that one is estranged from oneself.

If Adam and Eve have a unified self that has no projected self-image, they have no need of material things for the augmentation or attempted completion of the self. This shameless nakedness is a profoundly noneconomic self-relation and, therefore, a noneconomic relation between the two. A self that is incomplete desires to accumulate or dominate in order to project the self onto things or other people and thereby view the self in another. This person thus becomes economic by mediating personal value through material things. Value is thus objectified and thereby able to be exchanged. In the absence of clothing Adam and Eve do not enter into such a relationship. The other is not objectified, nor is the creation turned into use value.

That Adam and Eve are naked and shameless does indeed mean that they exist in a childlike naïveté. They do not have a mature conception of the

---

58. Rom 13:14.

self, but one that is blissfully ignorant of any possible division or lack within the self. Thus, we should not take their position as one that might be reattained by the re-creation of their behavior. One will not arrive at a noneconomic relationship merely by stripping naked, literally or figuratively. That is, not only is nudism absurd, a monkish nudism or renunciation of material goods is a similarly impossible attempt to regain what was lost. That is not to say that a certain self-discipline in clothing choice or accumulation of material goods cannot help one gain perspective on the influence these things play in one's life, but only that the innocence of Adam and Eve can never be regained, nor is regaining this ignorant innocence a desirable ethic. Paul in many places encourages believers to put on the armor of light, Jesus Christ, immortality in resurrection, a new self, the whole armor of God. Finally, also, the reconciled in Revelation are portrayed as wearing white robes. In all this there is no archaeological ethic, but an eschatological ethic. That is also to say that the initial naïve noneconomic relationship is unrecoverable.

CONCLUSION

Though many attempt to use the concept of God to establish and legitimize economic life, the God of the biblical creation account cannot be understood in this way. The Creator does not live in an economic relationship with his creation or his creatures, but in a personal relationship. Humans in the beginning likewise do not live in an economic relationship with the creation or with the Creator. Rather, as the *imago dei*, they represent the political authority of the Creator to the creation, exercising this dominion in a personal manner that cannot be the basis of an economy. Humans in creation are not *homo economicus*. Indeed, they are not understood ontologically or by species identity at all. Humans are defined by their relationship to God, to each other, and to the creation. In all of these relationships there is no hint of the traits of the economic relationship: scarcity, exchange, quantification of quality, objectivity, or mediation through matter.

All this is but the introduction to the biblical story, however, and it does not last. The understanding of the *imago dei* in terms of the kind of relationship the Creator has with the creation is irretrievably lost, and human self-understanding must therefore undergo radical alteration. Not only that, God becomes unknown and unknowable, and as a consequence, the world becomes boundless, chaotic, strange. It is in this strangeness that cosmos emerges, developing all relations into economic relations. Eden is lost and cannot be recovered, it thus cannot form the basis of any kind of positive ethic. It is, however, the introduction to the radical revision of the traditional religious story of cosmos being formed out of chaos and it is important to understand that, in the Bible, creation begins with a divine order expressed relationally. This divine order is lost to people, which gives rise to the need of a chaos—into—cosmos mythological structure. But, rather than God forming the foundation of the cosmic system, the God of Jesus Christ, as we shall see, is the God who brings subversion to cosmos in order to effect reconciliation. Our ethics of economy must therefore be held off until the proper theological story can be told so that ethics can be properly situated in the reality of the present cosmic-economic relationship with the truth of the relationship of reconciliation with God guiding our reflections.

4

Estrangement: Creating Cosmos

Following the biblical narrative, we quickly encounter the temptation and fall in Genesis 3, as well as the consequences of the Fall in Genesis 4–11. The Creator-creature relationship does not last, indeed it is confined to a very short part of the Bible. These few chapters in the beginning of Genesis are some of the most rich and profound texts the ancient world produced, but the details of this book are often sadly overlooked due to the mythical appearance of the genre and misguided debates related to modern science. These debates are misguided precisely because they misunderstand the genre of Genesis, especially 1–11, and they misunderstand the genre of scientific cosmology, which itself has a mythical structure to it as well.

The richness of these chapters merits some closer examination and, as we shall see, they provide us with an analysis of human relations and the human mind that are highly surprising given the lack of philosophical acumen of its author. I will first explain the story of the temptation before proceeding to investigate what is traditionally called *the Fall*. This term is loaded with ontological baggage that is nowhere present in Genesis. Instead I will use the term *the Estrangement*. We will look at some of the vignettes that Genesis provides after the Estrangement to examine its consequences. As we shall see, one of the major necessary consequences of a broken relationship with God is the creation of relationships mediated through material, or economic relationships. These relationships express themselves in the creation of alternative worlds that I will call *cosmos/cosmoi*, as the terms cosmos and chaos are themselves quite appropriate terms to use in relation to early Genesis. We shall see, however, that Genesis 1–11 is not a cosmology or cosmogony, it is a profoundly different type of story than both of these genres.

TEMPTATION

The Creator-creature relationship comes under attack quite rapidly in Genesis 3 with the appearance of the serpent. The serpent offers a specific temptation in 3:5, "When you eat of it [the fruit] your eyes will be opened and, you will be like God, knowing good and evil." There are several things to explain about this.

The serpent implies that Eve's eyes are now closed. She is not perceiving reality. Eve is living in a false world that is keeping her back from realizing her potential. This means that her relationship with God is put into question. If the Creator-creature relationship has priority, that means that the creature-creation relationship is mediated through the relationship with the Creator. And this, as we said, enabled the image of God to relate to the creation after the pattern of the Creator, in a benevolent and personal way. Now the serpent is saying that this situation blinds Eve. Like a child seeing everything through the eyes of the parent, so Eve is with God, according to the serpent. So the temptation is to reverse the relationship, mediating the relationship with God through the relationship with the creation.

This openness of the eyes will make Eve like God. God has a direct relationship with the creation, and so too could Eve. Note that this temptation has real content behind it. This is not a bluff as some imagine the serpent's words to be. Her eyes will indeed be opened and she will become like God by having a direct relationship with the creation. This is confirmed when the narrator says, "Then the eyes of both were opened" in verse 7.

The main content of this godlikeness is the knowledge of good and evil. Now traditionally this has been understood to be some content that is present in the mind of God to which this fruit somehow gives secret access. This would mean that in eating the fruit the content of the minds of Adam and Eve are expanded. There are major problems with this interpretation. Firstly, it implies that there is a good and an evil independent of God such that he would have knowledge of this, which is not simply knowledge of himself. Secondly, it implies that evil preexists the sin of Adam and Eve. But there is no attestation of this in the preceding story. This is the first mention of evil in the Bible. Thirdly, it implies that good and evil are some eternal and changeless concepts—metaphysical categories. It is unlikely that the author of Genesis, given the time and place of composition, had any knowledge of metaphysics living in the premonetary and pre-metaphysical ancient Near East.

Rather, the temptation here is to create the knowledge of good and evil. The temptation is not to enlightenment, which as we saw pertained to the monetary gospel, rather the temptation is to godlikeness in creativity. When God created things and saw that they were good, this is not moral goodness, but the correct result of the intention. It is the goodness that an architect would see standing in front of a finished building, and examining the initial blueprints for their correspondence. So God has not created good and evil in Genesis. Karl Barth notices this and writes his surprise:

> What the serpent has in mind is the establishment of ethics. ... It is surprising that in the Christian Church more offence is not taken at the fact—or have we simply read it away?—that in Gen. 3 the desire of man for a knowledge of good and evil is represented as an evil desire, indeed the one evil desire which is so characteristic and fatal for the whole race. The consequences for the theory and practice of Christian ethics—and not only that—would be incalculable if only we were to see this and accept it instead of regarding this very questionable knowledge—whether sought in the Bible or the rational nature of man or conscience—as the most basic of all the gifts of God.[1]

The serpent's temptation is for the establishment of ethics or morality. The church has indeed made a terrible mistake and continues to do so whenever it tries to explain good and evil in a metaphysical manner. There is great temptation to do so, for it provides common ground, but as we will see, this common ground cannot be refer back to God, and so good and evil are alienated from God, which was the whole point of the serpent's temptation in the first place. It is by means of encouraging Adam and Eve to take on the function of creator-judges that the serpent leads them away from God.

They eat of the fruit, of course, and their eyes are opened and they do become like God. They have created good and evil. But verse 6 is also quite telling in showing how the relationships of mediation transform in the process of looking at the fruit: "The woman saw that the tree was good for food, and that it was desirable to the eyes, and that the tree was desired to make one wise . . . ." The woman saw that the tree was good for food. Now it is not possible for Eve to make this decision on the basis of her own experience. Instead she must rely upon testimony. She has two competing witnesses. God says that it will kill her, the serpent says it will not, but will make her

1. Barth, *CD*, IV.1 448–49.

godlike. To decide that the fruit is good for food she must decide to favor the serpent's testimony, and it is at this point that the break with God has already happened, for Eve has acted out of distrust and unfaithfulness.

Furthermore, Eve is seeing the fruit as instrumental. It has become a resource to her. This is the first result of relating primarily to the material, it necessarily becomes identified for its use value. The fruit also has aesthetic value; it is a delight to the eyes. Eve is showing that her judgment is based, not only in the testimony of the serpent, but in the witness of her own unmediated vision. Is the fruit beautiful in itself or because its relationship to God makes it beautiful? Where is beauty located? There are three options: in the fruit itself, in the eyes and judgment of Eve, or in its relation to God. Eve thinks that the fruit is itself beautiful, and so she already is showing signs of what we will see as a projection and alienation mechanism that comes as a result of an immediate relationship with the creation and the creation of meaning.

Genesis seems to agree with Protagoras, yet without reference to money or metaphysics. Value and meaning are human creations, as are ethics or morality. The great temptation of humans is to judge for themselves what is right, what is good, what is beautiful. That is, humans are the measure of all things, they are the ones who create categories. This is a godlike creativity—it is how value and meaning is constructed. Yet this construction comes precisely by abandoning the Creator-creature relationship for an unmediated relationship with the creation.

ESTRANGEMENT

As said above, the traditional notion of the Fall needs to be challenged. Not only did the culture in which Genesis was written not possess the linguistic capacity for metaphysical expression, such a metaphysical expression of sin is troubling for a variety of reasons, not all of which are important for the theme of this book. Suffice it to say that sin that corrupts human nature can hardly allow for personal responsibility for that sin, and thus not allow for justice in punishment of that sin. So we end up with theologies that state rather boldly that Adam's sin deserves infinite punishment and that the sin of Adam is imputed into the nature of humanity. I was lectured in seminary that the denial of the imputation of Adam's sin is the gateway to theological liberalism that eventually denies the imputation of Christ's righteousness. And that may have some truth to it. But Adam's sin hardly seems worthy of eternal damnation for all humans who will ever be born. Such an idea makes God seem vindictive. It also closely aligns with other religious ideas of a debt of honor that is infinite because it is incommensurable.

If we pay greater attention to the linguistic and philosophical context of the authorship of Genesis we will have to challenge the view that human ontology is in question here. What this means is that instead of a good nature falling to corruption there is a Creator-creature relationship that becomes estranged. This is not the place to spell out my entire theology of original sin and how it differs in the details from an ontological or genetic sin. Suffice it to say that once the relationship is estranged and people mediate their relationship with God through their own cosmos (see below), it is impossible for them to repair this relationship of their own accord because it is not possible to return to God, to seek God, or find God through the cosmos, for the god of the cosmos is always a projection. God must initiate reconciliation. All this will be explained in greater detail as we continue. But for these reasons I will speak of the Estrangement, not the Fall.

Adam and Eve: Physical Estrangement and Irresponsibility

Returning to the text of Genesis we come to the immediate reaction of Adam and Eve after they eat of the fruit—the realization of their nakedness. The minute their eyes are opened they see one another, not as they did previously, but in a radically new way, in a shameful nakedness. Their relationship with one another is now mediated by external appearance. Previously Adam and Eve would have looked at one another's heart, as their own relationship was mediated through their own relationships with God. Now, without this mediation they look upon one another as foreign objects. And so they immediately fashion makeshift clothes. Clothing is a deeply profound theological reality as we've already seen. It protects a person from God's creation and from the gaze of others and the shame associated with the deep guilt that is created at the moment of their sin. But clothing is also about influencing the perception others have. In this dual aspect, clothing is a small example of the cosmos-creation that happens as a result of sin. Adam and Eve immediately create physical barriers of clothing between themselves to demonstrate that their previous relationship has been broken in some way. No longer are they really one flesh. The first technological innovation of human beings in the Bible is a result of brokenness and it reinforces this estrangement by building barriers of protection.

After hiding from one another by clothing themselves, they hide from God when he comes walking in the garden. Their hiding and creation of clothing in itself demonstrates their guilt to God. Their hiding, like their making of clothing, shows another major theme we see here in the Estrangement: their godlikeness is not met with a correlative courage to be self-responsible. God is subject to no law; he freely does as he wills with no accountability. And yet, God is responsible and freely takes responsibility for his creation. True godlikeness involves the taking on of responsibility, not its abandonment. What Adam and Eve begin to demonstrate here is an impulse that will return millennia later in the formation of the idea of the corporation. As discussed, the corporation exists precisely to limit responsibility and so reduce the personal risk in undertaking bold plans. In the same way Adam and Eve attempt to limit their responsibility by clothing their nakedness. Adam blames God and Eve, and Eve blames the serpent, each passing responsibility off of themselves.

When God says to Adam, "Because you have listened to the voice of your wife and have eaten . . ." he does not imply that Adam was wrong because he obeyed a woman, but because he listened to his wife over the command of God. Eve mediated her relationship with God through the creation, through her own judgment. Adam mediated his relationship with God through his personal relationship with his wife. Both of these orientations are expressions of estrangement from God, as they express distrust at the express command of God. Rather than trusting in the faithfulness of God they chose to trust the serpent, their own eyes, and the mimetic influence of each other.

Sin should not be seen as a corruption of human nature. There is no evidence of this in the text of Genesis. Instead original sin is the corruption of human relationships. Original sin is Adam and Eve's initial turning away from God that creates an entirely new epistemology. Adam and Eve were related to God's creation through their relationship with him, and this formed their thoughts. When they turn to the creation, they immediately begin to relate to God mediated through the creation. This is the birth of religion. This is the birth of natural law, of morality and ethics. By looking to God through what will thenceforth be understood as *nature* instead of *creation*, Adam and Eve can only understand God analogically. Hence any god they can know on their own terms will necessarily be a projection of something they experience in their milieu. The angel guards the way to the tree of life. God himself becomes wholly inaccessible to the human mind.

The Curse: Economic Life

After this incident God curses the man and woman. God makes normal life harder for them, as he will do again at Babel. In the previous chapter we said that the man and woman were brought to rest in the garden, to work it, and that this work should be understood more as a hobby than a survival mechanism. This is transformed by the Estrangement. No longer will they eat from the fruit of the trees that preexisted them, now they will have to work for food. Because they chose to mediate their relationship to God through the creation, God gave them what they wanted, a relationship with the world without God's intervention. This will be a bleaker existence where the majority of human life will be oriented to the ground, working it to eke out a living. Although this has changed by technology, the concept is similar, that we are defined by our labor and that work must happen for survival. The necessary connection between work and reward is established by the Estrangement. Whereas in the garden the work is its own reward, now work becomes instrumental and necessary. This, of course, gives birth to economics and technology. Because work is required and occupies the major part of life, it follows that any method that alleviates the harshness of this labor will be pursued. The division of labor will be based in this necessity of work and a desire to alleviate it. Economy is the fruit of the Estrangement.

Cain and Abel: The Birth of Religious Economics

Moving forward to Cain and Abel we come to the curious narrative about the two sacrifices. Note that this is the very first mention of any kind of religion in the Bible. It is amazing how often has it been missed that in this most essential and foundational of all supposedly religious texts there is no mention of prayer, sacrifice, priesthood, service to the gods, temples, or any other kind of religious language in Genesis 1–3. This is one of many reasons why John Walton's idea of the garden as a cosmic temple, although admirable in some ways, is a tragic concept.[2] The entire purpose of a temple is for mediation between the gods and people. But in the garden their relationship with God is immediate and thus there is no religion in this state, for there is no function that religion plays that is necessary when God and people are reconciled. These sacrifices, the first acts of religion, are a result of estrangement, demonstrating that religion is itself a product of the Estrangement. Indeed, religion exists to orient people to the milieu in which they live, and to ensure divine legitimation of their cosmos. Though it is nearly impossible to know for certain why Cain's sacrifice is rejected and Abel's accepted, one compelling theory that has basis in anthropology, is the division between farming and herding. Farming implies permanent settlement, the construction of cities, and the massive change in lifestyle that the city

---

2. Walton, *Lost World of Genesis One*.

creates. A few scholars have noted the general antiurban motif of Genesis.³ Every character in Genesis is on the move, never quite possessing a land of their own and ending up in Egypt. It is possible, then, that Cain's sacrifice is rejected because it shows his interest in the possession of land. We noted in the last chapter that property and ownership were not meaningful concepts when applied to Eden or to God. Instead of relating to God's creation as the image of God ought, Cain relates to it as a plunderer who gives to God the fruit of exploitation. The same could be said of herding, but not to the same extent as farming. In any case, God has not asked for a sacrifice. It is an important and necessary response of those estranged from God. It is the first attempt we see in Scripture of people engaging in economic relations with God.

The logic of sacrifice is thoroughly economic. As we saw in chapter 2 sacrifice was different in Greece and the ancient Near East, but both were methods of economic redistribution that reinforced social structures and hierarchies. The egalitarianism of the Homeric sacrifice helped to reduce tension related to unequal wealth from a tyranny, and yet it also provided the means whereby the wealthy could transform material wealth into social gravitas or honor. In classical Greece this became more explicit through *leitourgia*, or the massive public works and donations of wealthy patrons to create honor. In the ancient Near East sacrifice became part of a large system of temple complexes with an enormous number of employees. In all cases, sacrifice is a means to pay one's debt to the gods or create a debt which the god would have to repay. That both Cain and Able engage in this activity profoundly illustrates that economic relations with God have begun. Cain is upset, not that God does not like him, but that God chooses not to be in his debt. That God chose to accept Abel's sacrifice perhaps ought to be more surprising. But it demonstrates here what I will explain as the conclusion of this work: God works through human expressions to subversively transform relationships. God accepts Abel's sacrifice though there is nothing valid about sacrifice. God has not thereby legitimized sacrifice and has not justified sin, but justifies the sinner based on the intentions of the heart, not on the outward form of expression.

The outcome of Cain's estranged relationship with God is the murder of his brother Abel. Estrangement from God leads to estrangement between other people and between people and God's creation. God curses Cain, forbidding the earth to yield food after his farming. God condemns Cain to wandering, the very life his brother Abel would have led. God breaks Cain's relationship with the earth, leading him to a situation of disorientation. For

---

3. Ellul, *Meaning of the City*; Wenham, *Genesis 1–11*.

God has not reconciled Cain to himself forcefully, but nor will he allow Cain to express his estrangement by having such an immediate relationship with the earth.

In response, Cain complains that people will seek vengeance upon him. He knows that violence begets violence, estrangement begets estrangement. He has begun the vicious cycle of violence out of which there is no escape for the remainder of human history. What we see here is the firstfruits of original sin, and it is here that we begin to see how sin is transmitted from one generation to the next. It is not through biology, as though biology becomes broken by an act of disobedience. It is hard to understand how it could be that an isolated human act could immediately and wholly corrupt the entirety of God's creation. This is lazy metaphysical thinking. It makes far more sense to understand sin as something beginning and spreading through Adam and Eve relationally. Sin becomes cultural and systemic rather than biological. Furthermore, there are clearly other people at the time of Cain, Abel, and Seth. Otherwise who would get vengeance on Cain? His father, mother, and unborn brother? Who would Cain and Seth marry, unspoken sisters? There's no good textual reason to believe that Adam and Eve are the sole genetic forebears of the human species. Genesis is silent about the matter and it tacitly assumes the existence of other people. If we are to properly understand Genesis and this original sin we need to see it as relationship built upon relationship, experience upon experience that reinforces cultural and systematic estrangement from God. Cain shows a new kind of evil founded on a new estrangement from God. But this evil is not limited to the murder of Abel, Cain begins show his estrangement from God in his relationship with God's creation.

Cain's Estrangement: The City and Cosmos

God's creation is totally lost to humanity at the moment of the Estrangement. It is not as though the plants and trees suddenly die, but that epistemologically it becomes impossible to see God's creation. It is only through a relationship with God that one can conceive of creation instead of nature.[4] Thus it is that Cain becomes the first city builder. Cain rejects God's protection and instead builds a city to protect himself. We cannot escape that the first city in the Bible is built in direct response to a rejection of God. Cain performs two acts to counter God's curse. He "knows his wife" and builds a city. In producing children he satisfies his desire for eternal life and in

---

4. This is my major problem with Christian participation in non-Christian environmental movements and ideologies. The Christian voice is subverted from the beginning.

building a city he satisfies his desire for a place of his own that is secure, as Jacques Ellul observes.[5] The name Cain gives to the child and the city are the same, and this is important. *Chanakh* (Enoch) is related to the word for the dedication or consecration that one performs at the building of a new temple or city walls. Enoch is Cain's new beginning. Ellul wonderfully summarizes the importance of this:

> Cain dedicates a new world: "Enoch," as opposed to *Reshith* in Genesis 1:1. Inauguration, as opposed to creation. Initiation, as opposed to the garden paradise. The city as opposed to Eden. It is certainly not unawares that Cain gave this name to his creation. Now he also is going to make the world over again.... For in Cain's eyes it is not a beginning again, but a beginning. God's creation is seen as nothing. God did nothing, and in no case did he finish anything. Now a start is made, and it is no longer God beginning, but man. And thus Cain, with everything he does, digs a little deeper the abyss between himself and God.[6]

Cain, in response to rejection of God creates his own world. He is no longer able to see God's creation, instead he perceives a hostile and chaotic world, a world that needs ordering. Cain is feeling lost, like he will be a wanderer and vagabond in a land of *Nod* (wandering). And this is of vital importance, Genesis does not begin with chaos and God is not the one forming *the* cosmos. Chaos is a human experience, an emotion, that despairs in the face of disorder and thus meaninglessness. In that situation the only response can be the creation of order. This can occur through stories like cosmogonies, through metaphysical categorization, or through a blending of story and metaphysics as we find in modern scientific cosmology. Cain is the first cosmologist, not God. Whereas God created a creation *ex nihilo*, Cain creates a cosmos out of the repurposing of resources, and thus he creates purpose out of what was formerly viewed as purposeless. Recall that Aristotle views humans as the source of purpose in nature and this justifies their free use of all things. The major distinction between creation and cosmos is personal. Creation requires a creator and is entirely dependent upon its creator. A cosmos is impersonal, for it masks that the creators of a cosmos are human beings. Aristotle demonstrates the logic of the cosmos: humans give value to what is otherwise purposeless and thereby justly dominate a purposeless nature.[7]

---

5. Ellul, *Meaning of the City*, 5.

6. Ibid., 5–6.

7. The justification of oil exploitation has, in every case I have encountered, followed just such a logic: it's there and it's for us to make use of it. We give it purpose by

Cain's Descendants: Creativity and Violence

Cain's descendants are the font of civilization. Lamech, the seventh-generation descendant of Cain, demonstrates the perfection of the Cainite line by poetically boasting of the perfection of Cain's vengeance and violence in himself. Lamech's son Jubal is the father of those who play the lyre and pipe. Another of his sons, Tubal Cain, is the father of bronze and iron smiths. Genesis is making an important theological point. The estranged are violent, not only against other humans, but also as forgers of brazen implements, an essential part of civilized and imperial society. We might say that Cain's line was more self-expressive and thus engaged in the fine and industrial arts and we are fully accustomed to calling these things good. But Genesis places the origin of this self-expression in the line of people who do not walk with God but are given to violence. Self-expression is never solely about the self, of course, it is a projection of the self upon something or someone else. If one expresses himself he leaves an impression, he transforms the world and people around him. So music and smithing are ancient examples of this. The smith in forging, less so in casting, must violently work metal into shape. The smith creates objects that extend human power and desire beyond their own strength, objects that are used to conform the world to one's desires. Our examples of smithing gods in mythology— Hephaestus, Vulcan, Ptah, Wayland—all share a physical deformity. Hephaestus's leg or legs are improperly developed. Ptah, the Egyptian creator god revered by smiths for his association with underground fire, is sometimes portrayed as a dwarf. Wayland, the Germanic and Norse master smith, is hamstrung to be kept in servitude by a king. But these are all clever and creative gods. These gods are profoundly creative and most of them are also quite cunning. It seems that psychologically there is much to say about their disability and creativity and there is much speculation that could occur here, but I will constrain myself to simply noting that the potentiality that exists in their incomparably skillful creative ability is met with fear and distrust, leading to ostracism that is rationalized by attributing to them a physical defect. And it is these physically handicapped gods that are the most skillful in imposing themselves in a magical way on the world and on people. Tubal Cain is the son of the man who epitomizes violence; Tubal expresses this violence through his creative capacity.

And we should note that creation in the ancient mind is almost uniformly violent and/or sexual. These two concepts have a very thin dividing line in the ancient religious mind. Violence seems to be creative to the

---

using it, otherwise why is it there?

ancient mind, a notion also present in Hegelian and Marxist dialectic. The golden age is one of total potentiality and therefore also violent monstrosities.[8] Cosmogonies often begin with a violent monstrosity that is the parent of more reasonable gods who must kill their parent/monster and create the world out of its corpse. Tubal Cain is perhaps touching on this mythical background, tapping into this understanding that violence begets creativity.

Creativity and violence are linked, then, because the self that must express itself in ways that distinguish the individual as creative are naturally opposed to the common practice of their peers. This is not to say that Genesis is urging a strict uniformity that is dull, lifeless, and uncreative. Smithing is not itself the issue, nor are music and the arts, rather it is the motive behind this self-expression that is suspect. Those who are estranged from God engage in creating value by externalization, as is explained below in relation to the Babel narrative.

As the generations pass and evil, which is put almost solely in terms of violence in this narrative, grows, God regrets his creation of all things. Genesis states that it is because of human violence that the earth itself is full of violence, thus showing that it is human estrangement from God and its consequences that lead to the corruption of creation. It is not Adam and Eve's sin that somehow immediately transforms the moral ontology of the creation. The story of Noah will be covered in the next chapter as it is an insight into reconciliation, though it is judgment, and its importance will be covered there.

Babel: Cosmic Self-Creation

After Noah and his family exit the ark and some generations pass, we come to Babel. Babel, which means the "gateway of god," is a traditional expression of human religiosity. There is the building and consecration of a city that is there to solidify horizontal relationships. And there is a tower, likely in the center of town, that itself symbolizes the communion of heaven and earth. As the Greeks understood Delphi as the *omphalos* (navel) of the world, the meeting point of heaven and earth, so we ought to understand the tower of Babel, the *axis mundi*.[9] The city and tower of Babel are the paradigmatic expression of cosmology. Let us look somewhat carefully at this story and what it reveals about estrangement and economic relations.

The stated purpose of the construction of this city is twofold, that the people would not be scattered, and that they would make a name for

---

8. Caillois, *Man and the Sacred*, 105–7.
9. Latin: "axis of the world."

themselves. This first expression of community in Scripture is roundly condemned by God, precisely because there is solidarity in human counter-creation. The unity the people have is self-created and excludes God. The common good is thus the exact source of estrangement from God, and this is part of the reason for the harsh response by God. They have identified the good outside of relationship with God and, unified in this estrangement, "nothing will be impossible for them." The implied meaning of this statement, especially in context with the antediluvian superabundance of violence in Genesis 6, is that no evil will be impossible for a united group estranged from the source of all goodness. In this context it seems that God is actively taking steps to prevent the situation from escalating to the point it was in Noah's day.

In building Babel, the people also desire to make a name for themselves. This does not mean they are trying to gain a reputation as the phrase means to modern people, but that they would like to create their own identity. Names are of great importance throughout the ancient world and the one who gives a name is in every case a superior. Naming someone or something is to give that person or thing its identity and purpose. We can see in the Bible the importance of name-giving and name-changing to signify an important and life transforming event. God gives Adam permission to name the animals, which must be seen as the sharing of his own right, and this naming is perhaps the clearest expression we see in Genesis 1–3 of what the image of God really means in sense of it being delegated authority over creation. So when the builders of Babel desire to name themselves they are desiring to define themselves. Once again the result of estrangement from God is the creation of value. And just as for Adam, Eve, and Cain this creation was not *ex nihilo*, so too these Babelites build out of other substance. That is, the value they are looking to create, even though it comes entirely from within themselves, cannot take the bare form of this self-referential valuation. It must be projected, masked, and then derived from something now seemingly objective. In order to make a name or identity the builders feel like they must build. It is through the action and product of their construction that they will define themselves. Apart from themselves the city and tower has no value. And yet, this value must be objectified. Instead of simply naming themselves, they must alienate this value from themselves by projecting it into an object. In building the object some*thing* is created. A city has a life of its own, a spirit or identity of its own, and yet this identity comes solely from humans. Nevertheless once this object is alive in some sense it becomes capable of creating value independently of the people who created it.[10] It is in this way that humans create, mask, and derive value for themselves. This might be called cowardice. After all it was precisely this faculty of the creation of value that was expressed at the Estrangement. This is what makes humans godlike. And yet God does not need to create to give himself value. If God is truly *a se*, or content with himself, his value is not derived from anyone or anything outside of himself. To be truly godlike, then, is to create value out of the self and recognize it as such, without a need to externalize it.

And yet this almost never happens. For those who recognize this mechanism there is often an accompanying depression at realizing that everything has self-assigned value, that value is subjective or cultural, and that there is no access to, or no such thing as, an objective value. Others react in religious hatred against such an idea in order to preserve the sacrality of the cosmos they have inherited and legitimized in their own lives. Xenophanes identified the problem of projection, at least in terms of religion, and Protagoras went further to see that all categorical distinctions and attributions of being are created by humanity. Seaford makes a very compelling case that these observations could only come about, at least partly, by the advent of coinage, which forced the concept of fiduciarity on everyone. And yet, if Genesis is describing the self-assignation of value or identity, "let us make a name for ourselves," and Genesis was clearly authored in a premonetary society, we have a very unique narrative here, one that is profoundly desacralizing to its surrounding cultures and self-critical as well. Genesis thereby has quite a lot to say about a different genealogy of economic relations, in estrangement from God.

And the reaction of God at Babel bears further witness to this. It was not the objects, the city or the tower, that so offended God, for otherwise we imagine he would simply obliterate the city in some dramatic way, like Sodom. Rather it is this idea of making a name for themselves that is problematic, which is why the curse is a confusion of language. We need not look at Babel as an etiological myth for why there are different languages. Rather we can look at it as the destruction of the means by which a people were establishing a unity in naming themselves. It could be argued that this is the origin of the problem of interpretation. Where there is a total oneness of mind in linguistic expression interpretation does not exist. Interpretation only becomes a consideration when the same verbal expression leads to disagreement of intended meanings. This is far more profound than confusion of language, and it addresses the stated desire of the people. Instead of

---

10. This is very similar to the very common science fiction notion of a self-aware robot or android.

allowing themselves to assign themselves value together through common, large-scale undertakings, God hinders their ability to agree on what the value of the project is. They left off building, not because cooperation was technically impossible, as though one builder couldn't ask for a stone or hammer from another, but because they could no longer agree on the value and purpose of the project. Once again God becomes the author of chaos in the midst of cosmos-construction, leading to the destruction of forms of human meaning and significance, since these forms were nothing but projections anyway.

Babel demonstrates that humans are unable to construct value for themselves but must objectify it, give it a measure of independence so that they can derive value from this new objective source. Though this was the case for a people group of themselves, the consequence of this narrative for money and economic relations is evident. Money is a human assignation of value that takes on an objectivity beyond the person. This is why money, "the Economy," and "the Market" are reified. For us to create exchange value that can provide value beyond what the individual desires, there must be a communal solidarity in valuation. Everyone must play the same game and put fairly equivalent value in these humanly created objects. Once that happens, once trust is established, then money takes on the kind of status in which it can determine nearly the whole value of a person's life. The Babel narrative critiques the kind of valuation essential for the formation of money and economy in the first place, again demonstrating that the basis of the economic relationship is in an estranged relationship with God.

CONSTRUCTING COSMOS

We've looked at some key narratives in Genesis 1–11 and how they speak to the formation of economic relations. Let us here look at some of the commentary and further reflections in a more systematic way. I will do this under three headings of relational estrangement: Creator, creation, and other people. Finally, we will look at how the sum of these relations work toward the formation of a cosmos.

Creator

The Estrangement is primarily a relationship, or lack thereof, with God, and it is this relationship that determines all others. The image of God, if we understand it as political representation in the way described in chapter 3, is not disabled or disempowered by the Estrangement, but is delegitimized.

God created people with capacities, but these capacities or capabilities are not what comprise the meaning of the image of God. This would make God into a collection of abilities, the omnipotent (all-able) instead of the God of Abraham, Isaac, Jacob, and Jesus. The image of God is not creativity or love; it is the relationship that people have with God in Genesis 1–2. Adam and Eve's rule over the creation was mediated through their relationship with God, and thus the character of God was communicated by their relationship with him to the creation on God's behalf. In the Estrangement their capabilities are in no way diminished. But their rule over the creation is now no longer mediated by God and thus God's character of personal loving care is no longer communicated to the creation. The royal charter is rescinded and this makes human aspirations to godlikeness into usurpation, rebellion, and piracy.

In the Estrangement God becomes an enemy. Indeed, it is God who does the cursing of Adam, Eve, the serpent, Cain, Ham, and the Babelites. Genesis 3–11 almost seems like a series of stories of how people came to be cursed by God. He becomes humanity's great enemy because his rule is systematically interrupted by humans. This needs some explanation. In the creation God chose to establish highly complex causality. Since Newtonian physics people have tended to believe that we can think of causality in singular terms, like a billiards table. The cue hits the cue ball, which then rolls along, and strikes another ball. This understanding of causality is what gave rise to the once popular and still sometimes held view of deism, that God is like the divine watchmaker who constructs a complex instrument, winds it up, and lets it run on its own. But though a watch might seem complex, it is really quite simple on the scale of causality. Not only is physics far more complicated than Newtonian models, so causality is far more complicated. We can imagine that God created the world and all its guiding principles and forces, he then created human beings to be yet another source of causality, one that is heavily influenced by physical laws, but not fully determined by them. In this way God created instruments that can alter what we might otherwise consider a natural course of development. To humans God delegated his authority in Adam and Eve, removing this authority when they sin, but not removing their causal impact on the creation. But physical laws and human intent are not the only two factors of causality, God himself can and does engage in this complex symphony of causality. This is the source of what is normally called a miracle. It should not seem unusual for the Creator to interact with his creation, but it is important to recall that God rested on the seventh day and that the creation was completed. God is not actively creating and so can choose a level of active involvement. It is great in the flood, small in the four hundred years in Egypt.

Because there are many sources of causality there is never an either/or situation in cause-effect relationships. What this means is that, as humans are estranged from God, their own causal power is deeply altered in character. Instead of mediating this causality through their relationship with God, it is now misguided. Human causal power is unable to stand alone. This was made clear earlier in speaking about Adam and Eve's inability to fully embrace godlikeness in terms of responsibility, and at Babel where self-determination had to be projected, objectified, and derived. Human causal power requires inspiration from context and externalization in various forms (slavery, animal labor, technology). In no case can one identify human causality being as God's, *ex nihilo*.

God's rule is systematically interrupted by the Estrangement because God does not continue to work as he did at creation. That work finished, and he promised at the flood to not destroy all things again in a similar cataclysm. Human causality, no longer mediated through a relationship with God, engages in a vicious cycle of forming a cosmos and being determined by that cosmos. The story of reconciliation that occupies the remainder of the Bible from Genesis 12 onwards is a story of how God operates through human causality and very rarely acts dramatically through immediate exercise of his power. Because God committed himself to some human agency in his creation, and he stands by his decision, the consequence is that the humanly constructed worlds of sin and rebellion continue, with a minority working in its midst for its reconciliation. God so chooses human agency that he himself becomes human in Jesus Christ to work quiet, loving, subversive reconciliation.

Because humans recognize their causal power and technology augments this power, there is less need to posit a God-of-the-gaps for unknown sources of causality, though it certainly still happens through notions like chance. The God revealed in Jesus Christ is made an enemy of independent human causality, however, because he always and everywhere delegitimizes it. The rebellious image of God cannot accept God, because whenever God is present so too is the judgment that unmasks the piracy and usurpation of the deposed image of God.

Creation

By the Estrangement humans become pirates and plunderers of God's creation. Indeed, as I have said, the very notion of *creation* becomes impossible and *cosmos* must be constructed. In the premonetary societies of the Old Testament the world outside the self is understood in more personalized terms, through gods and goddesses. In monetary society the concept of *nature* and the *universe* become possible. We briefly reviewed the literature of both of these societies and saw that myth and paratactic epics described a cosmogony and a cosmology, but not one that was logically coherent. Such a *logos* was neither prioritized nor even conceptualized prior to the work of the pre-Socratic philosophers. None of these stories or philosophies understood God as the personal creator of all things in the way the Bible describes. Certainly Aristotle spoke of the unmoved mover, but his god is very different than the God revealed in Scripture. His is an aloof god who did not delegate authority. So neither the premonetary authors nor the monetary society authors spoke of creation. The Greek term *ktisis*, meaning "creation," seems to originate in the New Testament with it meaning "creature" in the Septuagint.[11] Creation is a uniquely biblical concept. Apart from the revelation of God this is an impossible concept.

It is impossible because there is nothing in experience that could lead to any firm knowledge of God. Paul explains the situation in Romans 1, that though it is conceivable that people know God, they cannot because of sin and the hardening of hearts. It is disobedience or rebellion that precludes knowledge of the creator, or the creation. Therefore, human relations with the creation are also estranged. No longer do people exercise their rule over the creation in a personal way, as Adam and Eve had done after the character of God, who knows and cares for each sparrow. After the Estrangement people rule in a variety of ways that pertain to the kind of society in which they live.

In premonetary societies there are numerous gods that demand certain things of people who obey. The external world is filled with all manner of creatures, both above and below humans, and it is the role of religion, ritual, and the sacred to maintain order in this world. Indeed, many rituals enable people to participate in the cosmogony on a yearly basis, as the year and the universe were often combined.[12] Every New Year was a new start in a new world and the people got to, had to, bring it out of chaos anew. Humans were viewed as integral participants in a larger order. Human rule was also social, expressed through proper social relations. People had predefined roles for them to fill as part of this larger order. The external world was at once a most intimate friend and a terrible foe depending on the mood of the god who had authority over a certain domain.

In monetary societies human rule over the creation becomes characteristically exploitative. As a personal world is depersonalized into a material

---

11. See LSJ.
12. Eliade, *Sacred and Profane*, 73.

world the fear of it decreases. Instead of participating in cosmogony, the individual can rightfully own and submit all his property to his will. Animals are given meaning by humans. The natural world is open to any use humans decide is best. So instead of personally relating to specific animals or plants, people think of universals and create value in categories of matter. Objects become resources, commodities, and capital that can be bought, traded, and sold without ever having to refer to their use value. Because matter and spirit are distinguished it is possible to turn to full scale exploitation of the natural world, for it is the human spirit that gives value to matter.

In the postmonetary society, in which we currently live, we again see a strange synthesis of these previous two ideas. Never before has the natural world been so exploited, and it is still humans that give value to all things by use and exploitation. Nevertheless, there is a strong reaction against such exploitation. There is a sense in which the world itself is being reinvigorated with a universal spirit of humanity, a spirit that feels some sense of guilt and compassion with the suffering of animals, or with the destruction of beauty for the sake of profit. However, the environmentalist reaction is based in precisely the same perspective of the world as the exploiters. Environmentalists, whether aware of it or not, still believe that humans give value to the world by their use of it. But instead of campaigning against all technology, there is a similar managerial position taken. The earth needs to be saved, protected, cared for. Many Christians, following the same economic logic but reinvesting it with Christian terms, speak of "creation care" as though Adam and Eve had not delegitimized their claim to management of the creation in their sin. It is easy to see that the grounds of this managerial perspective are laid out in Genesis 1–2. But precisely here is the problem of an ontological view of the image of God. By subtle logic it is thought that humans are godlike in their managerial capacity and their creativity. By combining these two things with a notion of stewardship, Christians are able to look progressive and justify a progressive political agenda by theological ideas. The problem is that this is nothing but self-justification. In any case, it does not make economic sense to unsustainably exploit the world's resources. Christians can join in the praise of ever new technologies that can and will be used to exploit the world, while urging stewardship, sustainability, and moderation, like Solon in the face of an unleashed tidal wave of greed rooted in the infinitude of money. Recall that it was only by the creation of money that the concept of moderation became tenable or expressible. Stewardship only makes sense if one already has abandoned the Creator-creature relationship, but is attempting some way to return to it, without abandoning the gains in power humans have made over the millennia. Like warmongering politicians, we attempt to parley with God, bargaining for peace with honor—keeping our spoils but cutting our losses. We want our world to become God's again. We want God to accept the world of human creation with all the despoiling that has occurred over the millennia, to justify human inventiveness.

But it is the Estrangement that creates the necessity that proves the mother of invention. It is only in a state of dissatisfaction, in the experience of scarcity, that people create new means of achieving similar ends. Scarcity, as we've seen, exists because of desire. It is because humans, like Cain, reject the protection and provision of God that they must take care of these things for themselves. Technology is not evil, it is the transfer of the sacred into technology that is evil, as Jacques Ellul says.[13] It is the total dependence on technique, not only for sustenance, but also for spiritual meaning that further deepens our estrangement from the God who promises abundance if we "seek first his kingdom and his righteousness." Our continual creation of and adaptation to our cosmos through technology only deepens our estrangement from God, because each new invention or technique reinforces the epistemology of the Estrangement. It is only when people have created the means of corporate self-sufficiency that the concept of God is obviated. And it is in this situation that Christians attempt to reintroduce a concept of God as an adornment or decoration, a jewel in the crown of human conquest.

Although there are attempts to reintroduce some level of personality to aspects of the world in the postmonetary world these are nothing but attempts to cover over the fact that value is a human concept and is given only by humans. There is a creation of the Other to mask the reality of fiat value. This is done through a reinvigorated sense of myth, a revivification of the sacred.

Estrangement from God creates estrangement from God's creation. The epistemology of the Estrangement, the turning from mediation through God to a material orientation of the mind, necessarily leads to an economic relationship with the world. It cannot but become resources, given meaning by humans in their religion, industry, trade, and management. There is not one part of creation that is untouched by the Estrangement because all aspects of creation lose their identity mediated through God and so transform into whatever identity humans assign.

The Estrangement also creates the notion of scarcity as something that exists in the world itself. Whereas God's creation was abundant, it can no longer be seen in this way. It is given value by quantification of its resources. Desire creates scarcity, which then creates value. But this scarcity is again a

---

13. Ellul, *New Demons*, 206.

masked projection. It is not reasonable to see scarcity as a human problem, and so it must be a problem with the world around us, a problem that must be solved by the creation of new technologies.

So the Estrangement creates an economic relationship between people and the world outside of themselves. Creation is lost and the earth is divided up into quantifiable blocks that are suitably scarce to be valuable enough to exploit and trade. But it is not the world itself that exists this way, it is the human mind separated from God.

Other People

The Estrangement also fundamentally transforms interpersonal relationships. The first reactions of Adam and Eve to eating the fruit are shame and hiding, even from one another, by improvised clothing. Their relationship is now mediated through material and the image they can project by invention. It is quite important that the Bible reports clothing as the first invention of humans as a response to the Estrangement. Genesis makes quite a lot of their shameless nakedness prior to the Estrangement, and so the clothing is also very conspicuous. They are not simply hiding. Were this the case they would have split up and run off. As it is they encounter God together. They are hiding by projection, not by separation but by unity in deception. Just as morality is created in the Estrangement, so also is shame. Shame is not a reality that exists outside human relations, and this means that clothing does nothing to actually conceal shame. Shame exists within them and no clothing can change that. But they can work to create dignity and honor by the projection of an alternative self through clothing. For it is in the Estrangement that identity becomes something constructed, something that the individual is responsible for. And for this the individual turns toward what surrounds them, in this case fig leaves, in other cases cotton, steel, fashions of various subgroups, to clothe themselves and create an identity. But because identity becomes mediated by the created products it is, again, a masked projection.

Because identity becomes constructed and found in human creations, it is thenceforth impossible to have the same naked and shameless relationship that Adam and Eve shared before. God accepts this, understands their shame, and himself makes clothing for them. God does not thereby legitimize clothing, or their constructed identity. But it is an example of mercy and grace. God, of course, does not look at the outside. Projections have no merit and no effect on God, before whom "all are naked and exposed"[14] Es-

14. Heb 4:13.

trangement from God necessarily leads to estrangement from others. And yet people must still relate and interact.

Clothing is in itself a very profound artifice, but it is simply a microcosm of an entire constructed cosmos. People must now figuratively clothe themselves. Human relations become artificial or constructed. Culture and society are created in ways that, unsurprisingly, dialectically are shaped by and shape their cosmos. But social relations cannot be self-consciously self-created. Just as in clothing, it is necessary to project and mask. Just as clothing both conceals the self and creates an image, so too societies conceal and project. Social roles and class structures, for example, must be placed back on the gods, the ancestors, nature, or natural law or rights. Gender roles are perhaps one of the best examples of this. One finds gender roles explained in cosmogonies. One sees models of sexuality and roles in nearly everything: in rain on furrowed ground, in other animals, in machinery, in architecture. Even in contemporary times the seeming confusion and redefinition of sexual and gender identities is little but a modeling of what has become for us our natural environment: technology. Technology tolerates all things that do not cause harm or inefficiency. We are no longer confined to the binary male or female identities so prevalent in previous human history, for little other reason than we do not spend time with plants and animals, and so our identity is more and more constructed in terms of what we construct.

Estrangement from God is not somehow the loss of objectivity, though. It is not as though God has given Adam and Eve a full account of gender roles. Genesis 1–3 has proven fertile ground for the projection of many different perspectives of social roles looking for biblical legitimation, and this is a helpful indication that Genesis does not itself describe the shape of these social roles. Though it presents a binary sexual division, there is not actually any sexual behavior in the garden of Eden, demonstrating that the identity of Adam and Eve is not primarily or even secondarily understood as sexual. The command to reproduce is equivalent to that given to other animals and so not an outstanding species trait. Genesis 1–2 is quite unique in its lack of social and religious roles. Male domination is part of the curse, not part of God's creation. It is on account of violence and estrangement, not because God sanctions it. But Genesis also gives no account of rights. Instead, the man and the woman relate to each other through the relationship they have with God. When this is abandoned, their relationship is transformed. Again, not because objectivity has been lost, but because their relationship is no longer mediated through God, but through projections. The subjectivity/objectivity divide is itself a perspective only possible by means of the Estrangement because it holds that there is some kind of wholly impersonal and nonhuman truth "out there" from which one can derive more valid ways of thinking and living. This is again masked projection.

Such masked projection is essential for the formation of notions of property and ownership, however. Just as clothing and other artifices are used to create identity, so also property becomes a crucial factor in the formation of identity. The notion of ownership is an entirely competitive concept and is little more than posturing. It is claiming something for oneself to the exclusion of all other people. Because property is exclusive, it is very powerful in the formation of identity, because it dramatically particularizes. This object only belongs to this person. And this person, especially in premonetary societies, inhabits history and adds to history precisely by means of possessing an heirloom. Its uniqueness conveys some gravitas to the possessor. This is most profoundly illustrated in the personal seal of a king. It can act as the king himself in his absence, conveying his authority to a document or emissary. It is through the object that the person is treated as one who has authority.

We saw that the introduction of coined money changed all that. Money is purposefully without a history and conveys no particular history. It is anonymous. Nevertheless, by means of money one can make a name for oneself by the acquisition of a comparatively larger sum.

In the postmonetary world we again live in a combination of the two other perspectives. We use anonymous money to buy products that give us meaning and identity. But these are not heirlooms. Like coined money they are mass produced and functionally identical. It is by superficial differentiation that people construct identities through their products, by selecting certain brands, colors, sizes, operating systems, etc., one can feel unique. This is most prevalent in teenagers, though it certainly is not confined to an age bracket. This differentiation is, once again, masked projection, because the differences are highly superficial. A car, for example, performs the same function, but nevertheless it becomes a chief means of self-identification. A family man has a minivan, a midlife crisis man has a sports car, a young single woman has a cute car. And all of this can be taken a step further with stickers, or personally with tattoos.

Estrangement necessitates relations mediated through artifice, and our projections through these artifices must be unique to give us personality and individual value. It's embarrassing to wear the same dress as another woman to the same event, unless it is specifically an event of solidarity, like bridesmaids, or the imposition of a new aspect of identity, like a graduation. Difference is never equal. "Separate but equal" has long been found a mistaken, though now ubiquitous belief. All differences have different value to different people. Hence there is exchange, and in exchange one can create profit. As time wears on people who have a keener insight into the mechanisms of economic relationships are able to advance on the backs and ignorance of others. Debt is created to meet social obligations and unpaid debts can transform into moral debts that alter a person's social position. And this leads to the formation of hierarchical relationships.

So Estrangement creates the contradictory ideas that so define social relations: equality and hierarchy. These concepts are codependent, revealing that they share the same economic perspective. Hierarchy requires equality amongst social equals. Equality requires a conscious rejection of hierarchical identity. Equality is a reactive position to the necessity of hierarchy in valuation. We have to know what separates us in order to know what can unite us. These concepts are both based in estrangement. For where people relate to one another mediated by their relationship with God, there can be no question of hierarchy or equality, because there is only one between them, and that one is the unique person of God. Estrangement, then, is the basis of economic identity, of class systems, of social hierarchy, and of created personal value by artifice. If this begins to sound like the Estrangement is the basis for the entire human world, then the task is nearly complete.

Cosmos

First of all, it is a mistake to refer to *the* cosmos, as though there were one. I am using the term to both refer to the world "out there" and to the humanly constructed conception of what is "out there." Again, the subjectivity/objectivity dichotomy is itself based in the epistemology of the Estrangement that the Greeks discovered in their differentiation between the way of seeming and the way of reality. Recall that the ancient Greek philosophers, like Parmenides, posed the idea that Being is singular. The fundamental unity of the universe is a unity that exists in the human mind, and it is an idea that is hard to account for without recourse to money, as we saw from the work of Richard Seaford. There is little so counterintuitive to human experience than monism. The notion of a natural system, popularized by ecology, is fruit of the invention of electrical systems. It is only by the creation of cybernetics that concepts like *the ecosystem* have become possible. So there are many *cosmoi*, because there are many possible constructions of a cosmos that have similarities and differences.

A cosmos is a humanly created universe projected and masked. It is a conception of the external world grounded in story and in metaphysics. The cosmos is inevitably formed out of chaos. Chaos is the experience of a radical sameness in which value, morality, and identity is nonexistent or amorphous. Mythological accounts of chaos and of the golden age support this in ancient literature, but it is also visible in modern historical narrative that emphasizes revolution as the chaos out of which springs a new and just order.

Cosmos is an account of everything. It is similar to the now popular concept of *weltanschauung*, "world view," but distinct in some significant ways. World view is a somewhat passive concept that has the person viewing an objective reality through a different lens, as though one were looking on a distant object through a telescope. Cosmos is constructed. World view implies a distinction between seeming and reality, that there is a reality "out there" of which different people have a different perception. The idea of cosmos as I am using does not acknowledge a distinction between seeming and reality. Cosmos is reality, but is humanly constructed. And though it is only a projection, that does not mean that it is any less real to those who live within it. In this way there are as many worlds, as many realities, as many *cosmoi* as there are social groups. The notion of world view does not acknowledge that it is a projection or construction, it simply acknowledges differences in perception, and so still can refer to a proper or master view. This tends to support an ontological view of God as the source of all objectivity, that, if one could gain access the divine perspective, one could know objectivity. This concept of world view is not much different from that of the pre-Socratics. Like Parmenides there is Being or the One, by somehow participating in that, by enlightenment, by transcending the particular, one can access the universal. Herein we see the basis of mysticism and philosophical religions of enlightenment, and unfortunately many well meaning Christians set forth just such a view. But, even if there is only some merit in the arguments set forth in chapter 2 on historic economics, that as Seaford argues, coined money is one major source and prerequisite for metaphysical speculation, then it becomes clear that the notion of world view is simply another expression of a metaphysical perspective grounded in the ontology of money and not of reality or of God.

Because of this I speak of cosmos, a term properly belonging to mythology, though now has been applied to a scientific field related to the speculative endeavor of hypothesizing about the origins of the "universe." I would argue that scientific cosmology is myth making dressed in scientific formulation, insofar as people use it to assign value, meaning, or purpose to aspects of, or the whole of, life. Though cosmos is a mythological term, I do not mean that we should be blissfully ignorant of our own projection mechanism, but instead own them and take responsibility for them. These are not simply views, but are creations. Indeed, they are counter-creations as we said with Cain's building of the city of Enoch.

Cosmos construction is not simply myth making. Myths have exceedingly practical and immediate consequences. For example, modern people cannot conceive of a world in which technological possibilities are purposefully not implemented. For the ancient Greeks, however, this happened in numerous ways. The structure of their stories enabled some of their brightest minds to shun praxis. The beginning of philosophy with Thales is one such example. The story goes, as Aristotle tells us, that someone challenged Thales saying philosophy was useless. It was totally impractical. Thales, apparently using some astronomical or climate knowledge, was able to predict a bumper crop in olives. He gathered money and bought shares in all of the local olive presses at a low price. When the bumper crop came in, Thales made a fortune by subletting the presses. But then he despised it, showing that the life of the mind disdains the commoner's or merchant's stupid interest in making money for money's sake.[15] Whether or not this happened we cannot know, and it does fit Aristotle's own perspective on philosophy and money very well. Philosophy was eminently practical, he believed, but to use it for purposes of making money or putting slaves out of a job was not fitting of an aristocrat.

A second example of the Greek's disdain of applied science is Hero's steam engine and a wide variety of other technological marvels the Greeks invented. Hero's engine is an extremely simple but profound machine, a bronze sphere mounted on a spit so that it could spin on the horizontal axis. On opposing sides of the sphere there were tapered ducts or pipes bent ninety degrees. When the sphere was filled with water and heated over a flame, the water would boil and steam would escape through these angled pipes. Their angle created rotation. Now, if one attached a pulley and rope system to this and scaled it up, one would have a functioning steam engine capable of replacing human labor. The technology was right at their fingertips for an industrial revolution. But there was none. The great minds were interested in the life of the mind, not in making life easier. Nearly all of the philosophers were ascetics of a sort, including Epicurus. Epicurus taught that life should be enjoyed while you have it. But for him the enjoyment of the intellect far surpassed that of the body, and so one would be more happy if one ate in moderation foods that were bland but nutritious. Epicurus, the inspiration for the modern word *Epicurean* meaning a food connoisseur, ate mostly bread, and some cheese on feast days. The intelligentsia of ancient Greece were mostly aristocrats who had no interest in making work easy, in democratizing their privilege, or in a crass gratification of the flesh. In such a cosmos technological advancement is more an enemy than a friend,

---

15. Aristotle, *Politics*, 1259a.

so although it is fully possible, it is not pursued because the ends it would create were undesirable.

The way in which a world is constructed, therefore, has profound implications on the shape of all things. We have already explained how the transition from a debt-based economy to a monetary economy transformed society. Beliefs about one aspect of life influences other aspects in very practical ways.

The very impulse to create a cosmos is the outcome of the Estrangement. When people are estranged from God they first enter into a situation of chaos, and out of this chaos comes cosmos, constructed by themselves in such a way that people cannot understand that it is self-constructed. A cosmos is not a personal invention, but a world that takes generations to build. One is born into a cosmos, imbibes it for an entire life, and if not challenged with chaotic elements, elements that do not fit or jar with the cosmos, then one will never question the cosmos; no division between seeming and reality could be possible. This means that foreigners tend to be viewed as not part of the same species, since they tell a story of a cosmos that is absurd, and the scapegoat mechanism is developed to ensure the health of the cosmos.

In the Estrangement creation is lost and so the impersonal cosmos is constructed. The creation was characterized not by anything intrinsic to itself, but by its relation to the Creator. Its form is the will of the Creator and it is an exact representation in material form of his idea. This is why God "saw that it was good." When Cain built a city, and humans continued to do the same throughout time, they have continued to create at the cost of God's creation. As cosmoi become larger and larger, with more education, more accounting for unexplained forces, challenges to the cosmoi become less regular, producing a deeper trust and allegiance. Any notion of God as a being external and removed from the cosmos is done away with if there are no forces that are inexplicable within a cosmos. Jacques Ellul says, speaking of Babel,

> It was there that his pretension of becoming a subject, never again to be an object, could be realized. The cities of our time are most certainly that place where man can with impunity declare himself master of nature. It is only in an urban civilization that man has the metaphysical possibility of saying, "I killed God."[16]

So, with the possibility of critique excluded, the cosmos becomes more and more complete the more people are surrounded by human creations of all kinds. For it is not just technology or architecture that is part of

---

16. Ellul, *Meaning of the City*, 16.

constructing a cosmos, but literature, art, music, and agricultural technique. It is in human society: in marriage and family, law, politics, race, tribe, gender roles, sexuality, war, justice, and work. Religion might be understood as the primary means of constructing the cosmos, but is important to see that it too exists in a dialectical relationship with all other areas of the cosmos. In all of this the role of economics should not be underestimated, nor overestimated. Capitalism, socialism, and more classical Marxism have tended to maximize the role that economics has played in shaping history, history being one major way in which a cosmos constructs and is constructed by an awareness of time. These schools of thought make economic or class relations to be *the* determining factor in history. This is an overly narrow view. And there are many other oversimplistic constructions of history, like technology (stone age, bronze age, iron age, space age, information age, etc.), great individuals, nations, war, *Geist*, sex. Certainly what is being presented in this book has the potential to be oversimplistic and I have emphasized that money and the economic relationship are not singular factors. And yet I am saying that there is one determinative factor that initiates and sustains the need for cosmos construction: the Estrangement. The Estrangement does not determine the precise shape that a cosmos takes, or that history takes. Sin is profoundly determinative and fatalistic, but not in any necessarily particular way. The Estrangement creates a trajectory and it is up to people to artfully and creatively operate within this trajectory. We might say that the Estrangement creates a near infinitude of possibilities, excepting the possibility of peace, reconciliation with God, with one another, and with God's creation. The angst of the Estrangement is the muse of human creativity. This is not a condemnation of creativity, but of its ground of expression. It is cosmos creation. It is the creation of a social group. It is self-creation. And all of this creativity operates mediated through matter, expressing itself by its relationship with its own projected and masked cosmos. A romantic poet who waxes lyrical about the wonders of nature is expressing herself by means of her own projected and masked understanding of nature. So human creation takes the form of the world, but this is a world that has already been constructed by people over generations.

In this notion of the Estrangement we begin to develop a very different concept of sin than traditional theology has held. Rather than obedience or disobedience to a law, rather than acting against "nature" (the cosmos), sin is nothing more and nothing less than estrangement from God. Now, sin manifests itself in disobedience to God who gives law as a boundary marker to show his people when they, like sheep, have gone astray. But if we confine sin to law we miss out on its most major and profound aspect—that our very world, our very conception of reality, is an expression of sin. To put this another way, sin transforms human epistemology, giving people access only to their own projection of the world. God is systematically excluded from human epistemology.

This also transforms the way we think about original sin and why it is that all humans die because of the sin of one man, as Paul explains it. Rather than having the idea of the imputation of Adam's sin, an idea that is difficult to understand on any conception of justice, sin is transmitted generationally through the cosmos. People are epistemologically incapable of escaping sin. There is no right and proper way to view or construct the world that is accessible to humans of their own will. And all people are responsible for the continuation of sin, passing it on, mostly unwillingly, to descendants, not biologically, but in every possible manifestation of human creativity. Again it's not the creativity that is problematic, it's the desire out of which the creativity happens and the means by which it happens. Therefore, original sin does not effect the ontology of humanity or of the creation. It is not as though Adam and Eve creating morality by eating the fruit somehow immediately corrupts the nature of all things. But humans are responsible for the ever increasing corruption of what God created by human creativity. So the creation is corrupted, not by the single act itself, but by the radical transformation of the mind that occurs when it is estranged from God.

If money is one of the major bases of metaphysics and Christians have almost universally viewed original sin in ontological terms, then it follows that the traditional Christian vision of original sin is based, not in Scripture, but in economic logic. We need to be careful here. Sin has not always been primarily understood in financial terms, though certainly this has happened. But an ontological version of sin is genealogically rooted in the metaphysics of money. Rather than having a story-based version of sin, ontological sin is something that exists in human nature. Therefore, to be human is to be flawed. This is part of our everyday language, whether Christian or not. "I'm only human" is a common justification for imperfection. This idea of sin as an imperfection, flaw, or fallenness of human nature is purely metaphysical and we see an almost exact correlation between this vision of sin and the Titanic sin of Orphic mystery religion. This kind of sin is based, as we saw, in thinking related to the formation of coined money, that allowed for the division between body and soul to be complete. The soul participates in the divine, in Being, if allowed to transcend or escape the body. The body, as a particular instantiation, is necessarily imperfect. For it to be perfect it would have to be equivalent with the ideal, and so no longer be particular. So heaven becomes the place of disembodied spirits communing with the divine.

One could interpret Augustine's understanding of sin as *homo incurvatus in se*[17] in light of these ideas. Augustine was himself deeply influenced by Neoplatonism with thinkers like Plotinus, who taught that all things were emanations of, or the overflowing of, divine Being. *Homo incurvatus in se* is not as good of a description, I think, as *people estranged from God, creating their own worlds*. This has the effect of humans curving in on themselves, but it's not a conscious inward curving, it's an outward orientation. It isn't pure selfishness, or self-centeredness, because this self-centeredness has to be masked in projections. And this is where we see the economic nature of sin come to the fore in a different way. Ontological sin is an idea rooted in the logic of a metaphysics heavily influenced by money. In the version of sin I am giving, sin creates economic relationships. It is not itself based in economic logic, it creates economic logic of all forms.

So it is that the Bible itself uses economic language to partially communicate the meaning of sin. Jesus speaks of sin as a debt in the Matthean version of the Lord's Prayer and in a number of his parables. Now, he is not equating sin with debt as though God is the great creditor in the sky. Debt is but an analogy for sin. As we shall see later, Jesus profoundly subverts economic relations, and so he cannot be understood as projecting debt onto the cosmos. Debt itself is sin, however, for it is, *par excellence,* a relationship of estrangement, as it mediates relationships through the external world.

CONCLUSION

The story related in Genesis 1–11 is very rich, and by a careful study, armed with the theory of the importance of money for the formation of metaphysics, we come to see a very different view of sin than has often been set forth. Rather than original sin having ontological implications, we saw that the break in relationship had epistemological results. Rather than oriented to the creation through a relationship with God, in their primal sin Adam and Eve oriented themselves to God through the external world. Because of this, God became nothing more than a projection of their desires shaped by the world around them. Henceforth, humans engaged in a dialectical relationship with the external world, shaping it and being shaped by it. Because of this broken relationship people are systematically unable to reach God.

---

17. Latin: "man curved in on himself."

5

Reconciliation: Subverting Economic Relations

The Bible was written in two of the three kinds of economy we investigated. Because of this, it is highly problematic to seek eternal truths about economic justice or ethics in a straightforward way from the biblical texts. We simply do not exist in either of the two kinds of societies or worlds in which the Bible was written. The Old Testament was written over quite a long span of time and in various locations, and depending on the dating of certain books we cannot simply say that it was all written in a premonetary society, though the vast majority was. Recall that the definition of money given in chapter 2 could not be based on the exchange of precious metals alone, to which we find reference throughout the Old Testament. Even in the later prophets a shekel clearly refers to weight, not to a specific coin or denomination.[1] Nehemiah 5:4 refers to a state tax paid in silver and the mortgaging of property to acquire silver to pay this tax. Archeologically, the first apparent Jewish coins were minted under the later Persian rule in the fourth century BC. This suggests that the transition from premonetary to monetary society would be largely confined to the postexilic period, with the New Testament firmly and clearly rooted in the monetary milieu.

---

1. See for example Jer 32:9–10. Jewish people would likely have first encountered coinage in Persian exile, but the Persians did not make widespread use of coinage for quite some time. Their coinage was initially derivative of Lydian coins, and later their Darics were too valuable for general circulation. Seaford, *Money and the Early Greek Mind*, 128–29.

Because of this it is anachronistic for translators to render *kesef* as "money" in many of its occurrences, especially in earlier books like the Pentateuch. The Torah and its approach to wealth should then be understood not in relation to a monetary economy, but to a debt-based society. And this will have some significant repercussions for how we understand certain key financial concepts that are often used today in churches, like stewardship, which I will explain in our ethical chapter.

Because we are dealing with a large period of time and different economies in the Bible, it is important to look both at narrative and systematic themes. Any systematic approach to money in the Bible that does not take into account the radical changes that coined money introduced will read preconceived principles into texts that cannot support such anachronistic interpretations, the tithe being an excellent example. This chapter will not be a complete investigation of all pertinent story points, nor of all systematic themes related to economics. Instead, we focus on the economic relationship and how the revelation of God's work of reconciliation subverts it.

STORY—OLD TESTAMENT

The narrative of Genesis quickly turns from estrangement to reconciliation. There are inklings of this in the *protoeuangellion*[2] of Genesis 3:15. The story of Noah and God's judgment on all of his estranged creation in Genesis 6–9 is a unique break in the story of estrangement. From Genesis 3–5 the rebellion of humanity becomes greater and more blatant. The violence of Cain grows to fullness in Lamech, his seventh generation descendant. There is some prohibited marriage that happens leading to the rise of the nephilim, who seem to embody violence. Violence is not itself the problem, as some theologians seem to suggest,[3] but it is the most apparent manifestation of estrangement possible. Violence is the prime example of a person or group of people judging for themselves what is right and wrong and meting out their own justice. Adam and Eve's sin of becoming like God in creating good and evil is manifest when close-knit social groups assert themselves over others and so take on godlikeness to the detriment of other people.

The rise in violence becomes too much for God to tolerate and God destroys humanity and much of his creation in the flood. It is important to recall that other ancient Near Eastern literature describes a similar deluge. Whether this is because of a similar experience, or a similar fear of the

2. Greek: "first gospel."
3. For example, Walter Wink's trilogy on the powers places violence at the heart of evil.

sea and the chaos it symbolizes, is hard to know. But once again Genesis is playing with preexisting material, purposefully changing it and subverting its original meaning. The facts of the flood are irrelevant; the theology is very relevant. Human violence has not only grown against other people, but against God's creation, so that even it is becoming corrupt. Humans are destroying God's creation in their estrangement from him. Genesis portrays God as frustrated with humanity and in desperation for his whole creation, even regretting that he made it. In other words, God is not impressed with humanity and will destroy it to prevent its corruption from spreading like a disease.

The Flood

But in the midst of this violence there is one man in particular who seems better than others, Noah. And through him and the famous ark, God will preserve a seed for a new beginning. This is the first picture of how God will work through chosen people to reconcile all creation to himself.

The story of the flood is also a contrasting narrative to the remainder of Scripture. After the flood, God, with the sign of the rainbow, promises to never undo his creation again in such a way. This promise is quite important because it contrasts the remainder of Scripture with notions of God as a judge who only visits judgment on people, a God who is the enemy of humanity and friend of only a select few. Taken out of context, as most popular interpretation is and has been, the flood narrative confirms a terrible God of the Old Testament that so many dislike. This is an unfortunate misunderstanding of the narrative function of this story in Genesis, the Pentateuch, and the remainder of Scripture. The flood really should be understood as speaking directly against such a view of God as vengeful by his promise at the conclusion. From a systematic theological perspective, and the perspective of the book of Hebrews (13:8), God does not change or repent. But God is presented as having done something unique in the flood that will not occur again, and if there is one character trait of God in the Old Testament it is God's covenant faithfulness. In being faithful to the covenant of Noah, God makes a covenant with Abraham, demonstrating that God will work through humans in an entirely different way than the gods of any other religion or faith. Instead of being for or against, instead of taking a stance of direct involvement, God begins the process of reconciliation mediated through people.

This should be reminiscent of the notion of the image of God as political representation as I framed it earlier. Indeed, it is by reconciliation that the image of God is, in some way, recovered. Just as God would work through Adam and Eve to rule his creation, so the reconciliation presented from Genesis 12 through the remainder of Scripture will be worked through people. The remainder of Scripture is a drama of God's faithfulness to this admittedly fragile and precarious arrangement. For the success of this arrangement is predicated on the faithfulness of individuals in whom this message and mission of reconciliation is entrusted.

Abraham

The covenant God makes with Abraham has a number of parts depending on how one separates them out. I will combine them into two main ideas. God makes and confirms his covenant with Abraham on four separate occasions, in Genesis 12, 15, 17, and 22. He promises that (1) Abraham's name would be great, that he would be a great nation, have numerous descendants, a promised land, and (2) would be a blessing to the other nations. The notion of a great nation must be understood properly in its ancient context. The modern concept of the nation-state, nationalism, and patriotism, is a creation of the eighteenth century. In the Old and New Testaments, the word we unfortunately render as "nation" ought to be understood as a people group related by some organic or familial tie. It is non-ideological and rarely primarily geographic in the modern sense of a fatherland, motherland, or homeland. God will make Abraham great, with the result that Abraham will use that blessing to bring others into reconciliation as well. And so the remainder of the Old Testament could be summarized as the continual interplay between God's faithfulness to blessing the descendants of Abraham, and the continued failure of the majority of these people to be faithful in being a blessing to the other peoples.

The Abrahamic covenant is one example of God subverting religio-economic contracts. In Genesis 15 God confirms the covenant with Abraham, then called Abram. They participate in a strange ritual wherein animals are killed and cut in two to demonstrate that God is faithful to his promises. In a vision Abram sees a smoking fire pot and a flaming torch pass between the carcasses. This is supposed to confirm to Abram that God will be true to his promise. To venture an educated guess at this scene we see sacrificial animals cut in two. The smoking pot and torch would suggest the acceptability of the sacrifices that would be consumed by these objects. Yet these items pass through the sacrifices without consuming them, suggesting that God is making an oath in the religious symbolism of Abram's world, that he would be cut in two, like these animals, for failure to keep his word. God is making a social contract with Abram, swearing an oath on his own life. This is given in language relevant to Abram. God condescends to speak the religious-contractual language of this ancient pagan. Much of ancient religion is bound up with vows or votive offerings—deals made with the gods. If the gods keep their part and bring success to the person's endeavor, then that person vowed to give a certain sacrifice or donation. Swearing these oaths and keeping them lies at the heart of piety. To be successful and forget one's vow invites disaster and the vengeance of the offended god.[4] But in this vow it is God who is swearing to Abram. The hierarchy is inverted. Instead of Abram vowing to God a sacrifice that God would give him success in his endeavors, God gives Abram a promise and confirms it with an oath sworn upon himself that he should be cut in two if proven wrong. Already in the Bible we see God condescending to people, to speak their language, to undergo their rituals, to enter into economic agreements with them. But these are not agreements on human terms as a normal vow is. God subverts this religio-economic contract by inverting the relationship, demonstrating that God does not respect human vows or work for people seeking repayment in sacrifice. Rather, Abram does the work of God and God makes the vow. In such a premonetary world as Abram inhabits, God's vow targets the very heart of the estrangement between God and people. The economic relationship between God and humans is turned on its head, not by demolishing the system, but by God condescending to invert the system and so empty it of meaning. God initiates reconciliation.

The content of the promise, to be a great nation, to receive a political and economic blessing, is not as an end in itself, but is part of God's plan of reconciliation through subversion. The promised land is only given for the purpose of drawing people in, to be reconciled to the one and true God. This is subversive, if understood properly, for it means that though the Jews posses the land, they do not own it. The economic status of the land is not the same as those who are estranged from God. It is not private property, but God's land. This is why Abraham, though he never possesses the land, journeys through it and sets up altars or shrines throughout, as though he were marking boundaries of space where God is Lord.

---

4. This can be seen quite well in Plutarch's biography of Camillus, a Roman general who made a vow to the god of Delphi of a tenth of the spoils of Veii if he was successful, a vow which he failed to satisfy. The booty was distributed to the soldiers. When he remembered his vow he told the senate and they decided that, since recovering the actual 10 percent would be nearly impossible, the soldiers who received the booty should give 10 percent to the public treasury, which was then used to make a massive bowl of gold and send it to Delphi. *Camillus*, 7.5–8.2.

Moses

The Hebrews are not allowed to take possession of the land because the sin of the Amorites has not yet reached its full measure, according to Genesis 15. But I think there must also be an element of preparation of God's people for the task of inheriting the land. Throughout Genesis we see a slow growth of the knowledge of who God is. Abraham knows little. Jacob has a variety of clearly pagan practices, like the establishment of standing stones, which are understood as the dwelling place of a god. This we see at Bethel, where he has the vision of angels ascending and descending. But when he wrestles with who he understands to be God at the River Jabbok, he quickly reforms his household's religious practices, abandoning all their idols, and himself reforming his character to now be reconciled to Esau. Moses himself must go through a process or a journey of learning about the character of God, such that it takes eighty years before he approaches Pharaoh with the demand to release his people so that they can go and worship this God. If the Hebrews do not know who God is, they cannot bring people to reconciliation with him. And thus it is important that God is understood in terms of his faithfulness to generations, that he is primarily understood in the Pentateuch as the "God of Abraham, Isaac, and Jacob." The long-standing covenant faithfulness (*ḥesed*) must be established as the basis of the occupation of a promised land. Only in response to this *ḥesed* will the Israelites achieve the sole purpose for which they were chosen: to be a blessing and thus bring others into reconciliation with God.

God blesses a people in a manner befitting a people of their own era and it is the task of that people to use this blessing to subvert the estranged way of life of their neighboring peoples. Some of the economic policies laid out in the Torah help us to understand this subversion. Though a detailed study of many specific biblical laws would be enlightening I will investigate only at the so-called Jubilee laws, as they are often referenced today.

Jubilee

The Jubilee laws given in Leviticus 25 and 27 are not entirely unique to the Torah, but resemble the practices of other ancient Near Eastern groups, as we saw earlier. What makes them unique is that they are not transformation of financial debts into debts of gratitude, honor, and fidelity to the human king. Given in Leviticus these laws are pre-monarchical. One could argue, of course, that this could be a later addition from Jewish experience in exile in Babylon where this kind of debt forgiveness was common practice,[5] but the text itself does not mediate this debt liberation through the king. So, regardless of the time in which this text was written it is significant that the Jubilee is not mediated through the king. In this way the Jewish Jubilee holds an implicit critique of the kind of debt forgiveness practiced in surrounding people groups. Their debt forgiveness is no forgiveness at all, it is deeply politically motivated. In a way it is buying the loyalty of the indebted masses at the price of the satisfaction of the aristocracy. It came about as the result of peasant revolts in the ancient Near East. It is shrewd monarchical policy to alienate the peasants from their landlords, for this increases the power of the king by decreasing the power of a landed aristocracy. The landed aristocracy must come to understand that they own land and have workers by the leave of the king, and so their power is derived.

In the Jewish Jubilee God forgives debts. Although this can produce the same kind of debt transformation, it cannot have the same political effect as it does for an earthly king. Rather than centralizing power and transforming economic debt into moral debt or honor debt, the biblical Jubilee is symbolic of a greater liberation available in the proper relationship with God. In a sense we might call the Jubilee an Old Testament sacrament, taking common elements like debt and debt forgiveness and using them as a sign and seal of the work that God has already done for his people, not only in the exodus, but even more so in the liberation of the bondage of sin. It is a means by which God reveals himself as a liberator. Because there is no king through which this is mediated, the people are not ironically enslaved by debt forgiveness, but are truly liberated. Of course one could object that this is simply a different form of bondage, to a religious priestly order who might mediate this. But the Jubilee in no way enhanced or enriched the priesthood. They received no greater offering on a Jubilee year. Indeed, though it is not mentioned, because there would be no sowing and therefore only a meagre harvest of what naturally grows, the tithe would itself be significantly smaller, and so the priesthood would suffer economically along with all landowners.

God himself does claim the kingship. All land is his property (Lev 25:23), and it is for this reason that it cannot be sold in perpetuity. Permanent private property is excluded because God himself owns all things. Of course God does not own anything, but it is yet another way of speaking the language of a people that itself critiques the notion of ownership. When the Jubilee year comes, the great economic redistribution is but a reminder that

5. Hudson, *Restructuring the Origins of Interest-Bearing Debt and the Logic of Clean Slates*; Graeber, *Debt*, 82.

God is Lord over all, and that it is borrowed, for his people are always sojourners. Thus, the Jubilee subverts the notions of property and homeland. Rather than establishing a debt of honor to a human king who might then call in that debt to conscript soldiers, the biblical Jubilee critiques the notion that any human king could own property at all. Within the Jubilee charter is a complete rejection of centralized power and authority. For without the possibility of a family acquiring over generations, which the Jubilee prevents, it becomes impossible, so long as the law is kept, for any one family to rise to aristocracy and pass on an inordinate amount of wealth to children. This, in turn, disables the formation of long-standing generational debt that leads to permanent enslavement or serfdom.

Kingship

When the Israelites do receive a king it signifies their complete rejection of the image of God. The royal charter to rule with God is abandoned in pusillanimity. Rather than learning responsibility through reconciliation with God, they desire their relationship with God be further alienated, not only by the already present religious mediation, but now also through political mediation. A king would be the image of God alone, and be it for all the people. The economic results of this are spelled out by Samuel: conscription, enslavement, land appropriation, and taxation.[6] The economic results of estrangement from God are made very clear: further human estrangement. Monarchy is not especially problematic, ancient and modern democracies have practiced all of these things as well.

Though the people ask for a king in order to imitate their neighboring people, God again is working subversively in a way people understand. Eventually the kingship and the kingdom is proclaimed by Jesus. Until that time most of the kings are corrupted by their neighbors. It is almost without fail that, at least the way the books of Kings present it, the "good" kings are poor rulers and the "bad" kings are successful in extending borders, in war, and in trade. Solomon himself is the shining example of a good man corrupted by external influences. But Solomon begins well, asking only for wisdom to rule God's people. He's a man who initially understands what is right and lives for that duty. God rewards him also with wealth. But it is up to Solomon what to do with this, and he turns it for his own pleasure, eventually employing press-gangs to build his great works, something very unbefitting the spirit of the Jubilee. But Solomon had potential to use his power and wealth to bless other nations, as was his charter as an inheritor,

---

6. 1 Sam 8:11–17.

and now representative, of the Abrahamic covenant. The Queen of Sheba comes to hear of Solomon's wisdom, in a scene of what ought to have happened with all nations coming to recognize the splendor of God. But she leaves with some of Solomon's wealth,[7] taking away a token of something quite different from wisdom. Later the nations will come and will plunder the temple on many occasions.

Ahab's acquisition of Naboth's vineyard[8] is an excellent example of the corruption that kingship creates in economic terms. Ahab attempts to exercise eminent domain and so demonstrates that he does not believe that all land belongs to God. Rather it must belong to him, for this is what a kingdom means. The kingship, then, has potential to bring God's offer of reconciliation and love to all nations, but it fails miserably in this task.

Prophets

But God does not abandon Israel and Judah to the fate of all kingdoms. Instead, prophets convey the voice of God. The very existence of the writings of the prophets is remarkable. Even more remarkable is their inclusion as Scripture. It was common to have religious figures present in court, to help read signs and portents, to interpret dreams, to perform wondrous acts, and to give advice. Each of these functions is seen in foreign courts in the Bible, in the story of Joseph, Moses, and Daniel. The prophets are once again performing a culturally common role in advising the kings, interpreting dreams, speaking to God, and performing wondrous acts. But in performing these functions the prophets speak frankly about the failures of the king. Rather than acting as the sycophants often portrayed in literature, or schemers who use the power of a weak king to exercise regency, the prophets derive no benefit from their service. And the king does not profit by their words. The words of the prophets are critical, and much of what they attack is economic. For example, when Isaiah prophesies about a future restoration of Israel he speaks of provision without cost: "Come, everyone who thirsts, come to the waters; and he who has no silver, come, buy and eat! Come, buy wine and milk without silver and without price."[9] In this way the prophets identify that money is inimical to a state of restoration with God.

The Minor Prophets have become selectively popular in more recent decades as the social justice movement has grown in popularity. But what is vital to understand about the prophets, especially in their cries for justice,

7. 1 Kgs 10; 2 Chr 9.
8. 1 Kgs 21.
9. Isa 55:1.

is that their goal is not human justice, but reconciliation with God. Amos 4, for example, has a litany of calamities that befell Israel that were designed to break the stubborn will of the people, so that they would return to God. Social injustices are a result of the estranged relationship with God, and the solution is to return to God. If the people would return to God, God would return to them.[10] The widows, the orphans, and the foreigners are not taken care of because the people are estranged from God. These are symptoms of a deeper problem. The prophets are recognizing an essential connection between economic injustice and impiety, and between reconciliation with God and the consequent human reconciliations. They are not demanding the establishment of social welfare policies for the widows and orphans, but are attacking the rich and powerful for their broken relationship with God that manifests itself in the misery and poverty of the widows and the orphans, who ought to be taken care of without needing recourse to state institutions.

The justice for which they call is nothing other than the reign of God himself. The term we translate as "justice" is, in Hebrew, indistinguishable from judgment. It is what a judge does. As we saw in the Estrangement, judgment is at the heart of that original sin. It was the decision to decide for themselves what is right and wrong that made them godlike. Judgment is a creative act, but also an act of authority. It is an act that rightly belongs to God alone. Therefore, the justice that the prophets seek is the same as returning to God. So long as they practice their own judgment and act as judges for themselves they will go astray, hence the refrain of the book of Judges: "A man did what was right in his own eyes."

The economic message of the prophets is quite subversive, then. Rather than advocating a certain vision of economic justice that is achievable through political structure, all justice must be a relational return to God. Justice is then the result, the fruit of this reconciliation with God. That order is essential. Economic justice cannot lead to reconciliation. Justice can never itself reconcile because reconciliation has nothing to do with achieving justice. Justice, to use an economic image, balances scales. It leads to a state of equilibrium. Reconciliation is something outside of this image. It has nothing to do with balanced scales or accounts. Reconciliation requires that both the victim and the criminal move beyond justice and accounting to love, and, "love keeps no record of wrongs."[11]

God began working reconciliation in the world through his promise to Abraham. That promise adapted to the formation of a kingdom and then

---

10. Zech 1:3; Mal 3:7.

11. 1 Cor 13:5, significantly using financial/judicial terms: οὐ λογίζεται τὸ κακόν.

two kingdoms. And yet the Old Testament is, if nothing else, a litany of human failure and disappointment. A skeptic must say that Jewish people were unique in the world of religion for being almost entirely self-critical, enshrining these ideas as Scripture. A believer would ascribe this uniqueness as revelation from God. For if the social function of religion is to justify a certain identity and to underwrite the structures of power, the Hebrew Scriptures fail at creating such a religion. But throughout this description of failure one theme comes to the fore: God's faithfulness in the midst of human unfaithfulness. God continues to honor his promise, and the ancient Israelites continued to believe in the Abrahamic promise in spite of disaster after disaster. The story of reconciliation in the Old Testament is seemingly a failure then. Certainly the world has not been brought back to God by the time Alexander the Great conquers it. But this is the point of the story of the Old Testament: God is working subversively in the human cosmoi to bring reconciliation to individuals. Though the estranged desire to form our own cosmos continually works to subvert the work of reconciliation, it is in the cosmos itself that God brings reconciliation to individual people.

The individual is of great importance because it is not in people making a name for themselves or defining themselves as a people that God is at work. The entire Old Testament narratives focus on single people. It is not a history of a people as a whole so much as it is the commentary of certain people within that larger history. A person is proven good or bad not on their worldly successes, but on their faithfulness to God. And so, even though God promises to bless Abraham with a great nation for descendants, it is by the faithfulness of Abraham that God works in the world for reconciliation.

STORY—NEW TESTAMENT

Jesus is the fulfillment of God's plan of reconciliation. In Jesus's life and teachings this reconciliation is pronounced in ways subversive to economic relations. There are a number of teachings to look at, as Jesus teaches through and against money on a great many occasions. We will not be able to look at all of them, but many create a clear picture of what his kingdom is like and how economic relations are irreconcilable with this kingdom.

Call of Discipleship

When Jesus calls his disciples, they lay down their livelihoods to follow him. But others leave him when they hear that foxes have holes and birds have nests, but that Jesus has no home. The cost of following Jesus is total: "So therefore, whoever of you does not give up all his possessions cannot be my disciple."[12] Following Jesus is the total abandonment of any relationship that is not mediated through him. Being a disciple means following someone and loving whom he loves, in the way he loves. If discipleship costs nothing, then it is worth nothing. If it does not cost family relationships, or honoring the dead,[13] then it is not real. The interesting thing about Jesus's call to discipleship is that it does *cost* everything. Until one has emptied oneself of what is valuable one cannot accept a different valuation. Discipleship is a subversion of economic relations because it costs everything. It leaves nothing left for the disciple to fall back upon. There is no alternative love that can be secretly tended.

Beatitudes

Jesus, in the Sermon on the Mount, reframes the concept of blessedness. The *makarioi*[14] statements are often translated as "blessed" but through long-term familiarity and millennia of Christendom, the ambiguity of this term has been lost. *Makarios* could reasonably be translated with "happy," an English word that has its root in an archaic word, *hap*. *Hap* is luck or fortune, and we see it in various terms: happy, happenstance, happen. These words initially had a notion of hidden agency. By this, there is a deep connection between the circumstances of one's life, hidden agency, and an emotional state of being. *Blessing* or *blessed* has a similar connection between external agency, good life circumstances, and emotion. *Favor* is a similar concept, leading to blessedness. In this way people of many cultures have identified happiness with divine agency. It is by enjoying the favor of the gods that one is successful and happy, and one can gain the favor of the gods by sacrifice. In the Beatitudes Jesus subverts these notions.

Instead of the material prosperity evident in the promise to Abraham, Jesus says that the poor are blessed. Rather than attacking wealth, Jesus explains that the poor are the ones who enjoy God's favor. Indeed, the kingdom of heaven belongs to the poor.

---

12. Luke 14:33. It is important that "all his possessions" is ὑπάρχουσιν, a participle of ὑπάρχω, which can mean "to be" or "to exist" with the extended meaning of "to possess." The connection between being and possessing is extremely close, such that the concept of being in itself is an extension of possession, as we saw with *ousia*.

13. Luke 14:26; Matt 8:22; Luke 9:60.

14. Plural Greek adjective usually translated as "blessed." Epicurus sometimes substituted his usual term, ἡδονή, "sweetness," for, μακαριότης, "blessedness."

Instead of the blessing of a great nation also promised to Abraham, Jesus says that the humble and persecuted are blessed. It is not by mediating identity through the great powers, through kings and kingdoms, or through large corporate identities that one is blessed. Those who are outcasts, who are mistreated and ostracized by the large identity, are actually those that God has shown favor towards. This should not be too surprising if we return to the problems we saw with Cain, Babel, and the Israelite desire for a king. The desire to seek identity mediated by external things: a city, a tower, a king or nation, is a desire to be estranged from God. And yet it is that very estrangement that leads to success in the economic world. For Jesus, economic success demonstrates estrangement from God.

So, the meek or gentle shall inherit the whole earth. What might at first appear to be a clear break with Old Testament patterns, "You have heard that it was said . . . , but I tell you . . ." turns out to be a fulfillment of what was intended all along. The Jewish people assumed it was through their corporate identities that God was at work blessing them. But Jesus clarifies that God's kingdom does not belong to kings and high priests, but to the lowly.

Lex Talionis

When Jesus comes to the *lex talionis*, he is not proclaiming that the Torah was wrong to demand an eye for an eye. Jesus is not here advocating a new kind of justice, but is actually explaining that those who follow him abandon justice. Throughout Matthew 5 Jesus is explaining the superiority of reconciliation to justice. Reconciliation is not justice; it goes well beyond justice. Justice is itself an economic concept, rooted in marketplace imagery. Justice has become inconceivable without reference to some measure of accounting. The *lex talionis* was a very basic accounting method of direct reciprocity. It seems inhumane today, but only because we are used to outsourcing justice to the state, which economizes justice and translates nearly every crime into a quantitative sentence that offers little or no compensation or restitution to the victim. The more justice is given to ever larger authorities, the more it depersonalizes and turns justice into a commodity that primarily benefits the state. But Jesus takes justice out of the hands of the powerful. He encourages people to work out their differences before reaching court.[15] Reconciliation belongs in the hands of each individual person. It cannot be outsourced, not even to religion. Jesus says that one must not offer a sacrifice if one has something against one's brother. Instead one must be reconciled

---

15. Matt 5:25–26.

first before offering sacrifice.[16] The whole point of the religious system in the Old Testament was to recall people to a reconciled relationship with God. Religion did not itself create reconciliation with God any more than the *lex talionis* did between people. But these laws provided means by which reconciliation could begin. They provided boundary markers to highlight brokenness and estrangement. When wrongly used, the *lex talionis*, and the religious system, were understood as means to justice and righteousness in themselves, thus making God superfluous and the performance of duty primary. Thus, these systems of justice and religion served their opposite purpose—creating further estrangement from God.

Treasure

Wealth itself is an impediment to one's relationship with God, whether it be for a poor or a rich person. Jesus teaches about not storing up treasure on earth, but in heaven. What one most values, one's "treasure," demands the love of the heart. Those who love wealth cannot love God. Those who identify themselves as poor depend just as much on the desire for wealth as the rich. In Jesus's teaching, poverty and wealth are related to worry or anxiety. But this love of wealth demands too much, and consequently further estranges people from God. The identification of oneself by relative wealth or poverty mediates identity through human creations. This is the self-deceptive error of creating identity by external objects that only have a value we give to them. It is systematically impossible to love God and money, they are two different and competing masters.

Judgment

"Do not judge, so that you will not be judged."[17] Here Jesus addresses the very heart of sin, as we discussed with Adam and Eve in the previous chapter. Just as Jesus is teaching an abandonment of justice, so he also teaches an abandonment of judgment. The initial sin, as we saw, was the judgment of deciding for oneself what is good and what is evil. This perceived independence of judgment was actually mediated through the creation, thereby inverting the relationship Adam and Eve had with God. This relationship has continued unabated. Judgment is the heart of sin and the heart of the economic relationship. Judgment mediates God through the world, but this

---

16. Matt 5:23–24.
17. Matt 7:1.

is a world that people construct. This systematically precludes the possibility of knowing God, because any knowledge of God that people discover can be nothing but a projection. To abandon valuation is to abandon economy and ethics simultaneously. Jesus teaches that the measure one uses in judgment will be applied to oneself. Here he is recognizing that judgment leads to reciprocity, whether one desires it or not. Judgment creates relationships of reciprocity, for good or ill. In this way the *lex talionis* arises because of sin, because of judgment. God works through systems that develop as a natural result of human sin without thereby legitimizing them. So it was with the *lex talionis*.

The Golden Rule

Jesus further subverts reciprocity by his interpretation of the Golden Rule, provided that we take the Sermon on the Mount as necessary context to properly interpret his teaching in Matthew 7:12. Jesus twice refers to the Law and the Prophets in his sermon, this being the second time. The first time was in reference to himself, that he did not come to abolish the Law and the Prophets, but to fulfill them.[18] Here the Golden Rule fulfills the Law and the Prophets. In this way Jesus is claiming himself to be the Golden Rule. If Jesus is the fulfillment of the Law and Prophets, and the Golden Rule is the Law and the Prophets, then we might understand Jesus to be saying that the positive form of reciprocity that summarizes the Old Testament is fulfilled in himself. Jesus is thus saying that his own life and ministry are God's answer to reciprocity. Rather than returning upon his people their rebellion and rejection, God does not count their transgressions, but sends Jesus to bring reconciliation. This is the opposite action of the flood. Jesus is God's doing unto others what he would have them do back to him, namely, be reconciled. Rather than a general teaching approving of reciprocity, which would not really make sense as it seems to contradict his earlier critique of the *lex talionis*, it is better to understand Jesus's version of the Golden Rule as a subversion of the Golden Rule itself. Rather than following the economy of justice, Jesus is teaching that people should go out of their way to be reconciled to one another, forgoing justice, and initiating acts of reconciliation as a response to understanding the reconciliation God has given through Jesus.

Such criticism of reciprocity undermines the mathematics of both justice and economics. Discipleship, therefore, requires a dramatic transformation of one's perspective and way of life. The disciple cannot see any system

18. Matt 5:17.

of justice or economics based on balanced scales, or notions of harmony as just, but as symbols of estrangement and sin. These are not to be openly opposed, but subverted. This is the point of his teachings on the "extra mile" and turning the other cheek. Rather than open warfare against sin manifest in bullying and violence, the disciple loves his enemy and does more than they ask, simply because this is what Jesus has done for the disciple. This kind of subversion is not new to Jesus; he is drawing on the theme of repaying evil with good found in the Old Testament in Proverbs 25:21–22. Now, one could say discipleship is a form of reciprocity, but the disciple can give nothing to God that God desires or could posses (for in a sense God cannot posses anything, and yet is Lord of all things). Rather than payback, and certainly not "paying it forward," the disciple no longer mediates relationships through economic metaphors. For the disciple no relationship can possibly be understood in terms of payment. This means, as I will discuss later, many modern forms of charity stand in need of subversion.

The Father's Provision

One final teaching of Jesus in the Sermon on the Mount is about his Father. The Father gives good things to those who ask, seek, and knock. In this Jesus reframes relations that people have with their material needs. Rather than pursuing means to create wealth, or at least daily bread, Jesus tells his disciples to simply ask of God. God will surely treat his children better than an earthly father would. Even earthly fathers care for their children and provide for their physical needs. God will do all the more, as he is not a sinner like human fathers are. Living in this childlike relationship with God will lead to needs being met. For those who must have the assurance of their provisions by their own means, God will always be mediated through this primary economic necessity, and God himself will be seen as a means to economic ends. God will once again become God the Economist.

Though more could be said of the Sermon on the Mount, this key text reveals a core truth of Jesus's teaching in word and deed: that evil is not to be openly resisted but met with a subversive love. Jesus demonstrated this love as a fulfillment of God's mission in reconciliation, initiating for us a life of discipleship in which we can follow this subversive love—proactively loving neighbors and enemies in the love of Jesus.

Paying Taxes

There are a few other select teaching of Jesus that are important for our task; let us look at some of these. When asked by the Pharisees whether paying Roman taxes is right, Jesus responds quite cleverly, as we saw in chapter 3. The question they ask is important. The Jewish people as vassals of the Roman Empire are required to pay taxes. Romans did not tax their citizens until late in their history. The Roman system of citizenship was quite remarkable in their intelligent method of incentivized integration. The Romans had a tiered system of citizenship for individuals, as well as a classification for cities that enabled cities as a whole to achieve rewards for exemplary allegiance or service to the Empire. In this way both individuals and cities would be able to escape taxes and tariffs, receive the right to appeal to a Caesar's centralized court as Paul does, reduce their requirements for military conscription, and other benefits. Thus, there was a strong incentive for the Jews, like any other people group, to conform to the rather reasonable demands of the Romans.

On the other hand, the Jews were unlike many other people groups in the Roman Empire. In not too distant memory were the Maccabean successes, and home rule. The Romans under Pompey had desecrated the temple by entering into it (63 BC). Though Pompey had regard for religion, he did not comprehend the nature of Jewish monotheism and so did dishonor by wanting to see the statue of their God and entering into the holy of holies. According to Josephus he intended to do right and, perceiving the negative reaction to his mistake, he ordered the temple cleansed.[19] This was, nevertheless, evidence that Rome did not honor the one God and so were inimical to Jewish religion. Pompey's intervention in Jewish affairs led to significant reductions in Jewish political prestige, bringing the Jews under Roman taxation.

Furthermore, the Roman method of tax collection was very open to corruption. Indeed, corruption was systematic as taxes were calculated and collected up front, leaving the tax collectors to recoup their costs and whatever extra they could obtain. So the tax system itself would certainly be resented for its corruption.

Thus, there are divided loyalties with regard to Rome and its tax for the Jews. The question, although designed to catch Jesus in a trap, was obviously a very prescient one. If Jesus were to answer that tax should not be paid to Caesar, the Pharisees would have solid evidence of criminal activity, even if they might secretly agree with him. But rather than being trapped in a false

---

19. Josephus, *Jewish War*, 14:70.

dichotomy, and rather than open rebellion, Jesus again chooses the subversive option. He refuses to accept the question or narrative as it is posed, a tactic that we will revisit in detail in the chapter on ethics. The Pharisees were looking for some grounding in the Torah or the Prophets for an ethical teaching on paying taxes. But the Torah does not address the issue and instead of engaging in a questionable interpretation, he turns to the nature of money itself. The money is Caesar's to begin with. It was minted for the purpose of taxation, distributed for the purpose of taxation, and had value because Caesar demanded it, and had the legions to back up his demand. Because the Romans at that time did not tax their citizens, taxation was equivalent to a tribute. Caesar's money was a method of control. Rather than simply rejecting this symbol of domination and entering into open rebellion, as many hoped the Messiah would do, and rather than legitimizing Caesar's dominance by acceptance of the coin "at face value," Jesus subverted the symbolism and meaning of money. If all the money is Caesar's, then it has no real value for God's people. It certainly is not God's money. Money never belongs to God, just like all human systems and symbols. Money is not the rightful property of an individual. Working for money is a mediated form of slavery because the goal of the work is a token whose value is given by the workers themselves to the benefit of the master. Certainly money gives a greater freedom to make purchasing decisions. But, in the end, it is a symbol of the authority of the master who benefits most from the money, not by the acquisition of the greatest amount of money, like a majority shareholder, but by being the god who guarantees its value. Such is the case for the modern world as well. When things are valued by the US dollar its political power is sealed and the government can be in perpetual astronomical debt. By his money Caesar establishes his political control over regions and peoples who would otherwise have no economic incentive to obedience, there would remain only the fear of punishment. That threat remains, and the Jews would taste Roman steel again on numerous occasions. By giving to Caesar what already is his, Jesus participates in the system while delegitimizing it. He obeys the letter of the law while overthrowing the spirit of the law.

In this episode the teaching of Jesus serves as a paradigmatic example of the attitude of the disciple toward human systems of estrangement. The most important thing is not the action, but the meaning of the act. This is what I mean by subversion: one can continue doing an act while changing or challenging its meaning, thus emptying the act of its intended result. By showing that money has only the value that the subjects of Caesar give to it, Jesus undermines its value and Caesar's authority at the same time, all without committing any crime.

Jesus teaches in the Sermon on the Mount that no one can serve God and money. They are two contrary masters.[20] Part of the reason for this is that money is a symbol of human authority. Money exists precisely because people are estranged from God. It is only by estrangement from God that the material world is commoditized, privatized, and marketed. And it is only by estrangement from God that humans rule over one another.

We saw that the development of money was deeply involved with religion and sacrifice, that it developed out of tokens of participation in a sacrifice. The movement, from iron spits that could represent this participation, to coins with the face of the emperor, is not all that difficult to imagine. Participation in a sacrifice creates community by submitting the group to the single purpose of worshipping a god or goddess, and their destruction of goods or of animal or human life joins them in a bond of destruction. Together the people have achieved the great task of propitiating the wrath of the gods. Together they have restored the cosmos to its proper order. As a symbol of this, to remind the people of their unity and the right ordering of the cosmos, each is given an item that is exactly the same as everyone else's. Money is rather similar. It binds people together in their common act of sacrifice at every transaction. Out of each transaction the authority takes a cut, a propitiation, that ensures the right ordering of the cosmos. Caesar, or whatever king or authority, represents the right ordering of the cosmos. Money is a token of this rule and a token of each individual's participation in the maintenance of this order. These monetary transactions are veiled religious ceremonies.

In serving money one serves human authorities and invented gods. In serving money one establishes and confirms human power structures. And in serving money one engages in a kind of worship that is necessarily opposed to God's rule. Now, modern nations have attempted to get around this, as I pointed out in chapter 3. I seriously doubt that the American motto, "In God We Trust" was chosen out of a conscious and conspiratorial attempt to get the American people to think that God was behind their economic system. The teachings of Jesus have been so perverted by Christendom that I'm sure the originators of this phrase were attempting to be pious and patriotic. But by the belief that God supports human authority structures, confirmed only by a decontextualized interpretation of Romans 13,[21] to the complete neglect of Jesus's teachings and the general thrust of Old Testament authors, those of Christendom unified the religious act of monetary transaction with the confirmation of American supremacy. Transactions of American money

20. Matt 6:24; Luke 16:13.
21. See explanation of Rom 13 below.

thereby symbolize the unification of God (whomever or whatever that is), the stability of the American economy, and the authority of the government.

America and many modern nations no longer put the faces of current leaders on their money, as democracy would hardly allow for this. The perception of government by the people is maintained by the establishment of a narrative, expressed by money. America honors previous presidents, national monuments, and a variety of patriotic symbols on its money to narrate a myth, complete with symbols, of national unity and identity through authority. England has an image of the queen, heroes of science, medicine, and economics, again to honor those who have contributed to the national identity. Of course, Adam Smith is one of those figures. In this way money is both a token of the unity shared and the propitiation itself. It is a propitiation because, if one does not pay the required percentage of each transaction to the government then one will be speedily punished.

To serve God and to serve money is impossible, not so much because serving money is about consumerism, though that is part of it, but because serving money is actively engaging in sacrifice to idols fashioned by the myth, symbolism, and order that money represents. We saw that estrangement led to the need to create a cosmos, that religion serves to create and help individuals participate in the work of the gods in the formation and annual re-creation of the cosmos, and that human authority derives its power from this system. Money is an integral part of this cosmogony, and serving money is to willingly support systems that estrange people from God.

There is another story about paying taxes in Matthew 17 as well that bears some elaboration. On this occasion Peter is approached by the collectors of the temple tax who ask whether Jesus pays it or not. Peter responded in the affirmative. When he next sees Jesus it is Jesus who speaks first and asks Peter whether kings tax their own sons or others. Peter responds, "From others." So Jesus says that the sons are free. By this he implies that the children of God need not pay the tax. So as to not cause offense he sends Peter to fish where he will find a fish with a *stater*[22] in it. In this way he pays the tax. One cannot help but find this a mockery of the tax. Jesus claims to be above the tax as the Son of God, but rather than cause a scene he has the creation yield up his share. We will investigate the tithe in depth in chapter 6.

Jesus's teaching on the temple tax is striking because Peter gets money to pay his share as well. It is understandable that the Son of God is exempt from the temple tax, but so also is Peter, according to Jesus. Peter is included

---

22. A Greek coin equivalent to Peter's and Jesus's share of the two drachma temple tax.

as a son of God, adopted through reconciliation in Jesus. Peter has no need of the temple. He need no longer pay for its services, for sacrifices on his behalf, or on anyone else's behalf. He is reconciled to God and has no need of sacrifice or religion any longer. The temple is obsolete, a shadow of what was to come, as is the Sabbath, festivals, laws regarding food and drink,[23] the priesthood, sacrifices, the law and the old covenant as a whole.[24] When the reality comes, the shadows, copies, and symbols pass away. They are useless. But again Jesus does not insist upon these things, causing offense to those who are not yet his disciples and who would not understand his teachings. Jesus participates in human systems and in the outmoded symbols of the temple, but he gives his disciples a different story to live by.

Cleansing the Temple

But Jesus also turns out the money lenders in the temple, seemingly offended by an act of desecration. Others still believed in the symbol of the temple. They had not been reconciled to God in Jesus yet. Jesus had not yet torn down the temple and rebuilt it in his body, so the temple still represented God's house to the people. Jesus works with them where they are. He enters into their cosmos, but upsets it. Rather than openly tearing down their cosmos, he uses their symbols, but shows how they are using them wrongly. So although Jesus does not really believe God lives in the temple, he is angry that the temple is being used for trade. Money has no place in God's house because one cannot serve both. Those who are selling animals have simply identified an obvious opportunity: selling sacrificial animals at a place of sacrifice. It would be far easier for a person to buy a lamb, properly raised, and sacrifice it, than to raise one himself. How could a city dweller, for example, be expected to perform an animal sacrifice if he owned no animals? But again, money transforms the relationship. Though the sacrifice was always an economic relationship between people and God, a relationship God tolerated in its proper time, money transformed the sacrifice. Merchants were profiting on the brokenness between God and his people, mediating worship of God by service to money.

---

23. Col 2:16–17.
24. Heb 8–10.

The Parable of the Hired Workers

Let us now turn to a few of Jesus's parables. The Parable of the Hired Workers[25] is a great offense to economic relations. The kingdom of heaven has no place for a direct relationship between work and reward. Workers who work differing amounts of time are rewarded similarly, and they understandably take offense at this. Jesus is teaching that working in his kingdom is not work, it is its own reward. Indeed, the payment that the master gives to the workers is a gift, according to Matthew 20:15. This parable is not teaching that communism is God's method of economics. This parable comes after the story of the rich ruler in Matthew, and, in this context, it is an elaboration of Jesus's teaching that the last will be first and the first will be last. The rich, those who love money, can only with great difficulty enter into his kingdom. Those who love money cannot love God. They perform religious rites as a duty, as work, in order to receive the promised reward. The wealthy serve God as part of a contractual agreement. They expect blessing in compensation for service. This is a traditional belief, especially in Roman religion. Votive offerings were performed if a person received what they requested. So the gods were useful and utilitarian. The Greeks were similar—piety was honoring one's vows or contracts, "Holiness [is] the art of commerce between gods and men," a definition of piety that Socrates trials with Euthyphro.[26] But Jesus teaches that those who work for the kingdom cannot be in such a relationship with God. When the workers who worked all or most of the day see that the ones who only worked one hour receive one denarius, they expect greater compensation, even though they agreed to one denarius for their own work. So when they receive one denarius as well, they are unhappy. But, as a subtle insult to those who make religious vows, Jesus teaches that the master gives them what they agreed to, and calls it generous. That is, God does not owe anyone compensation for anything. The disciples of Jesus must not imagine that economic relations have any place in his kingdom. The work of the kingdom is a joy and a privilege, a reward in itself. Anything further is extra generosity. So the last, those who are not successful by means of economic relationships, will be first. And the first, the rich, those committed to economic relationships, will be last in his kingdom. They cannot understand the kingdom and think they can earn favor and rewards from God like the religious do.

---

25. Matt 20:1–16.
26. *Euthyphro*, 14e. My translation.

The Parable of the Talents or Minas

In the Parable of the Talents[27] Jesus teaches a parable that uses what we might call a proto-capitalist metaphor to characterize the kingdom. He begins with a very common situation in his parables, a master who is going away for quite some time. This master divides his wealth to his servants so that they would care for it in his absence. One is given five talents, another two, and the other one, each according to his ability. At this point we can see how the English word "talent" has derived its meaning from this story. But it is a gross misunderstanding of this story to imagine Jesus is teaching that God gives each person skills or abilities and they need to use those for his kingdom. A close look at Matthew 25:15 clearly shows that the master gives a talent to those who already possess skill or ability. The talent is not the skill; the talent is something given to those who posses a skill. The talent is what Jesus is entrusting to his disciples as he prepares to leave them for a long time. The talent is his teaching—the gospel. The differing measures of the gospel should refer then to a leadership capacity, such as he gives to Peter. Indeed, we might even imagine Peter being the one to whom five talents were given, and Judas Iscariot the one.

The master departs and the first two invest their money with money lenders. The term often used in translation, "banker," is deeply anachronistic and unfortunate. There were no banking institutions. There were, however, people who were ready and willing to lend, to change currencies, to engage in investing. Recall that the premonetary society was based in debtor-creditor relations in a way that did not involve money. This kind of debt created and strengthened social bonds, because the creditor becomes very interested in the debtor's affairs to ensure repayment will eventually come. Personal credit, or honor, would be well known to a small community. But Jesus is operating in a monetary society and these close relationships had four or five centuries to be eroded by the isolation and anonymity of money. What this means is that the two servants who invest are taking an immense risk. And so we can understand why the third servant would bury the money to keep it safe. There was no FDIC or other investment insurance.

And yet it is striking that the servant buried the money. It was and is common practice to hide heirlooms, as Graeber shows in his work on value.[28] Heirlooms are objects that have value because of their history. The possession or stewardship of this object incorporates one's own history with what the object represents. The talent was precious to the servant, too pre-

---

27. In Matt 25 as talents and in Luke 19 as minas.
28. Graeber, *Toward an Anthropological Theory of Value*.

cious to share or invest. It is precious because it belongs to the master and bears the character of the master, whom this servant believes to be harsh, harvesting grain he does not sow. Gathering the produce that another has sown is an excellent metaphor for subversion, as is that of plundering Egypt. It is only this servant's interpretation, however, that the master is harsh or cruel. The other two do not appear to think so. The third servant's interpretation is confirmed by his treatment at the master's hands.

The other two servants do not think the master harsh. They do not think the gospel, or talents, are too precious to share and invest. Instead, understanding who the master is, they take a risk and invest the money for the master and return to him their profits. They are the ones who sow, but it is the master who reaps. Instead of this sounding cruel, this is the subversion of economizing the gospel. Jesus wants to see a profit from his teachings. He wants a return on his investment in his disciples. The one bad servant receives the talent, but does nothing with it, so proving that he does not really understand the master or the gospel. The other two, however, do understand that the master desires to see fruit from his teaching. They have received freely and so they freely deal shrewdly with it. They have been the beneficiaries of Jesus's tutelage and now they must become teachers and evangelists themselves, earning a return on Jesus's investment in them. The gospel is freely entrusted, not purchased, and so not rightly the property of the recipient.

But, if Jesus is subverting money and economic relations, why does he consciously use an economic metaphor to describe what he desires of his disciples? Certainly Jesus is speaking a language and using an image they can understand. But he is also only appealing to certain aspects of money in this parable, and not to others. A metaphor always breaks down at some point, which is what makes it a metaphor rather than an equivalent. The bad servant was treating the gospel/talent like an heirloom. The two good servants treat the gospel like money. This is not a legitimation of either system of valuation. But Jesus appeals to the fact that money must enter into the marketplace for it to have value. The gospel only has value if it is taken to the marketplace, if it is invested in others. If it is buried, held as precious, then the disciples would be no better than the history of the Jewish people in the Old Testament who treated their nationality and elect status as precious, and would not bless others.

Again, this parable has nothing to do with investing our God-given skills, but Jesus entrusting to his followers the gospel, each in a measure according to his or her abilities. So also it is not a lesson on the importance of investing. We should not hereby derive principles of sound financial advice. This would be to invert the meaning of the parable itself, making God's kingdom a metaphor for money. This places God's kingdom in a subservient role to the kingdoms of this world.

But this issue raises the question of Jesus's use of money metaphors elsewhere, for example, the Lord's Prayer in Matthew. Is the kingdom Jesus announces shaped by the realities of money, just as we saw with metaphysics? Is Jesus's kingdom only conceivable with the advent of money? Certainly we can interpret the kingdom that is not of this world,[29] but is present in the midst of his disciples,[30] as drawing a strong division between seeming and reality. The whole field of apocalyptic literature works on this division. But Jesus does not render the kingdoms of this world as illusory. For Jesus they are just as real as the kingdom of God. This means that they cannot peacefully coexist. If the notion of the kingdom was shaped by the notion of fiduciarity, then human kings would again represent the authority of God. But, for Jesus, they are competitive. One does not symbolize the other. If fiduciarity were the basis of the kingdom, then serving God and money would not be problematic, but would be the ideal situation. Once again Jesus is plundering money and its meaning without money thereby shaping his teachings.

The Parable of the Unforgiving Servant and Forgiveness in the Lord's Prayer

The final parable we will consider leads back into the Lord's Prayer, so we will consider them together. In Matthew 18:21–35 Jesus tells the Parable of the Unforgiving Servant to explain that forgiveness must be offered "seventy-seven times." A man owed ten thousand talents to a king. This amount is a great exaggeration intended to heighten the immense disparity between the first debt and the second. This would surpass the income of an entire nation. Obviously the man could never pay, so, as would be customary, the master ordered all his possessions sold, as well as his family. Most societies have allowed for people to be put up as security on a loan, including to this day. This has been a major source of slaves for slavery. The servant pled with the master and the master forgave his debt. But this servant went out to another servant who owed him one hundred denarii. This sum of money, though still a sizable amount for a workman, would be payable. But it is infinitesimal compared to the ten thousand talents. The forgiven servant did not forgive the other servant, and instead threw him into prison. But when the master heard about this, he threw the unforgiving servant into prison.

29. John 18:36.
30. Luke 17:21.

This is a parable of the kingdom. God is willing to forgive an infinite debt, but if the forgiven person does not extend this forgiveness to others, then that person will not be forgiven. Forgiveness, like we saw with the gospel or talents of the previous parable, must be given, invested. It is not something precious to hold on to, but only acquires value if it is circulated, like money. The only thing in the Lord's Prayer in Matthew that Jesus explains further is that forgiveness must be extended to others for it to be valid. Jesus often uses debt as a way of describing sin. But it is a continual danger to forget that money is a metaphor for sin and guilt, not an equivalent system. To build a theology of justice, sin, and guilt around the realities of money is highly problematic. Sin is not debt and God is not a creditor. Forgiveness is only one step in the process of reconciliation. If forgiveness remains alone, it bears no fruit, instead it treats the one who forgives with contempt, inverting the whole purpose of forgiveness. The person who accepts forgiveness but does not pass it on to others does not seek reconciliation, but profit. It is only by understanding forgiveness in terms of release from debt that one is able to conceive of accepting forgiveness but not offering it. And perhaps this is the very reason Jesus uses money as a metaphor in this case, to make it as clear as possible that forgiveness is not an economic relationship. It is only by means of money, money that conceals relationships, that someone can be forgiven but not forgive. In a premonetary society such a situation would be impossible, for it would completely undermine a person's credit in his social group. If he loses his credit in such a way, he would be effectively ostracized or exiled, and would lack the necessities of life. Forgiveness of a debt in such a society would go some distance to restoring a person's credit or honor, and so restore the person to the social group. But in a monetary society where money tells no tales, forgiveness does not necessarily lead to reconciliation. Indeed, one can simply look on forgiveness as profit. Is the unforgiving servant evil, or parsimonious? Of course, Jesus does not give enough information to tell. Jesus's parable is incredibly simple and subtle. He shows quite clearly that forgiveness received must be passed on. But he also subtly shows that forgiveness is and is not like money. It is only by mediating a relationship through economics that one is able to look on desperate pleading and still demand the repayment of a debt. Justice is justice, after all. Debts must be repaid. Graeber begins his book on debt with an anecdote highlighting that, in a time of such fluid values as our own, one commandment that seemingly cannot be broken is that "Surely, one has to pay one's debts."[31] But debts do not have to be repaid. This is an economically destructive concept and it is the heart of the gospel. Is this not what Jesus is teaching

---

31. Graeber, *Debt*, 4, 391.

here? A man who owed an impossibly immense sum does not have to repay. A person who sins against a brother can be forgiven seventy-seven times. This is the abandonment of the economic relationship, in finances and in justice, in order to achieve reconciliation.

But Jesus's parable has another important aspect. Forgiveness in the economic world is generally extended only to those who owe large sums. God is willing to forgive any amount, for to God all sin is an expression of estrangement from him. This does not mean all sins are equal, but that they all have a common root. God expects that the reconciliation he offers would be extended to others, for this is his mission. This is the reason for Jesus's life, death, and resurrection, that all would be reconciled to himself. This reconciliation happens one relationship at a time. And from there, if people understand and receive this forgiveness, and extend it to others, reconciliation grows exponentially. But in the cosmoi of economic relationships those who owe most are those who have built the largest power bases. Those who owe most are often forgiven to buy their loyalty, while the loyalty of those who do not matter—the weak, the poor, the laborer—are not forgiven but instilled with a deep-seated morality and sense of justice that one must pay what one owes. Certainly this is how the taxation that looks very much like tribute payment is legitimized. Economic relationships necessarily support and maintain power, keeping the weak enslaved by morality. We saw that this was the case with aristocracy who could transform long-standing debt into a social hierarchy. This was also the case with monarchs who would forgive debt as a way to purchase loyalty and power from a larger power base, centralizing authority at the expense of the aristocracy. In modern times the same happens with large corporations finding tax havens, lobbyists, and campaign donations. They are forgiven their debts, as many large institutions were in 2008. But this forgiveness was not passed on, instead there was large scale foreclosures on housing. Corporations were deemed "too big to fail." Certainly it is understandable that large corporations represent a means at creating a lot of capital that would eventually trickle down to the average person. Helping the rich helps everyone, so it would seem. But once again, this is the kind of relationship that economics creates. While individuals suffer catastrophic life events, such events are not allowed to destroy certain fictive persons whose existence depends entirely upon divestment of personal responsibility.

The Poor You Will Always Have with You

And so we come to one of Jesus's most controversial sayings, "The poor you will always have with you."[32] This statement has been used wrongly as an excuse to not be concerned with the poor. Others have been ashamed of it. Rightly understood, however, it follows on from Jesus's other teachings perfectly. Jesus is claiming to be more important than poverty. Poverty will always be there because its roots are in estrangement from God. Jesus is saying that there can be no solution to poverty because, without forgiveness and reconciliation, poverty must continue. So long as people relate to one another in economic terms there will always be poverty. In John it is Judas Iscariot who is most upset about the anointing with nard that Mary, the sister of Lazarus, gives to Jesus. The money could have been given to the poor. But what Judas misunderstands is that money cannot solve poverty. No matter how money is distributed it can only reinforce poverty by reinforcing the primary importance of economic distribution in human relations. Money creates and reinforces poverty. This again is because poverty must be understood primarily as a wealth disparity. Money only has value because it is unequally distributed. Scarcity creates value. If we attempt to define poverty in relation to material goods possessed or accessible, what I earlier called absolute poverty, we forget that money is not simply a means to livelihood, but a power relationship, and a religious ritual. Economic relations are an essential aspect of the creation of our various cosmoi. To believe that economics can provide a solution to any problem is, as we saw in our chapter on historic economics, to pose economics as the primary problem in human societies. The problem is that salvation comes through the same thing that enslaves. If poverty is the main problem, then redistribution of wealth is the obvious solution. But by redistributing wealth we make wealth the most important thing, which redoubles its social value, thus leading people to desire it more and more, creating further disparity by corruption or attempts at power. We forget that money is stored value and that the classic aristocratic economic maneuver is to store wealth, take it out of circulation, and thereby increase one's power through the potential results of committing that money in a certain way.

Poverty is symptomatic, Jesus is saying. When Luke tells this same story he does not include "the poor you will always have with you." Instead Jesus proceeds to forgive the woman her sins. Jesus says that she is so enamored with him because she has been forgiven much. What this woman needs is forgiveness, and thankfulness for that forgiveness by her anointing of Jesus

---

32. Matt 26:11; Mark 14:7; John 12:8.

is a right response. Certainly she must spread that forgiveness to others, but having a proper understanding of what Jesus has done for her is of great importance. Indeed, it is because she loves much that her sins are forgiven. For Jesus, love is the proper opposition to poverty. If we want to counter poverty in our world, it cannot be done systematically. So once again Jesus teaches subversion. Love transforms economic relationships, doing away with any concept of wealth or power disparity. What the disciples did not understand, and it seems few today do, is that money is nothing in itself but a system of corporate belief that forms and transforms the entire world in which we live and the relationships we have. The only way to break through this system is to tell a different story and to live in different relationships, not directly opposed to money or power, but in a loving subversion that makes all considerations of money or wealth to be of no worth, compared with the relationship one has with God in Jesus Christ.

For it is not love by itself that saves, or love that can undermine the rule of economics. Love can itself be subverted by transforming it into a universal concept. By removing God in Jesus from the relationship of love, one depersonalizes love. We make love understandable only by what we already value. We end up loving only what we value. This makes love into a powerful agent of economic relations. People can love money and so love one another through money. Systematic charity is just one obvious example of this. Judas wanted systematic charity, to help "the poor," a group of people who are problematic because they lack something. Jesus sees the individual as she is, and loves her, cutting through any mediation. Judas loved money and was enslaved to it, selling out someone he could have loved for more of it.

Pentecost

After Jesus sends the Holy Spirit to his followers, one of their major responses is to create a new way of life. People from a diversity of backgrounds came together, devoting themselves to the teaching of the apostles, fellowship, breaking of bread, and prayers. They were all together and had all things in common. They would sell their possessions and belongings so that any who had need were taken care of. In other words, the Holy Spirit led them to forsake economic relations, plundering their own livelihoods to care for one another. Their relationships were characterized by the love of God in Jesus Christ, and what money they had went to everyone as an expression of love. In this way their love was not mediated through money. Taking care of one another was an expression of love. It was not systematic. We know from the story of Ananias and Sapphira that there was no forced sale of property.

Their sin was to mediate relationships through money. They pretended to give the entirety of their proceeds, but held some back. This lie demonstrated that their giving was not an expression of love, but of show, a play at power and acceptance while maintaining a backup plan. The community of believers was important, but not so much that they would trust this group of people to care for them. This incident demonstrates the corruption that so easily intruded and did intrude into the life of the church. The church is only composed of those who love each other in the love of Jesus Christ. So it is not the giving of money that is the mark of the church, but the total devotion of one's life and livelihood to the love of God and his church.

Paul

Though Paul again does not directly address money as Jesus did, he speaks volumes about economic and hierarchical relationships. The letter to Philemon is an excellent exposition on the economic consequences of reconciliation. Philemon, the master, has a runaway slave, Onesimus. Onesimus had come to Paul and had become a believer. Paul was sending him back to Philemon to be reconciled. Reconciliation with God in Christ for Onesimus and Philemon meant that they had to be reconciled. But Paul wasn't simply sending a slave back to his master, he was sending a brother back to his brother. Rather than openly criticizing the institution of slavery, the hierarchy it reinforced, and the economic system that was built upon forced labor, Paul subverts it in Christ. For Philemon to be a brother with Onesimus, he can no longer treat him as chattel. Paul even exhorts Philemon to receive Onesimus as though it were Paul himself, with the clear subtext that Philemon would never treat Paul as a slave, but as a most honorable guest. Reconciliation with God in Christ subverts hierarchy, not directly leading to revolution, nor respecting authority as though it were all delegated by God, but expressing the love of God in individual relationships that create deep metaphysical crises. What would Philemon do with Onesimus? That was his choice, but Paul gives him the line of thinking he needs to follow to his own conclusion.

But aren't the Pauline writings full of submissive language, whether it is for wives, children, slaves, or subjects of the king? Certainly he commends submission of people who are in low social positions, but I think these texts actually confirm my point rather well, rather than detracting from it. Though we do not have the space for a detailed exposition of these supremely controversial texts, a few comments should suffice to show their proper interpretation in the broader context of the whole canon. Ephesians

5–6 exhorts wives to submit to their husbands. Many interpreters have focused on this practical teaching without understanding the reasoning behind it. Paul is neither reinforcing some natural law that God created, nor giving some trajectory for the categorical liberation of women and slaves. To argue this latter point logically requires us to teach that children should be liberated from their parents and subjects of all political authorities liberated from political authority. Paul is not here engaged in ethical teachings derived from some divine cosmos or world view. Again, it is impossible to have a godly world view, because to do so requires that one assume God's perspective, and so the description of a godly world view is nothing but that prime sin of estrangement of which Adam and Eve were first guilty.

In Ephesians 5–6, which is very similar to Colossians 4:5, Paul introduces his practical teachings thus: "Therefore, regard diligently how you walk, not as unwise people, but as wise ones. Redeem the time, because the days are evil."[33] Paul is giving wisdom for a time that is ruled by evil. He is not saying, "This then, is how you should build a society that will stand the test of time." But he is commanding one to be wise in such evil times, to behave in such a way that does not dishonor God, does not retreat from the evil time, nor raises undue scandal. Instead the time needs to be redeemed. It is tempting to play on the word Paul uses here, *exagorazomenoi*. This is a compound word from *ex*, which is the preposition for "out of," and *agorazo*, meaning "to buy," itself coming from the word for marketplace *agora*. One could stretch the meaning to be "Take back the time from the marketplace." The time is evil and so what must be done is not simply to make the best use of the time, but to change the times itself, not by immediate outward change of behavior, but by loving subversion. The time must be taken out of the marketplace and put in perspective of one's relationship with God.

Wives should submit to their husbands because this is a wise thing to do in a time in which this is required, so that a wife might love her husband in Christ and so subvert the social construction of the marital relationship, which would require her to do her duty. The husband, likewise, should love his wife as Christ loved the church. Christ gave up all claims to rights for the church and died for it. In this way the common structure and narrative of marriage is subverted. A husband cannot dominate his wife because Christ dominated no one. A husband cannot abuse, hit, divorce, or be unfaithful to his wife, because Christ did not and will never do these things to his church. A husband cannot lord it over his wife, because Christ came to serve, not to be served. Paul is rewriting what marriage is, all while maintaining an

---

33. Ephesians 5:15–16.

outward composure of respectability. The same is true of parents and children, slaves and their masters.

And the same is true of subjects and political authority. Just as Jesus did not come as the military and political messiah the Jews desired, so too the church is not a military or political power to force the world into the image of Christ. It is in this context that Romans 13 must be understood. Because versification is a later addition, people often miss the context of this infamous passage. In Romans 12 Paul is exhorting believers: to live in peace with everyone, not repaying evil with evil, but doing what is honorable; not seeking vengeance, echoing Jesus's Sermon on the Mount; being the willing victim by abandoning rights and claims to justice; taking care of one's enemy because by doing so "you will heap burning coals on his head";[34] and not being overcome by evil, but conquering evil with good. This is the same kind of subversive teaching as Jesus. Only once we understand this should we proceed to Romans 13. Paul exhorts every person to be subject to the authorities. Certainly God is allowing their reign. Just as Jesus himself submitted to the judgment of unrighteous and cowardly people, so too should believers submit to the powers. If you don't want to fear the authorities, do what they ask, Paul is saying. Yes, do it, but don't believe it. Pay your taxes, pay your debts, give respect to those whom society demands it be given. And then in Romans 13:8–10 where there is an unfortunate paragraph break in many modern versions, "Owe nothing to no one except love one another; for the one who loves the other has fulfilled the law. . . . Love for one's neighbor does no wrong; therefore, love is a fulfillment of the law." Such is the proper context in which we can interpret Romans 13.

This is my paraphrase of Paul's teaching in Romans 12–13 with inspiration from other Pauline themes:

> Love everyone and do not cause offense. The love you have in Christ transforms the love you have for one another. It is a fulfillment of all the commandments. It does no wrong to a neighbor. You are not to harm them even if you disagree and they do not honor God. Love your enemy and do good to them. Rome is your enemy as are all the powers of this present evil age. But God reigns over all nonetheless. So leave your vengeance to God. And when you are oppressed, do good to your enemy. Submit to the authorities out of this love. Live peaceably with all. Did not Jesus do this? Submit and love, and so subvert their perspective on the world. Participate in the world, but do not be conformed to its pattern. Be transformed by the renewing of your mind, and so be free of this world. We live in an evil age.

---

34. Rom 12:20. Paul here quotes from Prov 25:21–22.

What should we do about it? Take the time out of the hands of the marketplace. Pay your debts, but forgive your debtors. Give honor to those who demand it, but do not demand it for yourself. Pay your taxes and revenues. Walk in the light, in the daytime, honorably and openly. But above all, be clothed with Jesus Christ. Follow him. This is the way God is at work through his people.

Romans 13, taken in isolation, and according to traditional interpretations by those in power who are deeply motivated to use the Bible to give divine legitimation for their authority and violence, stands in stark contrast with nearly the entire canon of Scripture. The prophets, the writer of Samuel-Kings, the Pentateuch, Judges, Esther, Jesus, Revelation, all these thoroughly speak against human authority. If we read Romans 13 as divine right monarchy, we do so at the cost of the canon of Scripture. But if we understand it along the lines of my paraphrase above, it fits extraordinarily well with these other books and continues the theme of subversion to hierarchical relations.

Recall that hierarchical relations are brought about by means of debt, whether financial or moral. Paul in Romans 13:7 urges the payment of all taxes, revenue, respect, and honor. These are all alternative expressions of an economic relationship. But it is by their payment that Paul undermines the debtor-creditor relationship. Because Romans 13 must be read in the context that I described above, Paul is in full agreement with Jesus's teachings about payment of taxes and debts. Jesus paid taxes to Caesar because the money was already Caesar's. He refused to engage in the economic system that assigned an objective and hidden value to what was an instrument of power and domination by the Emperor. Paul, in encouraging the payment of all kinds of debts, likewise encourages an obedience to the letter of an agreement so that the possibility of questioning and undermining the spirit of the agreement remains. Jesus further teaches that debts must be forgiven, just as God forgave our metaphorical debts. In this way the believer should forgive but not expect others to do so as well. In situations in which the Christian is in power, that power must be set aside, just as Paul explains of Jesus in Philippians 2. But when the Christian owes money or honor, it should be paid. This kind of relationship is not fair, just, right, or an expression of reconciliation, but by means of satisfying the terms of an agreement one provides no excuse to reject the love that the believer then can offer if the tables are ever turned.

First Peter

If we needed further instruction in how to interpret Romans 13, we can turn to the book of First Peter, which follows a very similar line of reasoning. Peter explains the subversiveness of the gospel much more clearly than Paul does. In 2:11–12 he urges believers as "strangers and exiles," language almost identical to that of Hebrews 11:13, to keep their conduct honorable so that when authorities accuse believers they will be forced to acknowledge the believers' righteousness on the day of judgment. And in 2:13–17 he goes on to say that the believers should

> Be subject for the Lord's sake to every human creation because of the Lord, whether it be the king as supreme, or governors as sent by him to punish evil and praise the good. Because this doing good is the will of God to silence the ignorance of the foolish—as free people, not using your freedom as a pretext for evil, but as servants of God. Honor everyone, love the brotherhood, fear God, honor the Emperor.

So for Peter, submission to authority is done because of Jesus, because it is God's will that we submit to them to reveal to them their own foolishness. This is done precisely because we are free, and this freedom cannot be used as a pretext to do evil. Again, the Christian life is not one of violence and power grabbing to forcibly conform the world to an imagined image of God. Nor is it a resignation and abandonment. It is a freedom-for that chooses to honor an emperor who will persecute Christians for failing to worship him. Like Jesus before Pilate, who could see nothing wrong with him, so we should be before our leaders as well. The Christian life is subversive because it is about transforming the structure of peoples' beliefs through reasonableness, honor, and love. Peter acknowledges that this will not end well. There will be persecution and suffering. But he shows in chapters 3 and 4 that this is how Christ suffered. Instead of lamenting this, or using it as a pretext to turn to open warfare, we should rejoice that we can share in Christ's sufferings. First Peter, like Paul, offers clear grounds for a subversive love, modeled on Jesus's life, persecution, and death.

Conclusion

Paul doesn't much address money in a similarly forthright manner to Jesus. Indeed, in comparison to Jesus, whose teaching was saturated with reflections on money, the rest of the New Testament is rather silent on the issue. The books of First and Second Timothy command that Timothy should avoid the love of money, which is the root of all kinds of evils. And the book of Hebrews also speaks of avoiding the love of money. For these later authors the important thing is to be free from many kinds of alternative loves, whether the love of wine, of self, or money. Hebrews 13:5 backs up its prohibition of the love of money with the promise of Jesus, "I will never leave you nor forsake you." Contentedness has its roots in the promise that God will be faithful. The love of money, then, betrays a belief that God will not be faithful and so alternative arrangements must be made. In spite of the relative infrequency of money outside the Gospels in the New Testament, as we shall see in the next section, Pauline thought is unique in his description of the work of God as reconciliation, which is a very important point to contrast with economic relations. Paul, Peter, the author of Hebrews, all acknowledge that believers are strangers and exiles, and they all encourage subversively honorable living in an evil age instead of resorting to power or escapism. In this way they form the basis for an alternative lifestyle that the believer must adopt, a lifestyle that is constantly met with temptation to turn to one way or another, instead of keeping on the way of the cross. In this way they subvert the structure of human creations and undermine economic and power relations by subversive submission.

Throughout the Bible we also find a consistent teaching through the story itself, that God is working through individuals to achieve reconciliation and that this reconciliation is subversive to all economic relationships. It is not openly judgmental, condemning human cosmoi. Nor is this reconciliation a command to depart these cosmoi and live the monastic life of poverty and purity in some ideal cosmos with an exact and perfectly biblical world view. Instead reconciliation is subversive, working through the systems to challenge the stories and beliefs that are foundational to the economic relationship. In both the premonetary and monetary societies we find in the Old and New Testaments respectively, economic relationships are subverted by sharing the reconciliation of God with others. We will see also that this kind of subversion is easily extendible to our contemporary postmonetary world, and that the calling to challenge the stories that underwrite economic relations is just as strong in our own era. Let us now look at reconciliation through a systematic and synchronic lens.

SYSTEMATIC REFLECTIONS ON RECONCILIATION

From Creator to Judge and Reconciler

The kind of relationship we have with God determines the kind of relationship we have with each other, with the creation, and with our own creations. Throughout the Bible the kinds of relationships that God has with people changes. This does not mean God himself changes. We saw how God was the Creator, and this is where many people stop discussing who God is. It is pleasing to think of God as the Creator, because such a God is inoffensive, wholly positive, life giving, and can provide legitimation of our creative tendencies. The image of God, that most mercurial of theological concepts, is often used to forge an ontological link between the Creator and human creativity. From the Estrangement human relationships with God transform entirely. God relates to estranged people as their judge and as their reconciler. God judges the people in Noah's day, at Babel, and the nation of Israel. But we must be clear that his relationship of judgment and reconciliation are one and the same. God judges for the sake of reconciliation. But God's judgment is not made explicit except in special circumstances we find in the Bible. As in Jesus's Parable of the Wheat and the Tares, separation of good from bad does not happen in this life. God's judgment is postponed to the return of Christ, but there are foretastes of it whenever someone is encountered by the Holy Spirit.

God's judgment is for reconciliation. When a person is convicted by the Holy Spirit of rebellion and sin, those things that estrange people from God are brought into judgment. It is by conviction of sin and repentance that forgiveness and reconciliation can occur. A person must die to him or herself, effectively condemning the old self to death and enabling the resurrection and new creation that a reconciled relationship with God creates. But this cannot happen without an encounter with the Judge. The relationship people have with God throughout the remainder of Scripture could be described as *judgment for reconciliation*. In this relationship we come to know God personally in new and different ways. We can understand the love of God not only by his willingness to forgive, but in his desire to bring his people to maturity by reconciliation, which requires taking responsibility for systems of estrangement.

The incarnation is an act of judgment for reconciliation. The Gospel of John describes this very well when it speaks of Jesus as the light that has come into the world that the darkness has not comprehended. Light is a suitable image of judgment because it removes the darkness of shadow and ignorance. No longer can evil deeds of estrangement and oppression be hidden or cloaked, all lie naked and exposed.[35] God's entry into the world is not only a revelation of God, but also a revelation of people, their *cosmoi*, and their relationship to God. But this is a crucial point. Jesus does not actively judge, but all are judged in his presence by themselves. Encountering God leads to the realization of one's own estrangement and sin, as is seen on many occasions in Scripture like in Isaiah's vision. Like a child who has done wrong but feels compelled to confess at the gaze of his loving father, so also do those who encounter God behave.

And so we see that reconciliation is a new kind of relationship with God, one that Adam and Eve did not, and could not, have in Eden. Rather than being the image of God, the New Testament speaks of the followers of Jesus as children of God. This is achieved through adoption as Paul explains in Romans, Galatians, and Ephesians. God becomes our Father, not because he is essentially the Father. God is the Father because he eternally begets the Son, not because he is the Father of humanity. As we saw, this is a common religious belief of which Scripture is critical in the creation accounts. So although God is not ontologically the father of humanity, he is our Father through a relationship he chooses to initiate. Like an adoption, this happens solely by choice. This again means that this relationship does not communicate genetic data or predisposition to those who are adopted. Instead his children are formed by the judgment for reconciliation they encounter in this relationship.

If we have an adoptive relationship with God, this means that we are being transformed by the love of God. This is the kind of love that calls for and produces opportunities for growth to maturity. Instead of the weakness that has characterized so much of Christianity, God has desired that people grow. We saw that Adam and Eve were very childlike in their naïveté and in their inability to assume responsibility. Reconciliation with God requires that individuals take this responsibility, and much more beyond. Instead of looking for ways to minimize responsibility, the children of God investigate their lives and seek out opportunities to be responsible. This stands in direct contrast with the economic relation that developed at the Estrangement when Adam and Eve mediated the word of God through their perception of the fruit and the word of the serpent. They also resorted to blame when confronted by God. And this seeking of responsibility and maturity stands in direct contrast to the nature of money and the corporation. Money, as we saw, was purposefully nonhistoric. It has value as money only because its history is unknown. This fog that money creates spreads from itself to all aspects of transactions, concealing the provenance of a product. And so

---

35. Heb 4:13.

through money the consumer can oppress with no knowledge of oppression. Money sanitizes estrangement in ways that personal debts could not. Similarly, corporations are formed in order to avoid personal responsibility. We need not restate that argument again.

This means that God cannot relate to corporations or other fictive persons, like nation-states, in a reconciled way. It is systematically impossible for a corporation, nation, or institution to be reconciled to God. This reconciliation cannot be mediated, even through religion. Not even a family can be reconciled to God, unless each family member is individually reconciled. Only individual people are adopted as children of God. And only as individuals can we express the maturity that reconciliation must produce. Now this is not an argument against the church, but rather for it. For the church is the body of Christ, formed only of individuals who are reconciled to him, having their sole identity in him and not in family, nation, corporation, brand, or denomination.

So reconciliation with God transforms a person totally. And this has epistemological consequences. We saw that estrangement from the Creator meant that it was epistemologically impossible to interact with creation, and so people had to create their own *cosmoi*. Reconciliation is not an epistemological restoration of an untainted mind, but a new epistemological possibility of perceiving these *cosmoi* as rebellious, humanly constructed, and irredeemable. Reconciliation changes the possibilities of the human mind. Instead of perceiving creation, or Nature, the Universe, or private property as rightly exploited, the reconciled mind begins to see other people and things from the perspective of responsibility, love, and a consequent desire to initiate reconciliation. We saw that this was Jesus's teaching about the Golden Rule.

But this epistemological reconciliation also creates inaccessible concepts. Just as God's creation is an inaccessible concept for one estranged from the Creator, so the notion of objective reality becomes epistemologically impossible for one reconciled to God. The reconciled mind understands that God is related to people and his creation as a judge who is reconciling everything to himself. This is a relationship of love, not one of objectivity. God does not have a neutral perspective. So the good news of reconciliation is that there is no such thing as objectivity. God does not treat any of his creation as universal concepts, but as individuals.

This means that though God judges, he is not blind like our image of Lady Justice. God does not judge based on objective facts of an act, but on a relationship. In human society this is a perversion of justice, but with God this is good news because God is *pro nobis*.³⁶ Judgments rendered through this reconciled relationship are mediated through God's love for us.

There are many other epistemological inaccessible concepts. Whereas humans estranged from God must project themselves onto the shape of the cosmos and receive back from the cosmos an objective image of themselves in the form of universal concepts, like gods, governments, nature, etc., in a relationship reconciled to God these concepts are no longer possible to maintain. Money itself can then be understood as corporate belief, highly akin to a religion of its own, and so it can be emptied of its value. Epistemologically, fiduciarity becomes problematic because reconciliation with God eliminates universality, and so money as a symbol no longer points to a believed reality of value. Those reconciled to God do not just abandon the use of money and retreat into what everyone else would perceive as a utopian fantasy. Money is used, but emptied of meaning and power. Jesus's disciples are to make friends by means of unrighteous money,³⁷ to use money to form relationships that create opportunities to share God's reconciliation.

From Creation to Cosmos to New Creation

We explored the Creator-creation relationship previously and found that the concept of creation requires the Creator. Adam and Eve were given delegated authority, the image of God, to rule over the creation according to the relationship that they had with the Creator. Their rulership was explained as a royal charter, granting them the privilege of this authority. But when they broke their relationship with God they became usurpers. God's creation was lost to their minds and they had to create their own, plundering and pillaging God's creation in the process. We saw that notions of property and ownership depended upon an economic perspective rooted in the Estrangement. In response to estrangement, God works with his people to bring reconciliation, through subversion of the cosmos. Full reconciliation must await the *parousia* when the new creation will be brought to its fullness. There are foretastes of this new creation and the disciple lives in light of it.

The creation that was lost is not recovered, redeemed, or restored. As I explained, we should not call God's creation *perfect*, in the sense of being in accord with some ideal. For God there are innumerable possible good creations, and this is in no sense the "best of all possible worlds," for there is no ontologically real and objective category of "world" to which ours can

36. Latin: "for us."
37. Luke 16:9.

conform. Instead God's creation was good because it was in completion as it was in intention. When this creation is corrupted by humans, it is no longer good because it is out of accord with what God created. But because this is not the only possible good, God need not return his creation to its initial good state. Eden was not a golden age. Rather than doing away with human history, as in the flood, God works through human history for reconciliation. This is no less true of people as it is for the creation itself. We must be clear, however, that the creation was corrupted because of people and their exercise of dominion over the creation as usurpers and rebels, plundering creation to create a cosmos. For those who are reconciled to God it should follow that they are reconciled to his creation. But this creation is largely lost. Although there are preserves and wilderness areas remaining, the very fact that we must preserve them and manage them implies that they are our museums. The environmental movement is the reaction of a people who believe humans to be the only managers of the world, demonstrating again that, so long as we do not mediate our relationship with the external world through a reconciled relationship with God, our noblest efforts at care of nature betray the same attitude of usurpation as those who actively plunder resources for personal profit.

To the reconciled mind there is no longer simply a creation, but a creation corrupted by millennia of human cosmogony. This is not a simple relationship, because much of the original creation is lost and unrecoverable. And this is true epistemologically as well. Creation is not a concept we recover, because disciples do not live in the same Creator-creature relationship that Adam and Eve did. Our relationship with the Reconciler as the reconciled, as adopted children, is far closer than the Creator-creature relationship. Because of this, the kind of relationship we have with God determines the kind of relationship we have with the creation. God has promised a new creation, one that contains elements of Eden, but preserves all of history within it. Those reconciled to God cannot return to Eden, and so they live in an attitude of hope. Indeed, they must have an epistemology of faith, hope, and love. The new creation is not perceptible. It is not present. But it can be explained, pointed to, symbolized, and narrated.

The reconciled mind thus lives in an entirely negative present situation. Unable to perceive the creation because of our history, a history neither we, nor God abandons, we are also unable to fully perceive the coming new creation. Those who are reconciled to God must adopt the attitude he does—patient, quiet, loving, subversion of the *cosmoi*. We might call this a deconstructive epistemology. This is not deconstruction for its own sake, but deconstruction because of faith, hope, and love. By faith we look forward to a city[38] not built by human hands.[39] We set our hope in this city, and this new creation, and not in human cities and human creations. Nor do we vainly hope for a utopian return to nature, for there never was a golden age, and Adam and Eve are not enviable in their irresponsibility and immaturity. And, for the love of God, we remain in all the various human cities and creations, not legitimizing them, nor fully participating in ways that increase their power. Instead, reconciled people work subversively in human cities and creations to challenge belief in the narratives that construct these *cosmoi*. By telling the alternative story of the gospel while demonstrating commitment to individual neighbors in the love of God, the reconciled carry out God's task in the present time.

This means that those who are reconciled to God live on the precipice of a continual epistemological crisis sustained only by faith, hope, and love. Living between the *cosmoi* and the new creation means that we cannot believe in any kind of natural moral laws, since these will always be mediated through our present cosmos and will teach us only to be integrated into it, or some nostalgic version of it. We cannot perceive truth in the world or in nature, for there is only our *cosmoi*. The food we eat, the forests we admire, the mountains we climb—all are mediated by our own constructions. Our food is mostly grown industrially, and nearly all of it, even if organic, was long ago hybridized. Most of our animals are not as God made them, like domesticated dogs or cattle. Our forests are managed and, even in fairly wild places, have changed dramatically due to humans fighting natural forest fires. Even our ability to access the few remaining wild places must be mediated through travel. It is significant that we speak of the "outdoors," and so betray to ourselves that it is a foreign place cordoned off by walls, windows, and doors.

This epistemological crisis returns us again and again to dependence upon God in faith, not in knowledge. Reconciliation is a distasteful idea to us because of this implication. To be reconciled to God, a God who is not simply a projection or an ontological construction, means we acknowledge that our truths are our own constructions, as are our whole worlds. So even those who are reconciled are continually tempted to return to the stability of their contemporary cosmology. It is a continual effort to think in terms of reconciliation because it means that all things solid have become provisional and groundless. The deconstruction of all cosmologies that reconciliation brings leaves us feeling in the wilderness. And yet this is precisely

---

38. It is fitting to speak of the city here because the city has always been a *microcosmos*, an earthly replica of what people believe the structure of heaven/the universe to be. See Eliade, *Sacred and the Profane*.

39. Heb 11:10, 13–16.

where God would have us—depending upon him. The moment we attempt to mediate God through our world again, we are immediately estranged, making God to be ourselves, and having to start reconciliation anew.

The economic consequences of this epistemology are many. All the economic outcomes of cosmology are undone. As we saw with Jesus, money and Caesar's power are delegitimized without active rebellion. So although our world is full of property, strict laws about trespassing, use of property, water and mineral rights, we know that these are conventional only. They exist by faith alone. Although our cosmos is made of resources for exploitation, we see this as the response of estrangement that it is. In love we participate as ambassadors,[40] which is often a polite word for spy. And we work to subvert, not the systems themselves, but those who put value in those systems. The town of my early life, Cripple Creek, Colorado, was founded as a gold mining town and is still to this day. Old shaft mines are dotted all around, evidenced by the old entrances and wooden elevator head frames. But the major sight today is of an entire mountain reduced to rubble, blasted with explosives, leached with cyanide, hauled away by enormous trucks to be turned into what people think is the most valuable and stable of all resources. It is a paradigmatic example of resource exploitation demolishing what was once God's creation. Rather than picketing, performing sabotage, or committing violence on the miners, it is the responsibility of God's people to lovingly show their neighbors that accumulating wealth, or thinking gold a secure and reliable way to store our wealth against a time of trouble, is to be estranged from God who promises to care for us and who warns against storing up treasure on earth.[41] Rather than seeking to destroy physical wealth or property, it is our task as disciples to undermine the solidity of the cosmos in which we live, and this can only happen by exposing structures of mutual delusion that happens by mediating our relationships through the cosmos, rather than through God. Like Babel where the workers simply quit construction, so too the power of the gospel is not in destruction of the tower or mine, but in the transformation of the value of gold itself by transforming the stories that give value to gold or other earthly treasures.

Reconciled Human Relationships

Reconciliation with God leads to reconciliation with other people, just as estrangement from God lead immediately and necessarily to estrangement from other people. We saw that Jesus continually emphasized that

40. 2 Cor 5:20.
41. Matt 6:19–21; Luke 12:15–31.

forgiveness cannot just be received, it must also be given for it to be real. God will not forgive those who do not forgive. This is because reconciliation with other people is the fruit, the natural outcome, of being reconciled to God. If this fruit does not grow, then its source is not God.

One major result of the Estrangement is the epistemological inability to know oneself. Attempts are made continually through relationships with other people, through the use of certain products, clothing, affiliations, and beliefs to construct identity. But in the end the self is always in transition, always becoming. The more one seeks to know oneself, the more oneself changes, so that knowledge is always one step behind inquiry. This has begged the question as to whether or not there is such a thing as a person's identity that can be known. Metaphysics introduced the concept of an identity that is aspirational or ideal. There is an ideal Me, an ontological reality somewhere out there that, if I can just reach, I will be perfectly contented. Of course this is entirely solipsistic, believing that an individual identity exists in the isolation of an ideal realm. The relationship between money and metaphysics is fairly evident here. The introduction of money caused traditional societies to disintegrate as relationships sealed by personal debts gave way to more instantaneous and impersonal transactions. We saw that in premonetary societies the individual was dependent on the larger group for identity whereas in monetary societies the individual became isolated and had to choose to participate in relations mediated by marketplaces. The aristocrat and philosopher could consider the oracle of Delphi's command to "Know thyself" because he, in isolation, could consider his own nature. The aristocrat derives his identity by withdrawing from common life, participating through magnanimity rather than mutuality. But it is only when one is separate from common life that the question of individual identity even arises. One must experience alienation to consider a notion of identity.

By reconciliation with God the question of identity is sublimated to that of relationship with God. It is a very common and trite maneuver in theology today to say that being a Christian makes us more fully human. The thinking is that because God became a man, humanity itself is glorified in this union, and participation in the body of Christ leads to the glorification of human ontology for you. Like the poor theologies of the image of God, it often turns out that "more fully human" refers to a certain moral or political agenda. Reconciliation with God does not alter one's being or essence. Such concepts are irrelevant. Reconciliation with God fully individuates a person by reorienting notions of personal identity considered in isolation to a relational union with God in Christ. God does not have a relationship with *humanity*, but with individual people, and that makes every relationship that God has entirely unique. Though God is not different in each relationship, each person is. And so, unlike ontological universals, a relationship with God is profoundly individuating. By making this relationship primary, all other sources of identity and value are devalued. Jesus explains it in his typically stark terms, "If anyone comes to me and does not hate his own father and his mother and his wife and his children and his brothers and his sisters, yes even his own self, he is not able to be my disciple."[42] To be Jesus's disciple, then, requires the abandonment of natural relations and even a concept of the self. But, if the disciple does this, then each of these relations is re-created. Even natural relations are formed by the cosmos. Fatherhood, for example, has changed dramatically over space and time, as have motherhood, marriage, and brotherhood/sisterhood. Reconciliation with Christ is subversive to these kinds of relations and their formation of identity. This is just as true of the patriarchalism of the pastoral nomads in the Old Testament as it is of the variety of family arrangements present today.

Because reconciliation does not make people more fully human, bringing them into alignment with an ontological category, the very notion of humanity becomes increasingly irrelevant. There is no unification between people except in relationships of reconciliation. Ontological categories, or unification of ideologies, interests, genetic similarities, are all made meaningless in light of reconciliation with God. As we saw with the postmonetary society, the economic gospel upholds a universal humanity in which all must participate. This is a systematic exclusion of God and ultimately a rejection of interpersonal reconciliation in favor of superficial species unity, a species that is impossible to define. We believe in a species identity, but we must create such an identity, as it is impossible to have an objective position outside of humanity to arrive at any objective definition.

By contrast, reconciliation with God in Christ unifies believers by mediating their interpersonal relationships through Jesus Christ. As Jesus said above, even marriage must be submitted to discipleship. The union of man and wife, certainly in good marriages the most intimate and profound relationship possible, even this must be mediated through Jesus. It is only through Christ that such relationships can exist without the shame that characterizes Adam and Eve's own relationship after their sin. Only by understanding the forgiveness given in Christ can one be free to live one's life naked and exposed to one's spouse, and indeed to other believers as well. This is not vulnerability, however, because a true understanding of forgiveness means there is no shame. So this revealing of one's life, thoughts, and actions is a way of life for disciples.

---

42. Luke 14:26.

Now, this does not mean that these disciples should choose a life of nudism, literally or figuratively, freely revealing these things to everyone. This would be a naïve attempt at returning to Eden. Adam and Eve's nakedness is not a desirable situation, and it is certainly not the one which John describes in his vision in Revelation. Nudism, literal and figurative, does not understand the notion of subversion. It is an attempt at creating a utopian world now, and so is an anti-cosmos that exists only as an inversion of the dominant fascination with clothing and emotional masks.

The reconciled relationship also means that there can be no hierarchy. Jesus says it plainly: "You know that the rulers of the Gentiles lord it over them, and the great rule over them. This shall not be so amongst you, but whoever among you wants to be great has to become your servant . . . ."[43] As we saw in Peter and Paul, this means submitting to authorities and honoring those who demand it, not because this is right, but because this is loving. Jesus showed that discipleship is about abandoning claims to justice, and so it is with authorities and hierarchies. They are wrong, and amongst the reconciled there can be no hierarchies. But in the world there is abusive power to which we, in full freedom, choose to submit, as Jesus did. Hierarchy often comes from economic relations. Peter and Paul urged believers to pay their debts and their taxes, as Jesus did, not because they are right, nor because this is a way of legitimizing systems of estrangement, but because by doing so believers have the opportunity at delegitimizing the belief systems behind the outward actions. It is again obedience to the letter of the law to subvert its spirit.

Finally, reconciliation subverts ethics. Ethical norms require an appeal to a universal concept, or at least a concept that is higher than all parties involved. Ethics, in short, requires metaphysics. But if metaphysics has its basis, like money, in estranged relationships, in relationships mediated through the nonhuman world of stuff, then metaphysical reasoning is rendered irrelevant by reconciliation. In reconciled relationships there is no need to have recourse to universal concepts of the good. Indeed, this was the very problem that Adam and Eve faced in their creation of a good and evil independent of their relationship with God. Such thinking necessitates estrangement. Ethics, likewise, estranges. Perhaps contrary to its intention, ethical reasoning reinforces economic relationships by mediating these relationships through ontological categories independent of God. This makes rules, laws, principles, maxims, and ideal situations of primary importance, submitting relationships to concerns of justice and rightness. As we saw, not only did Jesus not seek justice in his own life, but he also taught his disciples in his Sermon on the Mount to

---

43. Matt 20:25–28; also Mark 10:42–45.

abandon personal claims to justice and rightness. Reconciliation cuts through justice, making justice itself irrelevant.

The life and death of Jesus is not a homogenous pointer to a class of action: love, selflessness, etc. His death was not an example of a virtue. The Gospel writers were not biographers like Plutarch who looked to the lives of noble Greeks and Romans to find virtue and wisdom for good living. Jesus's death was an act of God abandoning claims to justice, willingly suffering human injustice, as God's initiation of reconciliation with all people. Jesus is, as Karl Barth says, the Judge judged for us.[44] By this judgment, judgment itself is overturned. And so Jesus's death cannot be imitated as an ethical category or virtue, it can only be participated in. Jesus died once only[45] but his disciples participate in that death by being reconciled to him. This is a death of the self, a death to one's cosmos, and a death to all economic relationships because it is entering into the life of Christ. Jesus is not an example of a category of behavior, but his behavior is profoundly and only his, as God incarnate. And so this behavior cannot be imitated any more than the perspective of God can be achieved. Only Jesus can die the death of reconciliation, but his followers can participate in this death through his body, the church.

CONCLUSION

We have now seen that God is not an economist and does not exist to support or actively destroy human economic structures. We have seen that the Estrangement is composed of a judgment mediated through the creation, thus relating to God economically by the creation of morality in the determination of good and evil. The result of the Estrangement is that God and creation are now rendered epistemologically impossible to access, so humans must set to creating their own worlds or *cosmoi*. Each cosmos is entirely constructed by humans, but humans are dialectically formed by their relationship to the cosmos and each other, in terms demanded by the cosmos. These mediated relationships are economic, for they deal with quantities, commodities, property, possession, exchange, distribution, hierarchy, and debt. In response to this world, as we examined in this chapter, God works subversively through individual people to bring true reconciliation that destroys economic mediations. In the next chapter we consider some more practical ethical considerations as a result of this all too brief outline of a theology and its relationship to economic relationships.

44. Barth, *CD*, IV/1.
45. Rom 6:10.

6

Plundering Egypt: Ethics

The Christian is in Egypt, always-already in a world of estrangement, slavery, alienation. What then can and should the Christian do? What would it mean to plunder Egypt, to subvert its power, to lovingly undermine Egypt itself? These are the questions we investigate in this chapter.

Be Reconciled

There is no Christian ethic that can be divorced from a living and active relationship with God. The Bible cannot be read ethically. That is, it cannot be read with the primary intention of finding ethical norms for all people at all times. To do so necessarily decontextualizes passages from the Bible, or turns it into a book like Aesop's *Fables,* or Plutarch's *Parallel Lives,* in which he relates biographies for the purpose of moral education. Reading the Bible for ethics is a strange undertaking because one is met with a majority of story, not law, and the law itself intermixes things no one would consider enforcing today right next to moral commands we might cherish. Countless Christian ethical systems derive principles from the Decalogue, but it is an essential part of the covenant God made with Israel after he brought them out of Egypt. "I am the Lord your God who brought you out of the land of Egypt, out of the house of slavery. *Therefore,* you shall have no other gods before me ...."[1] The interpretative *therefore* helps clarify the logic of the

---

1. Exod 20:2–3.

commandments, for it shows how the commandments rest on a relationship of grace rather than being the precondition for divine acceptance or an exposition of eternal law for all peoples.

The more universal we make a principle, the more it has to be stripped of its particulars. But the more it is decontextualized, the further removed it is from being the revelation of the word of God. If the Ten Commandments are posted in a public place without the preface about God's liberation of the Israelites from Egyptian bondage, are they still Scripture? Furthermore, principles are not contained in a story whose author has made no mention of them. David fighting Goliath is a beloved story because we see the underdog gain victory over the giant. But even a cursory reading of the story reveals that the author highlights the weakness and unsuitability of Saul's kingship by his cowardice. The youth of David is used as a means not to glorify himself, but to show what God can do through even a youth. David in his youthful weakness trusts in God, and so is victorious. Saul the warrior king does not trust in God and will not go up to battle. This story doesn't teach the principle of courage, but shows the results of a right relationship with God. A right relationship is not a principle, for it cannot be universalized. It is particular in every case. It would not behoove youth to take up slings and rocks and attack people thinking God is on their side. David's action is inimitable because he is not acting on an ethical principle, but on a living relationship.

There is great temptation to abandon this relationship and create principles, however. Principles reinforce the cosmos. Ethics commends the good, which is integration into the cosmos. For example, our contemporary postmonetary society believes in universal humanity, as we've seen. And the one of the highest goods that all seek together is to provide opportunities to become self-sufficient economically in a global marketplace. This, of course, is what the very notion of a global marketplace demands of people. And so the good is simply obeying the "natural" laws of our cosmos: participate in the economy and so become fully and truly human. For Christians the temptation is to affirm this as well. Christians do as many other charities do: seeking opportunities to alleviate poverty, provide education, grant microloans, educate about and provide water treatment, and so on. Christians do this in the name of Jesus, but essentially are doing the same as other people who do it because of humanity. Christians do it because they think Jesus loves humanity, and we express love for universal humanity through economics. After all, this is what parents would do for their children as well. Nearly all of childhood is preparation for participation in the economic relations so the child will be self-sufficient. Higher education has had to adapt to this as well. So why would Christians need a theology for this ethic? We already know what good is because it's obvious, it's common sense. That is, the good exists in a common narrative that we leave unexamined and unspoken. This is the same narrative that creates our cosmos, and the good lies within the structure of our creations. Jesus is entirely superfluous to such a good. He provides no unique skill or teaching that integrates people into their social and economic lives.

The temptation in Eden was to create good and evil. To do this Adam and Eve turned to the fruit itself, using their sense perception of the fruit to question the faithfulness of God. The same is true today. The good is found in turning to the thing itself, so we think, to ontologies. But as we've seen, metaphysics and ontological thinking are human creations themselves. The thing itself is always-already constructed by ourselves and by the relationships we have with others, who teach us and integrate us from birth into a way of thinking, into a cosmos. So to construct the good we turn to our cosmos, in the process necessarily abandoning the word of God, which is truly revelation: an in-breaking of God into our worlds, interrupting and disorienting them. If we find God in the cosmos, we are simply exploring the concept of universality projected by ourselves. And if we find good in the cosmos we are only finding the means of integration and perpetuation of a total system of belief.

The kind of relationship one has with God determines the kind of relationship one has with other people and every other thing. Without a reconciled relationship there is no good approved by God. So the first step in a truly Christian ethic is receiving the appeal of God in the gospel, "We implore you on behalf of Christ, be reconciled to God."[2] Though it is terribly unacademic to say, the same is true for the reader of this work. The following ethical considerations are irrelevant until you are reconciled to God. They are only of interest for what someone reconciled to God would do.

Re-narration

Because the gospel is the revelation of God and is not the product of human projection from the cosmos, it follows that it is a foreign story in all times and all places. Reconciliation with God runs counter to all possible *cosmoi*. This means that the Christian cannot accept what anyone else considers good. There is no good outside of a reconciled relationship with God. Certainly the majority of people today prefer a certain lifestyle that most would call good: individual liberties, a plethora of opportunities, a choice of products, the feeling that however much money one has, one is exceptional

---

2. 2 Cor 5:20.

and meaningful. It is important to understand that I am not saying that not being killed or living under a dictator is an evil thing or that the common good is evil. This is not about good and evil. Evil is, most often, the inversion of what is good. It is nearly always a mirror image of the cosmos, such that it inevitably confirms the cosmos itself by its evilness. Like the yin-yang or the Manichean gods, evil and good live in a relationship of mutual dependence. What I am proposing is an alternative to this binary system.

For a Christian ethic the first part of rejecting all other narratives lies in rejecting the concepts of good and evil. These lie at the very heart of original sin. If the church would only realize that this knowledge of good and evil is the very problem instead of assuming it is the most precious gift of God, as Karl Barth says, "The consequences for the theory and practice of Christian ethics—and not only that—would be incalculable."[3] This chapter will do just that, explore some of these consequences.

After abandoning the belief that good and evil are from God and realizing that they are our own creations, we can begin, as Christians, to take responsibility for creating these ideas. We can begin to investigate where these ideas came from. Why is the good so different in different times? Christians who thrive in the natural law field of thought like to point to the timeless similarities of legal codes, from Hammurabi until this day, that things like murder are forbidden everywhere. Certainly, but what qualifies as murder has quite a lot to do with one's cosmos. Killing in war is exceptional, we somehow believe, as though when a leader of a nation makes a solemn declaration all morality changes. Now bombing civilians is acceptable when otherwise it is the most reprehensible terrorism. The same is true in some societies that had slaves. Killing a slave may not be considered murder because the slave is property and not a member of society and so does not possess the right to life, but exists at the grace of the master. God did not invent war, slavery, or murder. These are purely human creations, and so our moralities that surround them are our own. How can there be a just war, as though it were God's task to legitimize human "politics by other means"?[4] Our task is not look for ways to justify the world or excuse the necessities we have created. As Christians a major part of our ethical task is to call all people to account on their own terms. This is not judgment, but prophetic revelation of self-created morality. It is calling people to be responsible for themselves. This is a task they more than likely will not do. Even the best of people who recognize something of this, like Nietzsche, do not take responsibility or call others to responsibility, but instead use this knowledge

---

3. Refer again to Barth, *CD*, IV.1, 448–49.
4. This is, of course, Carl von Clausewitz's definition of war.

to legitimize power itself. Nietzsche's own philosophy is ironic because, as a good aristocrat who hates the herd, he depends upon the self-same herd for his own sense of superiority. I suppose that's why Zarathustra comes down from his cave. Zarathustra must preach and teach, he cannot be silent. Zarathustra depends on rejection.

If we are to be responsible for the creation of good and evil, we actually draw somewhat near philosophers like Nietzsche, who taught the transvaluation of value. Nietzsche's sharp criticisms of Christianity are often well aimed and quite correct, although they refer to the cultural Christendom beliefs rather than the teachings of Scripture. Indeed, Benson argues that Nietzsche sees in Jesus himself the key to his project of the revaluation of value. Nietzsche says, "Jesus said to his Jews: 'The law was for servants,—love God as I do, as his son! Why should we care about morals, we are sons of God?'"[5] Benson thus remarks, "In a text titled *Beyond Good and Evil*, Jesus is depicted as already *being* beyond!"[6] But where this line of thinking departs from Nietzsche is that he is still required to look for moral justification, which for him is in the celebration of life and power. Indeed, Benson convincingly argues that Nietzsche was deeply pious. He was devoted to his Dionysian way of life. Nietzsche's transvaluation of value was really only a questioning of the values of his day. He told his own narrative of reaction. He labels himself the antichrist, which we can really understand as the anti-Christian. He lives in reaction, dependent again on the herd for his values by inversion. As Christians we must break out of dichotomous thinking of good and evil, of right and left, of conservative and liberal. We must challenge every narrative that emerges as a reaction or as a progression, for both are twin shoots going in different directions from a common stalk.

In rejecting narratives, we come to understand the structure of peoples' thoughts. We understand whence ideas, faiths, beliefs come. This enables us to see the gospel for what it is. It is a story that meets people in their own *cosmoi*, but draws them outside as "strangers and exiles." The gospel provides an alternative story that does not construct a whole cosmos but inhabits any cosmos and works subversively within it by challenging the beliefs of people within. Also, by knowing the gospel, we come to understand the cosmos into which we were born and now inhabit, enabling us to speak to others in this cosmos as ambassadors for God, calling them to reconciliation with God in Christ.

The gospel is not a world view nor does it construct a cosmos. As we've seen, the Bible was written in a variety of social situations. It refers often to

---

5. Nietzsche, *Beyond Good and Evil*, 164.
6. Benson, *Pious Nietzsche*, 205. Italics original.

the cosmologies of other people groups, makes use of them, and subverts them. One of the major reasons Jesus was such a disappointment to the Jewish people was that he did not build a cosmos for them. Instead he continually challenged their own perceptions. He spoke about tearing down the temple and rebuilding it in his body. This would be a total disorientation for the Second Temple Jew. The temple and Jerusalem was the center of the universe. Everything revolved around it. God lived there. It was symbolic of God's presence, God's approval, and God's faithfulness to the Jewish people. Rebuilding a temple in his body does not really give people sacred space around which they can orient and organize their lives.

The Christian ethic cannot attempt to build a world. There is no utopia. People are God's agents in the revelation of the kingdom, but not in its foundation or construction. The kingdom is nothing but Jesus Christ, those who are his subjects, and the relationships they share. Since it is not of this world, it cannot be built in this world. All *cosmoi* must disappear before the coming of a new creation.

So the Christian story and ethic is one of active waiting. We must be critical of all cosmologies, all world views, even so-called Christian world views. We must be critical of all attempts to found the good and construct it. This is sin itself and the surest way to estrangement from God. One and a half millennia of Christendom is the clearest indication of the failure of a Christian cosmos. Christendom was nothing but the church existing to serve the world by legitimizing its wars, power structures, economics, and way of life. So we wait patiently in the sure hope of resurrection and new creation. But this is an active waiting, working as God's ambassadors or spies to subvert the world by the love of God. And the first thing an ambassador must do is get to know the people to whom he or she is sent. We must understand the stories, beliefs, and structures of our time and see them as foreigners. An ambassador is not native, and no matter how much he or she comes to love their assigned nation, she must remain loyal to her sending nation, serve its purposes, and deliver its messages. So let us turn to look at some common but problematic Christian narratives, and then we will look at some ethical narratives of our present cosmos.

FALSE NARRATIVES

There are many examples of false narratives that Christians are particularly prone to believe with regard to economics. If we are to understand the gospel and act on it then we must see the ways in which we use Jesus to legitimize the good of the cosmos rather than calling people to reconciliation with

God in Christ. Many of these bad narratives have already been discussed when we looked at historic economics and the alternative gospels they present, such as universal humanity and its correlative of altruism, the justice of economic opportunity and distribution, and human nature. Let us look briefly at two further false narratives: stewardship and redemption.

Stewardship

The first false narrative is the notion of stewardship. The story generally goes like this: God created everything and made humans as the crown of his creation. He gave humans dominion to rule over the creation. This has been called the "cultural imperative." So humans have stewardship of God's creation. Because we are made in the image of God, which means that we are creative like him, he wants us to express this creativity through technology and building. God created resources in this world for us to use responsibly. Money is one of these resources that God gives us and we need to be responsible in how we use it. God has entrusted us with these resources and we need to, as in the Parable of the Talents, invest them and see a profit.

There are many problems with this very common story. There is the free interpretation of the image of God to justify our cosmos that is addicted to technology and entirely shaped by it. This narrative has a typical lack of discussion of sin, except in irresponsible use of resources. In this story sin doesn't change the fact that God wants people to have dominion over the world, just that they should do it moderately. The very notion of moderation is problematic, as we saw, being dependent on the invention of coinage. Moderation didn't exist as a concept when Genesis 1–2 was written because the notion of infinite wealth is dependent on value detachable from physical objects. Resources themselves are also problematic, as we discussed earlier. The idea of a resource means that human use is what gives a thing its value. It has no value until people give it value, a concept we saw Aristotle express openly. Furthermore, money is neither a creation of, nor a gift of God. We know that money has conventional value. Aristotle says this and Jesus suggests it in his teaching on paying taxes to Caesar. Its value is not determined by God, but by people. It is a structure of human belief and human self-deception. We saw that Jesus makes the opposition between money and God as explicit as possible, "You cannot serve God and money."[7] So to think that money is somehow a gift of God makes little sense if they are opposed. Money has value because it is unequally distributed. Money is a mask for hierarchical power relations, but Jesus told his disciples that

---

7. Matt 6:24; Luke 16:13.

they cannot lord it over one another. We also saw that the early church's response to the Holy Spirit was to sell their possessions and live a common life. To think that God has gifted money to a person, of which they are the steward, is a subtle way of using God to legitimize economic relationships. And the notion of stewardship enables us to not worry about where the money came from. Money has value because it conceals its history, and in that concealment much abuse can and usually does occur, but we don't have to know about it.

The story of Edward Colston (1636–1721) is instructive. Colston was an English merchant operating out of Bristol. Colston's business was in trade with Africa, so it involved sugar and slaves. Colston was also a major benefactor and philanthropist. As the slave trade was not viewed with the same reprobation as today, few in his own day questioned the source of his money. He opened schools, orphanages, almshouses, and donated to churches, one of which was the Bristol Cathedral. In that church some of the major windows were provided as a memorial to Colston, windows filled with examples of good deeds that exemplified his philanthropy. Many of these windows were lost to damage in World War II. But they represent the notion of stewardship well. Colston did good works, paid for by the slave trade.[8] In his day this was not really questioned. In our day it is a supreme evil. Did God give Colston the money? Was God behind his business successes? Was he a good steward? Such questions obviously break down in this historical situation and so they should caution us against notions of stewardship in our own time. Where has the money come from? Money belongs to Caesar, not to God, and its ultimate origin and destination lies in the coffers of Caesar. It we are stewards of money then it is for Caesar, not for God.

God has not entrusted us with his creation. He did so, but because of the sin of Adam and Eve human dominion has changed its character dramatically. Divine legitimation of our dominion was revoked, so that its continued expression leads to further estrangement from God. Money is an entirely human creation for which we must take full responsibility. Money is not the gift of God, it is created and maintained by inequality and by corporate belief in structures of power. For Christians it is very tempting to baptize money. But the concept of economic stewardship must be purged from the church for it to have any future, now that it no longer has the privileged role of granting divine legitimacy to the state. The church can use

---

8. Thanks to the Very Revd. Dr. David Hoyle, dean of Bristol Cathedral for this story in his sermon on Luke 10:38–42, *At the Home of Martha and Mary* (sermon, Bristol Cathedral, Bristol, UK, July 21, 2013).

money, of course, making friends by means of unrighteous wealth, so long as it continues to understand that wealth is Mammon, and not a gift of God.

Plundering Egypt is a better image for the task of the church and Christians than stewardship. We live with money and must have it to operate in the cosmos to which we have been sent as ambassadors. We must use that money to devalue Mammon for others by announcing and living the reconciling love of God in Christ.

From Redemption to Reconciliation, From Ontology to Relationship

Our next problematic narrative is that of redemption and restoration. Many Christian theologians who have joined the narrative revolution have made some critical errors. Understanding the structure of a narrative is essential before forming a grand theology. Perhaps the foremost of these errors is that the story of the Bible ends with a *restoration*. The narrative of the Bible ends up being circular, exactly like the myths it was written to counter. Likewise, a number of theologians use the term *redemption*, an economic term, as the primary term to describe the work of God. In so doing these theologians have remythologized the biblical narrative, transforming it from something subversive into what it was designed to subvert. This is the nature of subversion; like espionage it is easy to be taken in by the conscious imitation of form the spy takes. But the spy is there to work through the systems, to infiltrate, and demolish subtly, quietly, secretly. The Bible is mythical espionage. Those who have not recognized this end up describing well the biblical narrative in classical literary form, missing the subversive edge, even in the structure of the narrative as a whole.

Redemption is an ancient concept that can be understood as buying something or someone back. In the Old Testament there are laws concerning debts and how, if a family member or a field was pledged as security on a loan, such could be redeemed, or bought back out of that indentured situation.[9] In monetary societies it has a similar meaning. To redeem something is an exchange of a promise for a product. A coupon or voucher is redeemed when it is used. Redemption, like most economic concepts, loses its personal aspects when money is introduced. Redemption in theology has come to refer to the work of Christ in buying back sinners from God's judgment of sin and the power of death and the devil. To put it crudely, Jesus's death was a coupon good for the lives of people. But is he giving this coupon to God or the devil? If to God, then this version of redemption incorporates

---

9. See Leviticus 25–27.

penal substitutionary atonement. If for death and Satan, then this version of redemption is a lot like the *Christus Victor* approach to atonement. But as most commonly used in theology and in church teaching, redemption has come to refer to the restoration that occurs after the atoning work of Christ is made effectual. Redemption in this context means God buying back all things, all of creation, from the corruption of sin, or the fixing of something broken.

The Bible is not a story of redemption, but a story of reconciliation. Now, redemption is certainly an analogy used in many places in both testaments to describe the work of God, and it is fitting, but not complete. Redemption is not a false image, but it is limited, and it is a means of describing the work of God in terms of human, especially premonetary, systems. Redemption is one way of describing reconciliation. However, many use this term now to speak of a restoration concept. So the shape of the narrative goes from Creation, to Fall, to Redemption, to Restoration. The reasoning for this seems to begin with the Creation as ontologically or morally perfect. Now, perfection is a concept that is only possible after metaphysics have been developed. Perfection requires the distinction between seeming and reality, between particular and universal or ideal. If the initial creation was perfect, once imperfection is introduced through sin, then only by purgation of sin is the ideal again achieved. The problem with this narrative is that it's circular. It might take the form of a Hegelian spiral, ever going from binary opposition to *Aufhebung*[10] or sublation, and then repeating this process over and over again.

This theological perspective, grounded as it is in metaphysical commitments, begins to look very similar to other narratives of progress toward the ideal. We saw the Orphic mystery religion had a concept of a Titanic Fall wherein the soul is trapped in the body. We saw that the soul is the ideal, ever attempting to rise upward to transcend the particular and so be unified with universality. Of course such a view of enlightenment is not confined to the Mediterranean. As money was invented in India and China at nearly the same time, it is not surprising to find Hinduism and Buddhism take on very similar concepts. *Maya* in the Hindu Upanishads describes a similar contradistinction between illusion and reality. *Atman* is reality, *Maya* is appearance. And so it is easy to see where that leads—one must seek *Atman* or *Brahman* through and behind *Maya*. And so a Christian perspective that begins with a perfect creation (reality) that is corrupted by the Fall, leads to a distinction between seeming and reality. There are all kinds of world views

---

10. This is a technical term from Hegel, also used in Barth's theology. Its exact translation is subject to debate. The idea is that two contrary things coming together produce a third thing, a synthesis.

out there, but one true world view that one has access to by God's revelation. There is one pathway to objectivity, to reality, and this is the enlightenment of taking on a gospel world view, so the reasoning goes.

If the work of God is redemption, that must mean that God has to enter into an economic relationship to exchange Jesus's life for something else to someone. To whom is Jesus sacrificed? To whom is humanity in debt? These are essential questions that are often left unanswered because redemption, like all economic terms, focuses on the thing itself rather than on relationships. "Jesus saves," but from what or whom? The simple answer is sin, but this turns sin into a thing, a force or power that exists apart from human rebellion, a reification of disobedience.

Instead of speaking of redemption and restoration, we must move from redemption to reconciliation. Reconciliation is not about restoring something that was lost. The Creator-creature relationship described in chapter 3 is lost, totally and completely. It is never recovered because it was not perfect or ideal. It was not what God always intended before his plan was thwarted by a woman eating a piece of fruit. I described Adam and Eve as childlike in many ways. They were untested, untried, naïve. Though conceivably they could become strong through testing, they did not, unlike Jesus in his temptation. Adam and Eve are pitiable. And their relationship with God, though real and profound, was less developed than that of a Christian, and far less developed than the relationship we shall have in the resurrection. Adam and Eve knew God as Creator, but did not know his manner of love. Love never enters into the creation accounts of the Bible. Adam and Eve did not know God as Father, Son, and Holy Spirit, nor understand the lengths to which God would go to involve himself in the human story. Likewise, those who believe that God can be known through nature desire the limited knowledge of Adam and Eve, rather than the full knowledge found in God's self-revelation in Jesus Christ. Throughout the story there is growth, not recovery. Characters develop through struggles. The more one reads the Bible, the harder it is to understand theologies that speak of ontologies: human nature, sin as its corruption, and Jesus as its glorification. Such a reading is very selective and heavily influenced by philosophical presuppositions.

The image of God is a notion of political representation, not a comment on human nature. It is a royal charter that is delegitimized in the Estrangement. Now the image of God is not the highest concept of humanity that the Bible presents, so that its restoration is not thereby the elevation of humanity to its ideal form. Rather the image of God only partially makes up life in the resurrection. It is an important part, but it is not based on human nature, or even on the nature of Christ, but on the kind of relationship that one has with God. Jesus is the image of God,[11] not because he was created that way. Jesus is uncreated. Rather, Jesus is the image of God because of his relationship with the Father. Jesus is the Son, and throughout the New Testament the language of filiation is far more prevalent than ontological ideas, even in the Johannine corpus. The filial relationship that Jesus has with the Father is the basis of his kingship, which is often spoken of in terms of inheritance. And so the Christian does not recover the image of God by participating in God through Jesus in a sort of deification, but the Christian becomes far more than the image of God by adoption through Jesus Christ. Christians become co-inheritors with Jesus of his kingdom. Thus the image of God, that delegated rule over the creation, is returned and increased, not through a recovery of "what it means to be human" but by reconciliation to God in Jesus Christ and the consequent adoption that takes place.

Rather than redemption and restoration, there is reconciliation and adoption. In this way those who follow Jesus, not his moral teachings, nor participants in some mystical union through enlightenment, but disciples, are glorified to something well beyond what Adam and Eve could have dreamed. And so we see that a proper Christian ethic is not archeological, but eschatological. It is not backwards looking to the golden age, to the time before the Fall that will one day come around again, but looks forward to a new relationship with God in the fullness of his kingdom.

RE-NARRATING A SUBVERSIVE GOSPEL

Every narrative must have characters, conflict, and resolution. As we saw with our (simplified) explanation of the three kinds of society, how one describes the problem determines how one describes the resolution or salvation. The gospel of Jesus Christ is not different in this regard, but it is distinct in a number of crucial ways. First of all, the solution is not the same as the problem. Humans are the authors of good, evil, sin, and rebellion. We ourselves create evil and are incapable of liberating ourselves. The problem is estrangement from God, so the solution is reconciliation with God. God is the solution, but not the author of the problem. In the other gospels economic relations are the cause and solution of the problem.

Secondly, the Bible is not a book of cosmology. Certainly Genesis 1–3 shares in crucial genre characteristics as other cosmologies, but as we saw, the differences were vital. Cosmology only accounts for a minute percentage of the Bible. The Bible is not a book written to describe the nature of humans, or of the world. Those who stubbornly try to do this in the modern

---

11. Heb 1:3.

scientific world, or any, eviscerate the power of the gospel by confusing ancient cosmology with the gospel itself, and so confuse the medium with the message. The Bible is not cosmology, it is a book about God, people, and their relationships. It is a book with a lot of little stories that fit together in a larger narrative. It doesn't actually tell us all that much about heaven, hell, or the eternal destiny of people. It doesn't affirm people, power, or a certain way of life. It is not a book of mythical heroes doing mighty deeds in a far off golden age. It is a collection of stories of people who interact with God, sometimes God working through them in miraculous ways, but never to their own glory or that of a way of life. Every hero is most heroic in pointing to God, their weaknesses and failures juxtaposed with God's faithfulness. It is a story of God working through people in their own worlds, drawing them out of their worlds, not to heaven, but to exile within their own lands.

Nor does the Bible tell us what to do with bioethics, complicated economic ethics, global warfare, nuclear power, or ideal political structures. All of these fields must form principles based on texts that nowhere claim to be giving principles. As I've said, to derive ethical principles from narrative, we first have to universalize the narrative. So we destroy the whole point of the narrative of the Bible: to show who the character of the unique triune God is by means of stories about his engagement with people. If we want to be faithful Christians and engage with the problems of our own day, we must first abandon the belief in an ideal world described by the Bible. It does not exist, nor is that a problem. In fact, the power of the gospel as a narrative is found in its radical distinction from any society in which it is read.

If we want to answer ethical questions, in our case about economics, by reference to the Bible, we must carefully understand what the Bible is and what it is not. One can find legitimation in the Bible for capitalism,[12] or communism.[13] There will always be a text that can be used to legitimize one's preconceived notions and thereby receive divine approbation. This has always been and will always be the temptation of religion—that the god we forgot that we invented approves of us and shows us the shape of the world we ourselves created. So long as the Bible is a book of ethical principles or cosmology, it is of no use except for historic interest and self-deception.

What then is the solution? We must continually start over with the story, recalling that this is the revelation of God. If we let it, it will search out our projections and inventions of gods. Like the incarnation, it is human and divine. It bears the appearance of its time and place and people. God

---

12. The Parable of the Talents is one example of a text that can be used this way. Michael Novak represents a Christian capitalist perspective.

13. One could refer to Acts 2, Matt 20, and others. There is a whole field of Marxist theology to which one could turn for examples.

speaks through people, works through people, and yet it is God working and God revealing himself. In order to communicate, God must condescend to human forms and human language. But in using people and their worlds, God does not affirm, justify, or sanctify them. Instead, the revelation of God liberates by critique. The revelation of God tells us an alternative story. It does not describe an ideal reality. The Bible does not teach a world view, or enable us to reach God's perspective of supposed objectivity. The Bible tells a compelling and powerful story that subverts every religious expression, every concept of sacredness, every human value, in short, it subverts all possible human *cosmoi*.

This book has been a retelling of two stories: the Bible, and human history. Economics is a necessary invention of the Estrangement. People express estrangement from one another through economic relationships, relationships mediated by material things and corporately constructed worlds based on a dialectical relationship with material things. Human epistemology is entirely determined by the kind of relationship individuals have with God. The very structure of our thinking, estranged from God, necessitates the creation of a cosmos and the alienation of this cosmos. We have to create a cosmos and mythologize it, creating gods, so that we forget we ourselves created that cosmos. The human mind is solipsistic, but through religion, myth, science, metaphysics, and other stories we tell ourselves, we vainly try to escape this confinement of our minds. Economics is not just the study of how people deal with money or capital, but it is a field, like many others, that carefully weaves stories that enable us to abandon responsibility for our own delusion. When we do ethics as Christians, we cannot simply accept the story as we are given it. We must offer an alternative account, written in the form of our own day, but entirely subversive by placing the revealed Christ at the center of the story.

The only properly Christian ethic must be based in a counterposed story to the ones that are being told in our contexts. Ethical problems, like legal cases, are expressed in stories, usually hypothetical ones, and this itself should inform Christians of a problem. Each of these stories implies a lot more than what is being said explicitly. Every one of these stories has some common ground left unexpressed. Even those that are not hypothetical carry a large number of presuppositions and shared beliefs. Let us take an example from my own situation as an illustration.

As a Presbyterian minister I have had many encounters with people who arrive in my office looking for financial assistance. I have a wealth of moral principles to inform me what to do, and they are often in deep competition. I could live by a maxim of "help the needy," which then would require me to judge whether the person is or is not needy by some standard about which that person and I may have a strong disagreement. I could work on consequentialist logic, thinking about what they would do with the money I may give them, and whether it would maximize their happiness, or that of the whole community. Another principle could be communistic, that such a person deserves a living and I must do what I can to make that happen. Or it could be capitalistic, considering whether the money would help them become a productive member of the economy or continue their leeching of resources others worked hard to gain. I could try to establish a system of microloans for the most "deserving" of the needy. Or I could establish a system of handouts for the necessities of life so they don't starve or freeze. In all of these options I could turn to some Scripture or other to make it seem like the right thing to do.

But what if the situation itself is problematic? The kind of relationship that is expressed by their coming to me, with their own needs clearly expressed in their minds, is purely economic. They have a problem and I may have a solution. If I give such a person money, they will leave and only come back when they need more and they feel like enough time has lapsed. They have the exact solution they want. But I succeed only in reinforcing their own narrative. And it is likely that their narrative is precisely what led them to my door. In coming to me they are seeking practical and external legitimation for their cosmos.

To describe someone as homeless is to problematize them in their identity, so that all interactions with that person must necessarily be economic; because to my mind, they are homeless, namely, without an economic necessity. Every homeless person is a victim and also responsible for being homeless, the same as anyone else in any situation. But if they seek out help as homeless, and those who help offer it because homelessness is inherently problematic, no matter what is done the two people will continue to be estranged. Whether I give money, shelter, food, clothing, or whatever, I communicate that they were correct in their narrative of identity. Even if I help a homeless person buy a house, become a successful person, and wean them off of dependencies, I have taught only the economic lessons and truths of the dominant narrative of the postmonetary society that defines humans as individuals who cannot be fully human if they are dependent.

The first thing to do is to subvert that narrative. This need not be deeply philosophical. Jesus does this in Mark 2 when the paralytic is let down through the roof. The man and his friends obviously want him to be healed, but Jesus forgives his sin, and subverts the reason he was brought in, as well as challenging the narrative of the scribes. I determined that I cannot offer help to homeless people as the minister of a small and elderly church because I do not get the opportunity to subvert their narrative. Instead it is usually a battle of wills and they leave at the first sight of not getting money. But my church helps through a local cooperative charity set up by the churches of the town. In that way I get the opportunity to see the same people regularly and have the chance to meet them in a more friendly way. Instead of them coming to me, I am going to them. And this in itself dramatically changes the narrative. Instead of meeting a narrative of bad news, I am offering good news. Instead of being a potential patron, I am being a servant. This is not a strategy for all churches everywhere, but seems best in my own context.

Subverting the narrative of a homeless person needs to be individualized to that person. There will be similarities, of course, but it is not formulaic. The homeless person must not be engaged as homeless or as problematic because of his or her economic situation. This is unnatural and very difficult to do, because subverting the narrative must happen in my mind first before I can challenge the terms of his or her story. Certainly a homeless person will likely be met through channels related to their economic situation. Like the revelation of God, the Christian must meet people on their terms, in their worlds, but then immediately challenge that. Let's call the homeless person George, because using a name is one way of beginning to cut through the economic relation and particularize the person. George will tell me a story of how he came to be homeless. Instead of directly responding to that story, I might ask about some other area of life. The goal is to help George understand that his problem is not economic, but in my estimation, relational. There will likely be stories of broken relationships that led to that situation, whether in his life, or his mother's, or someone else's. I might eventually tell him the story of a man who chose to be homeless and chose to be a victim of hatred because of his desire to bring reconciliation between God and myself, and George, if he would have it.

Though a critic could just say that this is simply proselytization, it is not. It is not disrespectful to challenge narratives, because the story George would tell me is not his own personal creation alone, but is the product of a vast number of influences throughout his life. It's not me vs. George, my Christian world view vs. his cosmology. Rather, George is living in a cosmos largely determined for him that he can either choose to accept or reject. If he accepts it, he is a victim, the lowest of the low, problematic in himself. There is no neutral narrative, only a narrative that the majority accepts, a narrative that integrates individuals into the world. Rather than proselytizing George, offering him an alternative narrative, not forcing it upon him, is offering him a great liberation. And the same could be said of a rich person addicted to wealth and seemingly righteous because of his wealth. This is what Jesus does with the rich young ruler. In the end, I may end up helping George get a job, but not because this will make him human again, or acceptable to society, but because he would have become responsible in Christ and desire to share with others the alternative story he has come to believe in. He may remain homeless as well, so long as we understand that as Christians it is not our task to judge on outward appearances and to integrate people into the dominant cosmos. If we do that, we subvert the gospel, turning Jesus into a force of social normalization, which he himself certainly was not.

On a larger scale, re-narrating the gospel of Jesus Christ in all of its subversive power can be done in a limitless number of ways and places. But if it remains general or universal it is itself subverted, turned into a cosmology that people should accept on principle. We should always refuse to narrate a *Christian perspective* on global poverty, for example. But we can explain *Christian problems with the narrative* of global poverty. There is no global solution and so, if you will, there is no Christian ethic.

This is the power of the gospel. It is a very tightly constrained story that cannot be applied to any and all situations by turning it into universal principles. The gospel speaks to one thing only: that people are estranged from God, that God desires to be reconciled, and works through people to accomplish this reconciliation, and that in Jesus Christ we have full reconciliation with God. The result is that reconciliation can spread to all our other relationships. But it cannot be universalized or made into principles.

Subverting the narrative will always involve this personalization, whether it be related to people, to animals, to "the environment," or whatever. Any ethic related to animals and species needs to be challenged. As we saw in my comments on Genesis 1–2, God, and therefore Adam and Eve, would relate to the animals personally, not as species. Any Christian ethic of species is problematic because it perpetuates an economic relationship with animals. Rather than mediating a relationship with particular animals through one's relationship with God, one will only perpetuate the very problem of the abuse animals face, that they are seen economically. Treating animals by species economizes them, whether we are interested in exploiting them or saving them. Love cannot be expressed for a species because the very notion of a species is a concept we create. Then, like Aristotle, we again give nature and animals their meaning by our use of them, whether "humane" or exploitative.

This subversion involves the very difficult task of self-limitation. To not judge other people, God's creation, animals, even ourselves, feels unnatural and entirely contrary to wisdom and experience. And it is, for the gospel requires that one daily take up one's cross, die to self, and die to the judgment that created estrangement in the first place.

Subversion is deconstructive, and that is profoundly scary to many people. But unlike existentialism or the deconstructionism of Jacques

Derrida, this subversion is rooted in relationship. Its source is precisely the opposite of Sartre's. Rather than highlighting the distance between people, times, texts, and communication in Derrida, the gospel is a story that highlights the profound nearness that love creates. Philosophers that many Christians love to hate—Nietzsche, Marx, Sartre, Derrida—offer great resources to be plundered. They examine the posturing of people, the stories they tell in bad faith, the projections they have, the structures of estrangement. Their description of problems are wonderful, their solutions are insipid or (purposefully) absurd. There is nowhere else for them to go. But the deconstruction of reconciliation has its source in love. Nietzsche realized that when one had deconstructed narratives and transcended value all that was left was power. Jesus knew this, but instead of expressing his power, he subverted power by love.

SUBVERTING STORIES AND THEOLOGIES

Readers of books on ethics are usually looking for action. Ethics is the question, "What should I do?" That, like other narratives, must be challenged. Ethics as a field is impossible for Christians who desire to live and show the love of Jesus because this love is entirely particular and never general. We should not give classes of actions that are always and everywhere good. But that means we can examine particular and popular stories and see how the gospel subverts them, enabling Christians to interact with people who believe in these stories in different ways, ways that challenge the centrality of economics, and will, as a side-effect of love, undermine economic relations on a more universal scale. The subversive gospel is radically transformative, but it transforms only by its own power, not by any universal or formulaic action or maxim.

Put another way, every action has symbolic content, whether it is watching a sporting event, brushing one's teeth, driving a car to see relatives, or eating special meals. The symbolic content is dialectical. That is, the actor is both the creator of the meaning and the participant in the meaning. Each individual involved in an action has his or her own version or interpretation that contributes to a shared meaning. Symbols are conventional and their referent is set, not just by individuals, but by larger groups as well. Individuals participate and so help create and reinforce the meaning. This is true of money, as we saw that coinage was distinct from all other symbols because it was the first symbol that was valuable only as a symbol in referent to an anonymous higher reality. Personal seals and tally sticks had existed long before, but these were like private languages. Money was the first real physical-symbolic *lingua franca*. But this knowledge, that people are helping to create and reinforce shared value and meaning, is difficult to accept for many. And so ethics becomes a field of action, as though the meaning of the actions were timeless. Indeed, they must be for the act to become primary. If the gospel is a subversive message, then it must do something very difficult—live into a preexisting context in a way that keeps external symbols but subverts their referent. A Christian ethic of this kind will always seem "relative." And this kind of talk deeply threatens many Christians who want to maintain the kingship of God over truth. That is understandable. But once we accept that all knowledge is knowledge-as, always knowledge-in-relationship, then this relativism is profoundly gospel centered. We can never know as God, but we can know in relationship with God. We can never have unmediated truth, but we can have our reasoning mediated through a relationship with God. And so, through reconciliation with God in Christ, there is an epistemological revolution. Instead of mediating knowledge through a supposedly objective world, which was the very heart of Adam and Eve's sin, Christians have knowledge mediated through the Reconciler. All things must be seen from the perspective of reconciliation. Let us look at some economic ethics from this perspective.

Charity

In our time it has become common to see, not only nonprofit organizations, but also profit-seeking corporations and national governments heavily participate in charity. This can be the very mission of an organization, it can be an advertising tactic to draw customers looking to soothe the increasing guilt of consumerism, it can be disaster or crisis relief, or a nation can provide foreign aid for less noble reasons. But what is new is that charity is outsourced to professionals. Corporate charity has become an embedded part of American and English culture.[14] And our contemporary version of charity matches perfectly the character of our postmonetary society. We want to care for people in need, but our first thought of how to do this is systematic, technological, entrepreneurial, and related to categories, rather than to individuals. Modern charity is fruit of our postmonetary metaphysic.

Charity is often understood as a debt that people owe. The common expression "giving back" demonstrates this. Those who donate are not giving freely, they are releasing themselves from a debt. Who owes what to whom in this situation is usually not investigated. There is almost never a

---

14. I speak for these countries having lived there. I'm sure this would be true of others as well.

direct debtor-creditor relationship here. Providing clean wells in Africa is not really giving back, since it is likely they haven't given me anything in the first place. The debtor-creditor relationship rather exists between me and some universal, like Humanity, or the Universe. But paying a debt is not charity. Doing one's duty or fulfilling an agreement is simply just, not excellent or praiseworthy. It is expected. But it makes sense to use contradictory language in speaking of this kind of charity because it provides double justification—economic and moral. We feel good about ourselves morally for doing what is demanded of us. We also feel good about ourselves on an economic level, like we're not throwing money away because, after all, we're just giving back. The Universe or God has blessed us with wealth and so we should give a bit here and there.

Charity comes from Latin, *caritas*, or love. The etymology and later development of this word is significant because the word itself traces how money has subverted relationships of love. *Caritas* was used by Jerome to translate Paul in 1 Corinthians 13, in the Vulgate, for example. Charity is patient, kind, not boastful or envious, not arrogant or rude. But "charity" can no longer be used to translate such a verse. Charity now specifically means the act of giving material aid, usually money, to someone in need, or an organization that does this. The Parable of the Good Samaritan is the classic example of charity. But that story is told as an illustration of who is one's neighbor. Whatever can be said about the definition of neighbor, it must include geographic proximity. The first part of our English word comes from *nigh*, near. The Greek *plēsion* also conveys this geographic proximity. This parable must not be understood as love for one's "fellow man" or some kind of altruism or philanthropy. Jesus's point in the parable is that although a Jew may be hurt and Jews pass him by, a true neighbor is one who loves, regardless of his or her social group. The good Samaritan is not a story about altruism or humanity, but loving one's social enemies, or at least outsiders. It's a love for individual people, not for humanity.

For the Christian, love of God must come before love of neighbor. This is a logical, not necessarily temporal priority. If one does not love God first, and others second, this love will necessarily be subverted, as we see done in charity today. It will not be love, but an expression of an economic relationship, which is always a relationship of estrangement. Such charity sees problems, not people, and so never really expresses love of a person, but love of a concept. Philanthropy is deeply problematic because it is the love of an ideal. A philanthropist can choose what aspects of humanity are lovable and support those financially, helping to construct humanity in his or her ideal image. A person who is reconciled to God will treat people as God does, as individuals, as involved in their lives on an intimate and personal level, and as loving even enemies. This is a relationship that exists over time, with character development. Philanthropy, on the other hand, loves an isolated, ideal, timeless invention. And so philanthropy is not love at all, but its perversion. It is isolation, expressing love for an idea through money. The love of God is superfluous to the philanthropist or altruist. It is unnecessary and even unwanted. This is why Christians have lost their market share of charity. It might have started with Christian impulses, though impulses based in a bad theological anthropology, and as charitable institutions have developed lives independent of their religious orders, they have discovered that they can perform their tasks and their mission without recourse to religion.

The same may be said of the state. Formerly the state depended upon churches to provide human services. But states have taken this on themselves. Like the mass debt forgiveness in the ancient world, making citizens dependent upon civil and social services creates debts of honor or gratitude that discourages rebellion.[15] That is not the only reason for national charity, social services, or welfare, of course. Many rulers feel deep responsibility for their subjects, but this again is confirmation of a hierarchical order dependent upon economic relations. This can be especially true in cases of foreign aid. But that is another complex matter. Suffice it to say that systematic charity creates relationships of dependence, both economic and moral, that reaffirm a system much like vassalage or patronage. It is quite possible for charity to become a vehicle of enslavement.

The love of God in Jesus Christ stands in deep contrast to this. Jesus said little to nothing about humanity in general, he did not give lectures on philanthropy, but attacked such charity as hypocrisy. The story of the publican and the Pharisee in Luke 18:9–14 illustrates this point. The Pharisee who does his economic duty of paying his tithes is not justified because he does not love, but despises. The tax collector is repentant and does not judge any but himself. The tax collector is the one whom God justifies. Likewise, Jesus asks the rich young ruler not to just sell all and give to the poor, but also to follow him. This is not great philanthropy, but the love of God. Or again, the church of Acts 2 that sells everything and lives a common life with common property does so as a result of being filled with the Holy Spirit, not out of a generic altruism, or out of the political goodness or utopian vision of communism. Communism as a political doctrine, like charity, is a deep perversion of the love of God because it treats people as primarily members of a class and seeks a classless society by domination and hatred, rather than love. Any love not mediated through the love of God in Jesus Christ will

---

15. Machiavelli recognized this: "Therefore a wise prince ought to adopt such a course that his citizens will always in every sort and kind of circumstance have need of the state and of him, and then he will always find them faithful." *The Prince*, ch. 9.

lead to perversions. Christians must see this, understand it, and have it form the basis of any action or scheme in engaging with society.

Practically this does not mean that Christians should not participate in charity or work for charitable organizations. But it also does not mean they should. Rather, in freedom, Christians must subvert economic charity, using it as an opportunity to express personal love. Charity is not love and we should not confuse it with love. Donating money to a charity in no way expresses the love of God because, as we've seen, it is the very nature of money to conceal its history, and this makes it inimical to creating relationships of reconciliation. God does not require money for his work, and it often subverts that work. God works through people and relationships, not through money and systems of economic redistribution.

Sacrifice

Sacrifice was, as we saw, a major method of economic redistribution in the ancient world. We will leave a detailed discussion of sacrifice and atonement for another work. Tracing the influence of economic thinking on Christian theology is perhaps nowhere more needed and prescient than in discussions of the meaning of Jesus's death. I would simply say here that Christ's death is the subversion of sacrifice. Though this is similar to the perspective of René Girard, I arrive at it from entirely different means, and with different results.

Jesus's death is a sacrifice to end sacrifice because it is God's ultimate subversion of human economic relationships, especially as expressed in religion. It demonstrates the absurdity of infinite debt. God provides a sacrifice that could cleanse an infinite debt, but such a debt never existed anyway. There is no moral debt to God, because God is not the one who created morality. Nor can humans be indebted to God, because this would make God a creditor who depends upon his debtors in some way, as this is a relationship of mutual dependency.

The sacrament of Communion, the Eucharist, or the Last Supper is the paramount symbol of this. In it we celebrate that God gave to us. It is a total inversion of sacrifice. God keeps his promise, his covenant, that his people will be a blessing, even if he has to do it for them, so fulfilling the covenant he made with Abraham. In religion people sacrifice to the gods in recognition of what the gods have done for them, giving them victory in battle, abundance in harvest, or to placate wrath when the gods are angry that people have done wrong. So Jesus is sacrificed in the most sinister and perverse act of human history. Jesus is killed as a sacrifice to the peace of Israel in their slavery to Rome, a total abandonment of the mission of God in Scripture, and a perfect example of relating economically to God. After all, the scapegoat mechanism that Caiaphas employed is perfectly economic: better to kill one man than for all to die because of a rebellion. This is wonderful consequentialist reasoning. The murder of Jesus is the acme of human rebellion because it is the total rejection of reconciliation in favor of economics, a rejection of the image of God as God's power sharing by killing God,[16] and a rejection of the mission to be a blessing. In Communion we acknowledge that we have betrayed God, are estranged from him, but that he is faithful and himself provides the means by which we can be reconciled to him. We even symbolically eat the flesh of God, rather than offering to God a human or animal sacrifice to placate his wrath. Though God does not kill Jesus and so it is not really a sacrifice, Communion reveals that, if we must use sacrificial imagery it is God sacrificing himself to placate our wrath, the ultimate expression of Jesus's *kenosis*. For us to understand Communion in this way we understand now that by partaking of the flesh and blood of Jesus we symbolically participate in the act that destroys economic relations between God and people expressed in religion. It is not just receiving a gift, but proclaiming Jesus's death as God's taking the initiative, in language we understand, to be reconciled to us. Again, this is how Jesus subverted the Golden Rule. Instead of demanding justice God did not consider his rights something necessary to achieve, and took the initiative in reconciliation.

This is not intended to be a full expression of my theology of the atonement or the sacraments, but it is an indication of a direction that I think can be wonderfully transformative. There is nothing more ethical for the Christian than liberating the gospel to work in the power of the Holy Spirit for the transformation of lives and the renewal of the mind. If we concentrate on "What should I do?" first, then this transformation is subverted from the fore. We can say here that, as Christians, we must cease all economic relationships with God, and bid other disciples to do so as well, which is another way of simply saying that we should tell each other the gospel regularly.

Tithe, Temple, Priesthood, and Transubstantiation

Christians know that they are required to give 10 percent of their income to the church or charitable organizations. Most churches are happy to continue this story without much question, given that this is the livelihood of the institution and its employees. But the tithe is a deeply problematic concept for the church. The tithe was instituted in the Torah to maintain one of the

---

16. Of course God cannot be killed, but the act of murder occurred against Jesus who is God, and therefore can rightly be considered deicide.

twelve tribes, the Levites, as a priesthood. The eleven other tribes possessed land and were able to feed themselves from their own produce. The Levites could not own land and could not grow their own food. The tithe enabled them have provision for their service rendered to God and the people of Israel. The tithe in the Old Testament is always of food or drink produce, never money or precious metals, as the Torah was clearly written in a pre-monetary society. The Levites could not grow rich off of a tithe because produce is perishable, and possessing an excess of food is only waste, unless of course they were corrupt and resold this food. Although it seems obvious to translate the produce of one's labor on a farm to one's profits in business, this is actually a fundamental transformation of the original tithe. Food has a consistent use value. People need a fairly constant supply of it throughout their lives. Money, on the other hand, derives its value from economic relationships, which are always relationships of estrangement. What was once a life-giving service to the priesthood subtly transforms the purpose of the priesthood and temple. Much of the value of money is in its ability to exist as stored value, as a guarantee of future value, and so an ability to be self-sufficient. The entire point of the tithe was to create relationships of dependence, so that the priests could not become self-sufficient. Jesus questions why people store value against the future, as it betrays a mistrust of God's fatherly provision. Indeed, his teaching about the provision of God follows directly on his teaching about not serving God and money.[17] A tithe of money subverts the temple or church because it in itself teaches its users to value what everyone else in the world values. Money transforms those who use it into its own image. No one can serve God and money, these are opposed masters and a tithe of money encourages service to money, not to God.

This doesn't mean the church cannot use money, of course, or that its ministers should not be paid a fair living, or that building maintenance should be abandoned. The tithe is problematic when it is transformed into money because it transforms relationships of mutual dependence into relations of independence. I am convinced that money will never be lacking where the mission of God deems it necessary. Like the modern understanding of the individual, we are tempted to think of church institutions as fictive persons that are truly right and mature when they are self-sufficient. But it is always possible that a church institution can be financially self-sufficient and have no connection to the mission of God. Money naturally works to subvert the church in this way.

17. Matt 6:24–25.

The Levites maintained a central tabernacle and temple complex established primarily for sacrifice. But the church is the body of Christ, not a temple complex in a physical location. It is decentralized physically because it is a spiritual body. The tithe emphasizes an inflow into the physical institution. People are added to the pews to contribute financially, so people are quantified and turned into statistics, which then represent institutional health. The church as the body of Christ, however, must grow in discipleship, not in quantity. Quantitative growth tends to kill discipleship, whereas discipleship will produce growth of a vastly different sort. Instead of emphasizing a duty for people to give money, they must hear the call of Jesus to take up their crosses, not their 10 percent. The cost of discipleship is total. Disciples must be asked to leave all behind and count all their previous gains as loss for the sake of Christ.[18] For only then will they actually follow Jesus and not use Jesus to legitimize their financial lives. One cannot love God and money. The church as building or institution is not a temple in any meaningful sense of the word. The church consists of relationships mediated by reconciliation with God in Jesus Christ. Money cannot produce or aid these relationships, because the church is not a fictive person. It is a real person: Jesus Christ.

The tithe was established to maintain a large centralized complex with a professional caste of priests, as was usual in the ancient Near East. Certain church traditions have turned the Eucharist into a priestly act of sacrifice, namely the transubstantiationalists, turning the body of Christ into a metaphysical reality based quite clearly on the principle of fiduciarity. The bread that becomes the body of Christ in essence, if not in form, is valuable because it participates in the universal. The value of the bread is greater than its intrinsic bread-ness because the words of institution have transformed it. It is now a token, often taking the very form of a coin-like wafer. Transubstantiation itself shows the development of money as we saw in chapter 2 with the formation of a mass-produced object, indistinct from one another, that would commemorate the participation in sacrifice and so remind the participants of the benefits conferred by the sacrifice: economic redistribution (almsgiving, the tithe, the reception of equivalent amount of the sacrifice guaranteed by the mass-produced wafer), and community formation. Although I would not argue for a Zwinglian view of Communion either, by placing the efficacy of the sacrament in the presence of the Holy Spirit, as Calvin does, we participate in the body of Christ by personal relationship, not by metaphysical transformation. Furthermore, our participation in the body of Christ is not in the meal itself, in the transaction, distribution, and

---

18. Phil 3:7–8.

consumption of the elements. These must only symbolize the living relationships of reconciliation present in those who celebrate the Eucharist together as they have been reconciled in Christ. So instead of reinforcing the hierarchy of priesthood, the Eucharist, as I suggest it, undermines hierarchy because the only way God is present amongst the people is through living and active relationships of reconciliation with God and neighbor.

Much language and theology of the church has been profoundly shaped by economic relationships to its terrible detriment. The examples given here through the tithe, temple, and Eucharist are only a few examples of a false narrative that radically transforms what a church is and what its mission is.

Freedom, Liberty, and Justice

The story of modern times is bound up with talk of individual rights and liberties. The United States of America was founded on this kind of language, as well as that of the social contract. We have already discussed the social contract and individual rights and need not pick up that discussion again. This narrative, as we saw, was created as a conscious attempt to secularize Augustine's theology of original sin. Self-love was transformed into self-interest and so a kind of personal relationship is now mediated through economic interest. This narrative lies at the heart of contemporary conceptions of freedom, of humanity, of individuality, and lies at the heart of much ethical discussion. As Christians we must reject this narrative and work to subvert it because it offers us a vision of freedom far too small compared with that of Jesus Christ. Prioritizing the sovereignty of the individual is, ironically, an infantilizing narrative, because it tends to absolve people of personal responsibility by making them sovereign to themselves in isolation from preexisting relationships. Each person has the right to the "pursuit of happiness" however the sovereign individual conceives of that. I am not advocating the opposite of this view, and suggesting dictatorship or some such oligarchy is right. No human political system of thought can rightly express the kingdom of God. Nevertheless, the sovereignty of the self and freedom from others is a narrative inimical to the gospel of Jesus Christ, and so must be challenged.

Reconciliation is the abandonment of personal rights as a concept. As we saw, especially in the Sermon on the Mount, Jesus tells his disciples to give up claims to justice and rightness for themselves. Instead of gaining revenge for a harm, they are to turn the other cheek. Instead of settling disagreements by appeal to court, they should settle out of court and be reconciled. The disciple must take the initiative in reconciliation, which means that they must suffer more and willingly accept injustices committed upon themselves. The freedom of the Christian is not to be free from the influence of other people, and the possibility of their injustices, but the purposeful abandonment of justice for reconciliation. Justice itself, as we've seen, is profoundly economic, as is our idea of individual liberties. In order to subvert this, we must first be treated unjustly. Jesus is, of course, the best example of this.

Translating this giving up of personal rights into an ethical principle is highly problematic. This is the error of nonviolence as an ethic, for example. Nonviolence treats methodology as problematic, not addressing the underlying reasons for violence. Nonviolence is a means, but to what end is not always specified. In Christ there is reconciliation with God and with one another. Violence as a method is unlikely to achieve reconciliation. But nonviolence can also lead nowhere of itself. Giving up of personal rights is not, in itself, the gospel. It can be a way to a false humility and victimhood. In the economic field this translates exactly into what Jesus, Peter, and Paul were talking about in paying taxes and debts, even debts of honor. The whole structure of debt reinforces estrangement so the very existence of debtor-creditor relationships is problematic. Nevertheless, for the sake of subverting the relationship one should pay what one owes. Taxes, tributes, and debts are a kind of economic violence. If one doesn't pay one will suffer consequences of intimidation at least and possibly even physical violence.

But what about when it comes to other people? Often it is not oneself that is facing violence or debt collection, but a neighbor. The trouble with nonviolence is that it can lead to a tacit cooperation in violence if one is able to prevent it. It is one thing for an individual believer to abandon his or her own rights and willingly be a victim, another to watch injustice and do nothing. Shall we not defend those who cannot speak for or defend themselves? Absolutely. Recall that the prophetic literature of the Bible is full of calls to do justice, to speak for the voiceless, to defend the widow and the orphan. But this defense must seek reconciliation, not justice alone. Justice can be a means to reconciliation, but in itself it remains economic. Therefore, the pursuit of justice, of upholding peoples' rights and liberties can and does actively subvert reconciliation. Justice is a blind woman holding balanced scales and a sword. God's love is deeply personal and interested, it breaks scales by not seeking retribution but taking the first step in reconciliation, and it bears a cross instead of a sword. These are entirely different symbols of entirely different narratives.

This means that in seeking justice for someone other than ourselves, the disciple will use the opportunity to personalize the situation. There is no crime against the State, against the Universe, or other universal. There are only injuries to people. Only people suffer and only people can love. One concrete action a disciple could take would be to become involved in victim's advocacy, not pleading their rights, but working for reconciliation in the love of Christ.

All of this is inimical to notions of the common good, of course. One cannot found or build a nation on love. The kingdom of God is founded on just those grounds, but entry into that kingdom can only come by being reconciled to its king. We cannot impose love by power. Many are those who do not believe and will not believe, and Christians do not claim rights to tell them what to do or how to live. Non-Christians have thrived for millennia all across the world with ideas of justice, goodness, beauty. Christians do not have a monopoly on the good. In fact, based on our reading of Genesis 1–3, we see that being reconciled to God means the abandonment of humanly created concepts of good and evil. It was the act of creating the common good that was the Estrangement, especially evident in the Babel narrative of Genesis 11.

To advance a common good is to find principles upon which all can agree regardless of religious perspective. But the only good a disciple can recognize is to be reconciled with God. All other goods lead to estrangement, which is why they can be held by people of various belief systems in the first place. Like ideas of the social contract and individual rights and liberties, the notion of the common good is based on a problematic narrative that makes God entirely superfluous to ethical conversation. And God is entirely superfluous to ethics. Ethics are simply the description of what an individual must do to be sure his or her life is tune with the cosmos. This could be a summary of Kant's Categorical Imperative. Whatever gods are part of this cosmos will be the gods that demand this behavior. The Christian does not advance universal concepts of goodness, but seeks to create personal relationships of reconciliation in the love of God. This cannot be legislated or commanded, it can only be done.

Vocation and Calling

Protestants have classically reacted negatively to an understanding of special callings that create a priestly hierarchy, and rightly so. But Luther and his followers made a disastrous move in sanctifying all manner of economic life and extending the notion of a divine calling to all fields of work. Economic life is the fruit of estrangement from God. Jesus himself is critical of farmers who sow, reap, and store away, when God feeds the birds. Rather than legitimizing all fields of labor and valorizing the laborer, the gospel holds up all kinds of economic activity to critique. None are sanctified, not even priesthood. Though this is not the place for a full investigation or explanation of calling in Scripture, let it suffice to say that whenever the term is used by Paul he uses it to refer specifically to the gospel. The calling of Jesus is to reconciliation and to share reconciliation. The priesthood of all believers is not a way of sanctifying all work, but is a way of making all people engaged in gospel work, wherever they find themselves.

It is an implicit belief in the notion of vocation that God has legitimized such work for his people and that such work is therefore honorable. But some work is dishonorable. The Word of God does not exist to affirm human orders of existence in their structures of estrangement. If one does not work, one does not eat,[19] but that does not justify that work. Nevertheless, such work can be redeemed, bought back as it were, from service to economic relationships by using it as an opportunity for reconciliation. There is only one calling in Scripture, and it is given equally to all, to be reconciled to God and to share this reconciliation with others, so pointing them to the reconciliation God offers to them. Christian workers are ambassadors, placed in their fields, not because their fields are good and honorable ways of serving God, but because people spend the majority of their lives toiling in fields of labor and God has sent his church into their midst.

Fictive Persons: Getting Involved with Structures of Estrangement

It's complicated. We live in an age dominated by corporations and fictive persons of all kinds. Personal relationships are mediated, not only through governments and businesses, but also through technologies that transform the character of our relationships. How can a Christian engage in business and nonprofits, neither abandoning the world, nor baptizing it?

As we discussed, the corporation structurally demands economic relationships. Its very purpose is to release individuals from responsibility for the purpose of taking larger economic risks. It has been very successful in this and has been one of the major forces in creating our contemporary cosmos. The gospel of reconciliation stands in direct contrast with the narrative of the corporation. But to say that Christians cannot and should not own or operate businesses would be to create an alternative cosmos or "Christian world view." It is equally problematic to justify the world and say that business can be used for the kingdom. One cannot serve God and money, and God's kingdom was founded and can be best demonstrated without money.

19. 2 Thess 3:10.

Nor is it the case that we need to find a golden mean, somewhere between total condemnation and total legitimation. Moderation is an economic virtue.

Instead Christians participate to lovingly subvert. It is impossible to express love through money, but money can be used as an excuse to create relationships: as Jesus says, "Make friends for yourselves by means of unrighteous wealth."[20] A Christian is free and I'll not place limits on what he or she can or cannot do that Jesus himself did not create. Nevertheless, those who find themselves in positions of power and authority must take great care to continually keep the mission of reconciliation at the forefront of their minds. It is hard for a rich man to enter the kingdom of heaven. His time is more economically valuable and precious. Her acquaintances are more likely to have economic motives in friendship. The same would be equally true of government figures. But the CEO or the president could use his or her position of power to subvert the narratives of power in dramatic ways. Just as Jesus did not take advantage of his divinity to win people over, but chose to divest himself of his power, so too a CEO could make every effort to love people personally. But again, this is extremely difficult. Furthermore, it is difficult to make it to the top of a field without heavily investing into the structure and narrative that underlies it. Jesus told the rich man to sell all he had. A CEO must be willing to do likewise, and a ruler must be willing to step down for the sake of Jesus's call, having the mind of Jesus Christ that Paul explains in Philippians 2. In Christ wealth and power are nothing and of no value, but they are powerful temptations away from relationships of reconciliation.

On the other side are people who feel oppressed by the vast income inequalities we now see. The Occupy Movement was a curious protest movement that spread without leadership throughout the world in the space of a few days. It raised the issue of income inequalities, but it was itself subverted by its own means of communication, demonstrating the deep connection and vast structures of global capitalism. One major means of spreading this and other protests has become internet social media, such as Facebook. Now, the CEO and founder of Facebook belongs to the "1 percent." And he makes money whenever people use Facebook by advertising. So, as those protesting the 1 percent use Facebook, they are ironically funding the 1 percent. And the devices they use to communicate (smartphones, cameras) are a similar story. Although greed may be part of the problem, it is certainly only a part. The enormous global structures necessary for the development, manufacture, distribution, retail, support, and service providing of relatively

---

20. Luke 16:9.

inexpensive mobile devices could never be done without corporations who naturally see no problem in making profits. Due to an economy of scale, their profits are astronomic. And because no one is personally responsible for the actions of the corporation by design, it is easy to see how this is a recipe for immense personal wealth.

But the CEO's are not the problem. The relationship between the corporation, people, and their products is problematic. No one is responsible and no one person can make much difference. Again, this is by design. This design is further complicated by technologies that further remove a human element from the system. Such is the case, again, with Bitcoin and other virtual currencies. In our supposed democratic or anarchic freedom, we are simply enslaving ourselves to systems beyond the control of anyone. In such a situation, the gospel of Jesus Christ may seem to have nothing to say. It doesn't really address these issues. But the opposite is true. The subversive effects of love are more profound the more impersonal mediation people experience. This makes personal love all the more difficult, however. As people have less and less reason to be personally responsible, depending upon corporations, insurance, and government services, the task of discipleship is perhaps more difficult than ever. More has to be left behind. Discipleship is more costly and is a longer road. But with God nothing is impossible.

What then can a Christian do in this deeply complicated situation? The Christian can work to subvert the desire for money and power that corporations and technologies promise. The Christian can live in a way that undermines the value of technology, using it as a means to create interpersonal, face-to-face, and local relationships, whether it be in a protest, an office building, a high-power meeting room, or a homeless shelter.

The situation in nonprofits may seem somewhat different. But the existence of nonprofits that exist to limit responsibility and pool resources for greater effect can only be a desirable situation when the problem they identify as their mission is economic. The only reason to pool resources is to more effectively use resources. But the gospel is not about resource distribution. Now again there are people living in desperate situations and many are led by compassion to help. Here we need to again question the nature of the problem. No one lives in a bad economic situation where there is not also a failure of love. But people need help, so a charity is established that will alleviate this or that problem and people who have compassion but no means to reach these people in far away places can give money. This compassion is not love of individuals, but a love of humanity, a constructed image of "us." This enables us to identify the worthy and unworthy recipients of charity. But none are outside the love of God. Nevertheless, such a charity can be a great means to the expression of personal love, not for the donors, but for the workers who do meet people face to face. Certainly the workers or missionaries can return to the donors and tell stories and try to express this connection that has been made, and perhaps this can create a relationship between the worker and the donor. But the donor has not loved the recipient of aid. Love cannot be mediated or communicated by money. Money has value because it is impersonal, and it tends to transform those who use it into its own image. So again, we should not say that nonprofits are good or bad as nonprofits. There are dangers inherent in their structure. There is a danger in believing that donating money can be an expression of love and so confirming the economic gospel of our era. Charities and nonprofits can serve as wonderful opportunity creators for the expression of God's love in Jesus Christ, but they themselves cannot, corporately, express the personal love of God for individuals. And there is always the danger that systematic charity replaces personal, face-to-face relationships of love.

Hierarchy and Equality

One theme that has continued throughout this book is the dichotomy of hierarchy and equality, of the aristocrat and the demagogue. The socio-economic position of a person plays a large role in how their cosmos is constructed and the ethical ideals they prescribe. What should the Christian do? It is easy today to cry out for equality in societies that demand it, but, as we saw, equality, with its emphasis on rights, has its own problems. The language of hierarchy is inescapable in Scripture, and its authors speak very positively about such hierarchies. What do we do with that?

As in the above, the answer must be found in breaking through the false dichotomy of hierarchy and equality. The Christian, in seeking to share the reconciliation of God in Jesus Christ, can work through this eternal debate of economic relations. The story of Scripture and the three kinds of relationship we discussed has a lot to say about hierarchy and equality. We saw that in the Creator-creature relationship there was a clear hierarchy and language of dominion. This dominion was not violent, but was characterized by the character of the Creator. Human dominion was mediated through their personal relationship with the Creator, ruling in the same fashion. This was the *imago dei*. There was a kind of equality as well, Adam and Eve were not given specific gender roles in Eden, and male domination was part of the curse of Genesis 3.

In the Estrangement hierarchy becomes violent and abusive precisely because it was no longer mediated through God. Instead, by an inversion of trust and epistemological hierarchy, good and evil are self-created notions that are through matter. But the Estrangement also perverts equality by the exact same epistemological mediation. Rather than Adam and Eve being equals because of their role as the image of God, all equality must now be self-created and mediated through material reality. Tribe, family, race, species, nation, social class, gender, sexuality, all become relationships of equality that create equality by an exclusive hierarchy. Modern attempts to equalize these relationships can only do so by the same method: providing an exclusive hierarchy that seeks maximal inclusion of certain people at the cost of others. Hierarchy and equality are mutually dependent concepts, as pointed out earlier, and everyone participates in relationships of both kinds. Our equalities exist for selfish and economic reasons. We join together to face down common enemies in order to confirm identities we have created for ourselves, and this creates equality. We democratize all forms of expression by submitting them to the power of technology and techniques.

In the relationship of reconciliation, we again come to a difficulty. Eden is irrecoverable. We cannot go back, nor should we try. Our ethic is not archaeological, but eschatological. We live in relationships of estranged hierarchies and estranged equalities. Neither option represents reconciliation. Neither the pursuit of equality or hierarchy can reveal or lead to God. Rather, God revealed himself in Jesus Christ, as one who subverts these structures of estrangement. Philippians 2 is the great *kenosis* passage where Paul highlights that the attitude of Christians must be like that of God in Christ Jesus who did not seek self-glorification, but gave up his divine prerogatives to serve and give his life. When Jesus called his disciples, he demanded that they not call anyone else "teacher" or "father" because they were all made brothers in him.[21] By being reconciled to God through Jesus, the disciple joins a new equality that is not based on the exclusion of the unworthy, but on the inclusion of the unworthy who have received the gospel and given up self-created identities for an identity in Christ. This creates a fraternity mediated by Jesus, so that the attitude of Jesus carries through to the disciples. So this fraternity is not the basis for a dominating hierarchy, but one of love and service. Christians are adopted into the family of God through brotherhood with the king, Jesus. As such they are coheirs of his kingdom. But this is a kingdom not built by human hands or minds, unlike human cosmoi. It is a kingdom where relationships are intentionally hierarchical. That is, all relationships are mediated once again through one's relationship with the king. But we know this king as Jesus, the one who washed his disciples' feet and gave his life.

21. Matt 23:8–12.

So as with all other ethical aspects of this story, the Christian performs very specific tasks that are not possible for anyone else. The Christian is to subvert the common narratives of hierarchy and equality. Those places in which people seek justification by placing themselves above others are as false as those by which people seek equality. The Christian can stand boldly for a kind of hierarchy in a world that believes itself to be destroying hierarchies, by becoming the servant of all. The task of the Christian is not to replace an oppressive monarchy with a democracy, or a degenerate republic with a righteous dictatorship, but to tell and live an alternative story about a king who became servant of all, making us coheirs with him of his kingdom. In love the Christian submits to the reigning system to challenge the belief that people place in the system. The Christian ethic is storytelling in word and deed, a re-narration of the way things are and the way they could be. The Christian ethic in the economic world is, quite simply, subverting economics itself by love mediated through Christ. By undermining the value of identities mediated through material things, economic relationships are themselves devalued, opening the potential for reconciliation.

Conclusion

There are many other things that could be said here related to the nature of money and economic relations. These all too brief intimations of an ethic must be filled out by each person in his or her own context, for that is the power of the gospel. If the gospel gives us a cosmos, or a world view, it will inevitably fail as perspectives change. If the gospel remains attached to one of the many economic metaphors that the writers of Scripture used, it will eventually start to sound like bad news as our form of economy changes. Certainly many think this way about the Anselmic perspective of the atonement. Anselm used the notion of a debt of honor, perfectly acceptable in his time, to describe the atoning work of Jesus. But to preach a gospel centered in feudal economic relationships has proved difficult and increasingly unattractive. The same can be said of innumerable other aspects of the Christian faith. If the gospel is the revelation of God then it must communicate in language people can understand in their own contexts, and yet it must also transcend this context, drawing people out of their world by a relationship of reconciliation with God. This enables them to be a witness to the work of God in their own time, which always requires that they neither justify the world nor wholly reject it. God has done neither. But God loved the world, not as a universal concept that he would save by the revelation of metaphysical truths or mysteries (with an accompanying ethic), but as a human man who loved individual people. God's love is not expressed in metaphysical truths or in ethics, but in loving particular individual people.

By mediating relationships with our neighbors and our enemies through the reconciliation we have with God in Jesus Christ, economic relationships are naturally undone. Like a defunct currency, they simply lose all value. Our world is like the Egyptian slavery of the ancient Hebrew people. We are oppressed by relationships of estrangement that manifest themselves in economic forms. There can be no escape of our own. It is impossible for a person to be reconciled to God by rationality, or ethics rooted in a certain cosmos, because our rationality is mediated through the material world, and so our relationship to the gods or God will always be conceptual, metaphorical, and ultimately projected. But God sent his servant, Jesus, like Moses, to liberate people from captivity.

How, then, do we plunder Egypt? Not like the ancient Hebrews who took the treasure of Egypt with them, a treasure that corrupted them and led them to make an idol, but as Christians who can live with the treasure of Egypt as valueless. The gold of Egypt is like the sand. But the Egyptians value it, and so it provides us with a means to engage with them. Can we use the treasure of Egypt to subversively love the Egyptians? Certainly, if it provides us with an opportunity to tell them and show them the love of God in Christ in a way that Moses failed to do as a younger man. But there is a continual danger that this wealth will corrupt us as well. "Make friends for yourselves by means of unrighteous wealth"[22]; but, "You cannot serve both God and money."[23]

---

22. Luke 16:9.
23. Matt 6:24; Luke 16:13.

7

Conclusion: The Great Commission

There is a lot of work to be done, both in the formulation of a theology of relationship that I set out at the beginning, and in the investigation of how economic relationships have influenced and shaped Christian theology. Through this dialectical method, pioneered by Jacques Ellul, we are more and more able to understand the revelation of God in Jesus Christ for *what it is not*, in our time, and in times before. We are able to see how different and unique this gospel is, using the forms of its context to subvert the context and bring people back to God, and then to each other and God's creation. It retains this power in every cosmos.

It is the task of the theologian, I believe, to ferret out covert shared values and the philosophies and theologies that undergird them. Every theology has natural behavioral outcomes, whether covert or overt. Jesus says that a tree must be judged by its fruit. A theology must be judged by the ethics it produces. Any theology that ends up giving the same or similar ethics to the dominant narrative of a society, whether for or against, invents a god who will legitimize or condemn common belief. If there was a theistic, metaphysical prime-mover God who created all things, I imagine the last thing he would care to do is congratulate petty little humans in their pride for thinking they've finally arrived at the good, that they've finally ascended to heaven and found him out where he and his notions of goodness were hiding. Aristotle's God is more reasonable, remote, alone—a self-contented aristocrat. But theology has long been subjected to power and to economics, to kings, to merchants all looking for legitimation for their plunder and their oppression, looking to a god of their own construction to give them the confidence to do what otherwise their fear and cowardice prevents. Christian theology and ethics have long been held in Egyptian bondage, twisted into a slave mentality to serve the oppression of the Egyptians.

It is time for the church to exit Egypt under the banner of the gospel of Jesus Christ, our new Moses, who will deliver us from the slavery we have come to know and to love. The church's bondage has been in the nearly complete subversion of its guiding narrative. When Jesus says that no one can serve two masters, God and money, we imagine that he means that everyone can work forty hours in a week serving money and give an hour of worship to God. The church continues to ask people for tithes, that 10 percent temple tax to maintain a stolid and venerable institution. Its popular and successful leaders continually turn to economic models of success, of mission, of marketing, thinking that the church is a fictive person like a corporation rather than the body of Christ filled with the Holy Spirit. It is not surprising that our megachurch leaders have falls befitting Shakespearean or Greek tragedy, because the entire movement has built itself in the image of a corporation, which is established for the primary purpose of removing individual responsibility.

We live in a time when Christians believe that voting can enforce a Christian ethic in our nations, seeking to reestablish Christendom *de facto* and turn the gospel into a world view crusade. Egypt will not be converted by force and power, even by the power of the ballot. There is no Christian cosmos that we can build. Jesus gives a new command, that we love one another as he has loved us. And he gives all his disciples a commission to be his witnesses, to continue his preaching, teaching, and loving of individual people who are like lost sheep. Our one task, as a church, and as individually members of it, is to be the body of Christ, to carry out this great commission.

But Christians have turned the Great Commission into the Great Crusade, subverting the gospel with power and money. The Great Crusade sought to give ethics, metaphysics, politics: a universal church with universal power. But one cannot seek power and serve God. One cannot love one's enemies by killing them, forcibly converting them, or instilling in children a deep sense of guilt and fear that being in infinite debt to an eternal and omnipotent deity brings. The love of God empowers people to be Christ's witness. But the Great Crusade disempowered people, showing everyone their proper place and carefully delimiting appropriate behavior, while dressing it up in language of pride, nationalism, freedom, duty, entrepreneurship.

The Great Commission of Jesus will lead to the plundering of Egypt. His disciples are people who seek out others who are in relationships of estrangement, debt, slavery, wealth, and seek to love people without regard to money or power. These are people who listen to the stories of their neighbors, neither legitimizing them nor rejecting them, neither judging them good or judging them evil, but subverting such categories with the love of God.

The Great Crusade legitimizes Egypt. All Christian ethics that operate in the common narrative do this. Any conception of God as a being who engages in or validates economic relations is not a god worthy of worship, for this is a god that demands worship, who needs it, who has desires that can be satisfied by his creation. The God revealed in Jesus Christ does not come to demand worship. When his disciples finally see him in his resurrection body, about to ascend to heaven, some do worship him. Jesus does not commend them and so confirm this relationship of servitude, but he tells them:

> All authority in heaven and on earth has been given to me. Therefore, make disciples, going to all peoples, baptizing them in the name of the Father, and the Son, and the Holy Spirit, teaching them to keep all that I commanded you. And behold I am with you always unto the ends of the age.[1]

Instead of receiving their worship, Jesus commissions them with the very authority of God. Instead of reveling in their praise, he shares his power. And instead of demanding that they come to him and worship, he sends them away, empowered to continue his work by making disciples of individual people from every tribe, not just Jews. They are to make others into followers of Jesus who keep his command to love one another as he loved them. This was the subversion of justice, of the Golden Rule, as we saw, and the subversion of economic relationships as a whole. Adam and Eve were the image of God, having a royal charter for the shared rule of the creation with the Creator. In their estrangement from God this charter was revoked, people exercising their capabilities for domination and exploitation of each other and the creation, creating economic relationships. In Christ there is reconciliation with God. Now Jesus extends a new royal charter, a Great Commission, to his followers. They are to join in the work of God in bringing reconciliation to all. This is not the restoration of the image of God in its original content, as they are not joining with the Creator ruling the creation, but joining in with the Reconciler to bring reconciliation. This reconciliation is entirely opposed to any relationship mediated through anything or anyone but God himself. This means reconciliation is opposed to any and all economic relationships. Indeed, the economic relationship is itself to blame for much of the desolation of God's creation and enslavement

---

1. Matt 28:18–20.

CONCLUSION: THE GREAT COMMISSION

of God's creatures, human and nonhuman. So the follower of Jesus joins in combat with the economic relationship, but not openly, not in a crusade. The only means to reconciliation is reconciliation itself, and someone must take the first step in loving one's enemies. Jesus is God taking the initiative, and now Jesus tasks his followers with taking the same initiative.

Our present cosmos has taken systematic estrangement to new heights in the name of good things: freedom, opportunity, individual rights and liberties, democratization through technology. It is the task of Jesus's followers to tell an alternative gospel, not so much in the public square, but in the lives of individual people who are ever more alone in the great crowd of humanity. The more we interact with our neighbors through technological devices, the fewer opportunities for demonstration of love. And yet for precisely that reason our small acts of love have a proportionally greater impact. The declining churches of our formerly Christendom Western civilization have a wonderful opportunity to reflect on their own subversions by economic relationships. But they must decide to cut ties with their former *modus operandi*—legitimizing structures of economics and power. God is not an economist, not a capitalist, nor a socialist. It is time for our churches to cease preaching the same gospel of our cosmos and rediscover its unique voice and its unique gift—taking the first step to be reconciled with neighbors and enemies by a reconciled relationship with the triune God of Jesus Christ. This task will be most difficult and hard to bear. Every cosmos will regard subversive elements as chaotic and will seek to purge them or sacrifice them for the peace and prosperity of the people at large. This was Caiaphas's reasoning, and that of many who have followed. Many more will say, as church attenders have said to me, "I like your sermon, but I can't sell everything I have." Our churches are filled with rich young rulers who have kept the commandments and want to know what more they must do to inherit eternal life and they will not be willing to part with their wealth individually or as congregations. Nevertheless, the fields are ripe with the harvest, generations of people ever more connected technologically, but never so deeply alone and estranged. Discipleship costs everything, and yet it liberates us from the value of those very things that must be given up.

It may seem strange to conclude a work of academic theology with so sermonic a message. But for theology to be separate from an actual call to action renders it again nothing more than metaphysical speculation. Theology that reflects on the revelation of God cannot help but engender action. It is my hope that this work will do just that.

Bibliography

Anscombe, G. E. M. "Modern Moral Philosophy." *Philosophy* 33 (1958) 1–19. Online: http://www.philosophy.uncc.edu/mleldrid/cmt/mmp.html.
Barker, Margaret. *Creation: The Biblical Vision for the Environment.* London: T & T Clark, 2009.
Barth, Karl. *Church Dogmatics.* Edited by Frank McCombie. Translated by Geoffrey W. Bromiley and Thomas F. Torrance. London: T & T Clark, 2009.
———. *The Epistle to the Romans.* 6th ed. Translated by Edwin C. Hoskyns. London: Oxford University Press, 1968.
———. *On Religion.* Translated by Garrett Green. London: T & T Clark, 2006.
Bauckham, Richard. *Bible and Ecology: Rediscovering the Community of Creation.* London: Darton, Longman & Todd, 2010.
Bell, Daniel M. *The Economy of Desire: Christianity and Capitalism in a Postmodern World.* Grand Rapids: Baker Academic, 2012.
Benson, Bruce Ellis. *Pious Nietzsche: Decadence and Dionysian Faith.* Bloomington: Indiana University Press, 2008.
Berger, Peter L., and Thomas Luckmann. *The Social Construction of Reality: A Treatise in the Sociology of Knowledge.* New York: Anchor, 1990.
Bonhoeffer, Dietrich. *Creation and Fall: A Theological Exposition of Genesis 1–3.* Translated by Douglas S. Bax. Edited by John W. De Gruchy. Minneapolis: Fortress, 1997.
———. *Discipleship.* Edited by Geoffrey B. Kelly and John D. Godsey. Translated by Barbara Green and Reinhard Krauss. Minneapolis: Fortress, 2001.
———. *Ethics.* Edited by Clifford J. Green. Translated by Reinhard Krauss, Charles C. West, and Douglas W. Stott. Minneapolis: Fortress, 2005.
———. *Letters and Papers from Prison.* Edited by John W. De Gruchy. Translated by Isabel Best et al. Minneapolis: Fortress, 2009.
Buber, Martin. *I and Thou.* Translated by Ronald Gregor Smith. London: Bloomsbury, 2013.
Caillois, Roger. *Man and the Sacred.* Translated by Meyer Barash. Urbana, IL: University of Illinois Press, 2001.
Calvin, John. *Institutes of the Christian Religion: In Two Volumes.* Edited by John Thomas MacNeill. Translated by Ford Lewis Battles. Philadelphia: Westminster John Knox, 2001.
Case, Karl E. *Principles of Economics.* Edited by Ray C. Fair. Upper Saddle River, NJ: Prentice Hall, 1996.

Curd, Patricia, and Richard D. McKirahan. *A Presocratics Reader.* Indianapolis: Hackett, 1996.

Descartes, René. *Meditations on First Philosophy: In Which the Existence of God and the Distinction of the Soul from the Body Are Demonstrated.* Translated by Donald A. Cress. Indianapolis: Hackett, 1993.

Drury, Shadia B. *Alexandre Kojève: The Roots of Postmodern Politics.* Basingstoke, UK: Macmillan, 1994.

Dumézil, Georges. *Archaic Roman Religion.* Baltimore: Johns Hopkins University Press, 1996.

Durkheim, Emile. *The Elementary Forms of Religious Life.* Edited by Mark Sydney Cladis. Translated by Carol Cosman. Oxford: Oxford University Press, 2001.

Eliade, Mircea. *A History of Religious Ideas: From the Stone Age to the Eleusinian Mysteries.* Translated by Willard R. Trask. Chicago: University of Chicago Press, 1978.

———. *The Sacred and the Profane: The Nature of Religion.* Translated by Willard R. Trask. New York: Harcourt Brace, 1959.

Ellul, Jacques. *Anarchy and Christianity.* Translated by Geoffrey W. Bromiley. Grand Rapids: Eerdmans, 1991.

———. *The Ethics of Freedom.* Translated by Geoffrey W. Bromiley. Grand Rapids: Eerdmans, 1976.

———. *False Presence of the Kingdom.* Translated by C. Edward Hopkin. New York: Seabury, 1972.

———. *The Humiliation of the Word.* Translated by Joyce Main Hanks. Grand Rapids: Eerdmans, 1985.

———. *Jesus and Marx: From Gospel to Ideology.* Translated by Joyce Main Hanks. Grand Rapids: Eerdmans, 1988.

———. *The Meaning of the City.* Translated by Dennis Pardee. Grand Rapids: Eerdmans, 1970.

———. *Money & Power.* Translated by LaVonne Neff. Downers Grove, IL: IVP, 1984.

———. "Le mythe de l'environnment." *Economies et Sociétés: Cahiers de l'E.S.E.A.* 7, no. 9 (1973) 1539–54.

———. *The New Demons.* Translated by C. Edward Hopkin. New York: Seabury, 1975.

———. *The Political Illusion.* Translated by Konrad Kellen. New York: Vintage, 1972.

———. *The Politics of God and the Politics of Man.* Translated by Geoffrey W. Bromiley. Grand Rapids: Eerdmans, 1972.

———. "Si tu es le fils de Dieu: souffrances et tentations de Jésus" In *Le défi et le nouveau: Oeuvres théologiques 1948–1991,* 973–1016. Paris: La Table Ronde, 2007.

———. *The Subversion of Christianity.* Translated by Geoffrey W. Bromiley. Grand Rapids: Eerdmans, 1986.

———. "Technique and the Opening Chapters of Genesis." In *Theology and Technology: Essays in Christian Analysis and Exegesis,* edited by Carl Mitcham et al., 123–37. New York: University Press of America, 1984.

———. *The Technological Bluff.* Translated by Geoffrey W. Bromiley. Grand Rapids: Eerdmans, 1990.

———. *The Technological Society.* Translated by John Wilkinson. New York: Knopf, 1964.

———. *The Technological System.* Translated by Joachim Neugroschel. New York: Continuum, 1980.

———. *To Will & to Do: An Ethical Research for Christians.* Translated by C. Edward Hopkin. Philadelphia: Pilgrim, 1969.

———. *Violence: Reflections from a Christian Perspective.* Translated by Cecilia Gaul. London: SCM, 1970.

Franke, William. "A Critical Negative Theology of Dialogue: The Coincidence of Reason and Revelation in Communicative Openness." *Journal of Religion* 88, no. 3 (2008) 365–92.

Freuchen, Peter. *Book of the Eskimos.* Cleveland, OH: World, 1961.

Fukuyama, Francis. *End of History and the Last Man.* London: Penguin, 1993.

Girard, René. *The Scapegoat.* Baltimore: Johns Hopkins University Press, 1986.

———. *Violence and the Sacred.* Baltimore: Johns Hopkins University Press, 1977.

Goodchild, Philip. *Theology of Money.* Durham, NC: Duke University Press, 2009.

Gorringe, Timothy. *Capital and the Kingdom: Theological Ethics and Economic Order.* Maryknoll, NY: Orbis, 1994.

———. *A Theology of the Built Environment: Justice, Empowerment, Redemption.* Cambridge: Cambridge University Press, 2002.

Graeber, David. *Debt: The First 5,000 Years.* Brooklyn, NY: Melville House, 2012.

———. *Toward an Anthropological Theory of Value: The False Coin of Our Own Dreams.* New York: Palgrave, 2001.

Greggs, Tom. *Theology Against Religion: Constructive Dialogues with Bonhoeffer and Barth.* London: T & T Clark, 2011.

Hector, Kevin. *Theology Without Metaphysics: God, Language, and the Spirit of Recognition.* New York: Cambridge University Press, 2011.

Heidegger, Martin. *Being and Time.* Translated by John Macquarrie and Edward Robinson. New York: Harper, 2008.

Hobbes, Thomas. *Leviathan.* New York: Barnes & Noble, 2004.

Hosseini, Hamid S. "Seeking the Roots of Adam Smith's Division of Labor in Medieval Persia." *History of Political Economy* 30, no. 4 (1998) 653–81.

Hoyle, David. "At the Home of Martha and Mary." Sermon delivered at Bristol Cathedral, Bristol, UK, July 21, 2013. Online: http://bristol-cathedral.co.uk/images/uploads/Luke_10.pdf.

Hudson, Michael. "Restructuring the Origins of Interest-Bearing Debt and the Logic of Clean Slates." In *Debt and Economic Renewal in the Ancient Near East,* edited by Michael Hudson and Marc Van de Mieroop. Bethesda, MD: CDL, 2002.

Humphrey, Caroline. "Barter and Economic Disintegration." *Man* 20, no. 1 (1985) 48–72.

Jenson, Matt. *The Gravity of Sin: Augustine, Luther, and Barth on Homo Incurvatus in Se.* London: T & T Clark, 2006.

Jersak, Brad, et al. *Stricken by God? Nonviolent Identification and the Victory of Christ.* Grand Rapids: Eerdmans, 2007.

Kallet, Lisa. "The Athenian Economy." In *The Cambridge Companion to the Age of Pericles,* edited by Loren J. Samons, 70–95. Cambridge: Cambridge University Press, 2007.

Kantorowicz, Ernst H. *The King's Two Bodies: A Study of Medieval Political Theology.* Princeton: Princeton University Press, 1957.

Kenny, Anthony. *A New History of Western Philosophy: In Four Parts.* Oxford: Clarendon, 2012.

Kierkegaard, Søren. *Fear and Trembling.* Edited by C. Stephen Evans. Translated by Sylvia Walsh. Cambridge: Cambridge University Press, 2006.

———. *The Moment and Late Writings.* Translated and Edited by Edna Hatlestad Hong and Howard Vincent Hong. Princeton: Princeton University Press, 1998.

Krueger, Alan B. "Introduction." In *The Wealth of Nations,* edited by Edwin Cannan, xi–xxv. New York: Bantam Classic, 2003.

Liddell, Henry George, Robert Scott, and Henry Stuart Jones. *A Greek-English Lexicon.* 9th ed. Oxford: Clarendon, 1996.

Lynch, Gordon. *The Sacred in the Modern World: A Cultural Sociological Approach.* New York: Oxford University Press, 2012.

Lyotard, Jean-François. *The Postmodern Condition: A Report on Knowledge.* Translated by Geoff Bennington and Brian Massumi. Minneapolis: University of Minnesota Press, 1984.

Marx, Karl. *Capital: A Critique of Political Economy.* Translated by Ben Fowkes. Harmondsworth, UK: Penguin, 1988.

Marx, Karl, and Frederick Engels. *The Marx-Engels Reader.* Edited by Robert Tucker. New York: Princeton University Press, 1978.

Mauss, Marcel. *The Gift: The Form and Reason for Exchange in Archaic Societies.* Translated by W. D. Halls. New York: Norton, 1990.

May, William F. *Testing the National Covenant: Fears and Appetites in American Politics.* Washington, DC: Georgetown University Press, 2011.

Meeks, M. Douglas. *God the Economist: The Doctrine of God and Political Economy.* Minneapolis: Fortress, 1989.

Milbank, John. *Theology and Social Theory: Beyond Secular Reason.* Oxford: Blackwell, 1993.

Moltmann, Jürgen. *God in Creation: An Ecological Doctrine of Creation: The Gifford Lectures 1984–1985.* London: SCM, 1985.

Murray, Gilbert. *Five Stages of Greek Religion.* Westport, CT: Greenwood, 1976.

Nielsen, Karen Margrethe. "Economy and Private Property." In *The Cambridge Companion to Aristotle's Politics,* edited by Marguerite Deslauriers, 67–91. Cambridge: Cambridge University Press, 2013.

Nietzsche, Friedrich Wilhelm. *Beyond Good and Evil: Prelude to a Philosophy of the Future.* Edited by Rolf-Peter Horstmann. Translated by Judith Norman. Cambridge: Cambridge University Press, 2002.

———. *On the Genealogy of Morals.* Translated by Douglas Smith. Oxford: Oxford University Press, 2008.

———. *Thus Spake Zarathustra: A Book for Everyone and No One.* Translated by R. J. Hollingdale. London: Penguin, 1969.

———. *Twilight of the Idols.* Translated by Richard Polt. Indianapolis: Hackett, 1997.

———. *The Will to Power.* Edited by Walter Kaufmann. Translated by R. J. Hollingdale and Walter Kaufmann. New York: Vintage, 1967.

Novak, Michael. *Business as a Calling: Work and the Examined Life.* New York: Free Press, 1996.

———. *The Catholic Ethic and the Spirit of Capitalism.* New York: Macmillan, 1993.

———. *The Spirit of Democratic Capitalism.* Lanham, MD: Madison, 1991.

Polanyi, Karl. *The Great Transformation: The Political and Economic Origins of Our Time.* Boston: Beacon, 2001.

Rives, James B. *Religion in the Roman Empire.* Malden, MA: Blackwell, 2007.

Rousseau, Jean-Jacques. *The Social Contract*. Translated by J. H. Brumfitt. New York: Barnes & Noble, 2005.

Russell, Bertrand. *A History of Western Philosophy*. New York: Simon and Schuster, 1945.

Sackery, Charles, et al. *Introduction to Political Economy*. Boston: Dollars and Sense, 2010.

Scheidel, Walter. "Slavery." In *Cambridge Companion to the Roman Economy*, edited by Walter Scheidel, 89–113, Cambridge: Cambridge University Press, 2012.

Seaford, Richard. *Money and the Early Greek Mind: Homer, Philosophy, Tragedy*. Cambridge: Cambridge University Press, 2004.

———. "Tragic Tyranny." In *Popular Tyranny*, edited by Kathryn A. Morgan, 95–116. Austin: University of Texas, 2003.

Servet, Jean-Michel. "Le troc primitif, un mythe fondateur d'une approche économiste de la monnaie." *Revue numismatique* 6, no. 157 (2001) 15–32.

Shelmerdine, Cynthia W., and John Bennet. "Aegean Economy." In *The Cambridge Companion to the Aegean Bronze Age*, edited by Cynthia W. Shelmerdine, 289–309. Cambridge: Cambridge University Press, 2008.

Simmel, Georg. *The Philosophy of Money*. Translated and Edited by David Frisby. New York: Routledge, 2011.

Smith, Adam. *The Wealth of Nations*. Edited by Edwin Cannan. New York: Bantam Classic, 2003.

Trotsky, Leon, et al. *Terrorism and Communism: A Reply to Karl Kautsky*. London: Verso, 2007.

Veitch, J. A. "Revelation and Religion in the Theology of Karl Barth." *Scottish Journal of Theology* 24, no. 1 (1971) 1–22.

Vivenza, Gloria. "Roman Economic Thought." In *Cambridge Companion to the Roman Economy*, edited by Walter Scheidel, 25–44. Cambridge: Cambridge University Press, 2012.

Wagenfuhr, G. P. "Postmodernity, the Phenomenal Mistake: Sacred, Myth and Environment." In *Jacques Ellul and the Technological Society in the 21st Century*, edited by Helena M. Jerónimo et al., 229–42. Dordrecht: Springer, 2013.

———. "Religion comme jeu: la situation au XXIème siècle." In *Comment peut-on (encore) être Ellulien au XXIe siècle*, edited by Patrick Troude-Chastenet, 209–10. Paris: La Table Ronde, 2014.

Walton, John H. *The Lost World of Genesis One: Ancient Cosmology and the Origins Debate*. Downers Grove, IL: IVP Academic, 2009.

Ward, Graham. *Barth, Derrida and the Language of Theology*. Cambridge: Cambridge University Press, 1998.

———. "Deconstructive Theology." In *The Cambridge Companion to Postmodern Theology*, edited by Kevin J. Vanhoozer, 76–91. Cambridge: Cambridge University Press, 2003.

Weber, Max. *The Protestant Ethic and the Spirit of Capitalism*. New York: Scribner, 1958.

Wenham, Gordon J. *Genesis 1–11*. Word Biblical Commentary 1. Waco, TX: Word, 1987.

Westermann, Claus. *Genesis 1–11*. Translated by John J. Scullion, SJ. London: SPCK, 1984.

White, Jenny B. *Money Makes Us Relatives: Women's Labor in Urban Turkey*. New York: Routledge, 2004.

Wilson, Andrew. "Raw Materials and Energy." In *Cambridge Companion to the Roman Economy*, edited by Walter Scheidel, 135–55. Cambridge: Cambridge University Press, 2012.

Wink, Walter. *Engaging the Powers: Discernment and Resistance in a World of Domination*. Minneapolis: Fortress, 1992.

———. *Naming the Powers: The Language of Power in the New Testament*. Philadelphia: Fortress, 1984.

———. *Unmasking the Powers: The Invisible Forces That Determine Human Existence*. Philadelphia: Fortress, 1986.

Wolters, Albert M. *Creation Regained: Biblical Basics for Reformational Worldview*. 2nd ed. Grand Rapids: Eerdmans, 2005.

Yar, Majid. "Alexandre Kojève." *Internet Encyclopedia of Philosophy*. 2001. Online: http://www.iep.utm.edu/kojeve/.

Zizioulas, John D. *Communion and Otherness: Further Studies in Personhood and the Church*. Edited by Paul McPartlan. London: T & T Clark, 2006.

———. "On Being a Person: Towards an Ontology of Personhood." In *Persons, Divine and Human: King's College Essays in Theological Anthropology*, edited by Christoph Schwöbel and Colin E. Gunton, 33–46. Edinburgh: T & T Clark, 1991.

Name Index

Anaximader, 21, 27–30, 32
Anaximenes, 27–28
Anselm of Canterbury, 230
Aristophanes, 20
Aristotle, 37–40, 44, 45, 46, 146; ethics, 57; and theology, 43, 73, 138, 232; and humans giving meaning to nature, 84, 99, 101, 130, 203, 213
Augustine of Hippo, Saint, x, 11, 62–64, 150, 222

Barth, Karl, 9, 10, 96, 97, 123, 196, 200, 206
Bell, Daniel, 103n37
Benson, Bruce Ellis, 201
Buber, Martin, 107

Caillois, Roger, 97 n24, 105n40–41, 112, 132n8
Calvin, John, 221

Derrida, Jacques, 214
Descartes, Renée, 43, 62, 78, 108, 116–17
Durkheim, Emile, 83

Eliade, Mircea, 98n24, 95n105, 109, 111n48, 191n38,
Ellul, Jacques, 1, 69, 77, 102, 103, 130, 140, 147, 232
Epicurus, 39, 45, 146, 162n14

Feuerbach, Ludwig, 3, 30
Fereuchen, Peter, 55n69

Fukuyama, Francis, 74n90

Girard, Renée, 24n16, 50, 218
Goodchild, Philip, 67
Graeber, David, 6n2, 16, 19, 22n10, 47, 48, 50–51, 54–58, 62, 63, 68, 157n5, 173, 176
Guicciardini, Francesco 63, 64

Hector, Kevin, 7
Heidegger, Martin, 5
Heraclitus, 21, 32–34, 39, 42, 44, 58
Hesiod, 29, 43
Hobbes, Thomas, 65
Homer, 17, 22–24, 48–49, 76, 128
Hosseini, Hamid, 6n2
Hoyle, David, 204n8
Hudson, Michael, 53n66, 157n5,
Humphrey, Caroline, 63n81

Josephus, 167

Kant, Immanuel, 4, 108, 224
Kantorowicz, Ernst, 61n76
Kierkegaard, Søren, 10
Kenny, Anthony, 34n35
Keynes, John Maynard, 18
Kojève, Alexandre, 74n90

Locke, John, 65
Luther, Martin, 224
Lyotard, Jean-François 60n74

Marx, Karl, 30, 214
Mauss, Marcel, 47

May, William F., 65
Meeks, M. Douglas, 88n2, 97, 99n26, 103n37

Nietzsche, Friedrich, 3, 48, 56, 200–201, 214
Novak, Michael, 209n12

Otto, Rudolf, 109

Parmenides, 21, 34, 36–37, 39, 44–45, 73, 144–45
Paul, 119, 149, 167, 180–85, 187, 195, 223, 225
Plato, 33, 35, 36–37, 39–40, 42, 43–45, 57, 70
Plotinus, 150
Plutarch, 25, 155n4, 196, 197
Pompey, 167
Protagoras, 35–36, 37, 38, 73, 124, 134
Pythagoras, 31–32, 39

Rousseau, Jean-Jacques, 65

Sartre, Jean-Paul, 5, 214
Schleiermacher, Friedrich, 109
Seaford, Richard, 15–42 *passim*, 52, 134, 144, 145, 151n1
Servet, Jean-Michel, 59
Sextus Empiricus, 35
Smith, Adam, ix, 6, 20, 38, 46, 49, 60, 63–64, 66, 170
Solon, 21, 53, 139
Sophocles, 20

Thales, 27, 28, 146
Trotsky, Leon, 54n67

Walton, John, 96n19, 110n45, 127n2
Wenham, Gordon, 128n3
White, Jenny B., 56n70
Wilson, Andrew, 102n32
Wink, Walter, 88n3, 152n3

Xenophanes, 30, 32, 134

Yar, Majid, 74n90

Subject Index

Abraham/Abram, 111, 136, 153–56, 160–63, 218
abundance, 103–5, 110, 113, 140
Achilles, 22, 48–49
acquisitiveness, 37
Adam and Eve: as image of God, 107–8, 136–69, 154, 187, 189–91, 213, 228–29, 234; and innocence or naïveté, 118–19, 207–8; and knowledge or epistemology, 13, 125–26, 215; and knowledge of good and evil or ethics, 122–24, 199; and shame or clothing, 141–42, 194–95; and sin, 129, 132–33, 149–50, 152, 164, 181, 187, 204; and work, 110–15
altruism, 203, 216, 217
ambassadorship, 192, 201–2, 205, 225
America: and charity, 215; and creation, 101; as empire, 68; and freedom, 222; and identity, 65; and money, 86–87, 169–70; the *Pledge of Allegiance*, 87
ancient Near Eastern: creation myths 94, 97; debt forgiveness or Jubilee, 53, 156–57; kings, 105; literature 41, 152; names, 52; precious metal exchange, 25; as pre-metaphysical, 123; temples and sacrifice, 23, 128, 221
angels, 61, 80, 100, 108, 126, 156
animals: humans as, 5, 6, 63; human domination of, 37–38, 84, 139, 142, 191; and metaphysics 2, 3; in reconciled relationship, 213; relation to Creator, 105; relation to image of God, 133; as sacrifice, 24, 154, 171
apeiron, 21, 27–30, 32, 71
aristocracy: aversion to market, 20, 178; and debt forgiveness, 157–58, 177; and history, 52–55; of philosophers 31, 34, 39, 44–46, 53, 57, 146, 193, 232; and self-sufficiency, 34, 64, 79, 81, 94, 201
aseity: *see* self-sufficiency
atheism/atheists, 10–11
Atomists, 28, 39, 54, 70
atonement, ix–x, 218–19, 230
Aufhebung or sublation, 206

Babel, 126, 132–35, 136, 137, 147, 163, 186, 192, 224
Bank of England, 67–68
barter: and Adam Smith, 6, 49, 63, 66; with the gods, ix, 95; in the Middle Ages, 75; and money, 17; Myth of, 6, 14, 46–47, 66
Beatitudes, 162–63
being, 2, 5–8, 10, 34, 35, 37, 45, 144, 145, 149–50, 193; see ontology, *ousia*
bloodguilt, 28
Brahmanas, 54
Buddhism, 55–56, 68, 206

Caesar, 53, 86–87, 167–69, 183, 192, 203–4

Cain, 52, 111, 127–32, 136, 140, 145, 147, 152, 163
calling: *see* vocation
capitalism, x, 70, 84, 99, 107, 148, 209, 226
causality, 102, 136–37
chaos: vs. creation, 97–98, 101–2; vs. cosmos, 121, 144; as experience 50, 54, 60, 135, 147; in Genesis, 104n38, 130, 153; in mythology, 29, 94, 111n48, 112–13, 120, 138, 145
Chaoskampf, 97
charity, 72, 76, 166, 179, 215–18, 227–28
China, 15, 47, 206
Christus Victor, 206
church: character of, 182, 188, 196, 221; Christendom, ix, 202; and ethics, x, 123, 200, 217–18; and love of God, 180–81; mission of, 233, 235; separation from state, 87; and stewardship/tithing, 152, 180, 204–5, 219–22
city, the, 111, 129–30, 132–34, 145, 147
clothing, 118–19, 125–26, 141–43, 193, 195
cogito, 62, 116
coinage: and fiduciarity, 35, 134; history of, 15, 16, 22–27, 31, 151n1; and metaphysics, xv, 5, 70; and moderation, 78, 203; other uses 31, 38, 214
commensurability and incommensurability, 19, 27, 37, 48–49, 53, 56, 58, 125
commodification, 103, 106
common good, 12, 24, 64, 88, 95, 133, 200, 224
commonwealth, x, xi, 12, 64, 75, 80–81, 88, 95
Communion, sacrament of, 50, 218–19, 221–22
Communism, x, 57, 172, 209, 217
Confucianism, 66
consequentialism, 57

corporation, 60–62, 68–73, 76, 81, 126, 177, 187–89, 215, 225–27, 233
cosmology: mythical, 33–34, 110, 132, 138; philosophical/metaphysical, 41, 44, 62, 89; scientific, 121, 130, 145; subversion of, xvi, 122, 191–92, 202, 208–9, 213
cosmos/cosmoi: arising out of chaos, 120, 130, 144–45, 147; vs. creation, 100, 102–4, 119, 137–38; and debt, 54–57, 58–59, 150; defined, xv–xvi, 121, 144; and ethics, 198–202, 224, 231; as humanly created, 121–50, 191–92, 196, 199, 210; and identity, 78, 91, 196; and money, 29, 31–32, 33, 39–40, 46, 169–70, 189; postmonetary, 70, 225, 228, 235; subversion of, 120, 161, 171, 185, 189–92, 194, 199–202, 208–14, 233, 235
creation: corruption of, xvi, 132, 137–41, 149, 152–53, 192, 234; as epistemologically inaccessible, 137–38, 140, 147, 150, 188, 196; estrangement from, 13, 121–30, 135–37; and ethics, 88, 203–5; human: *see cosmos*; and the image of God, 105–9, 110–20, 135–36, 234; new, 186, 189–92, 202; not a resource, 101–3; and perfection, 99, 189, 206–7; and relation to Creator, 10, 13, 88–105, 119–20, 147; *see also* abundance
creativity, 99, 123–24, 131–32, 136, 139, 148–49, 186, 203

David, king of Israel, 111, 198
debt, 48–59; criminal, 28; and god(s), 57, 95, 125, 128, 176, 218, 230; infinite, 55, 58, 218, 233; longstanding, 49, 51, 64, 69, 158, 177; milk, 56; modern and corporate, 61–62, 67–71, 76, 80; moral, 48, 53, 56, 58–59, 62, 67, 69, 144, 218; NT teaching on, 150,

175–76, 182, 183, 195, 223; and social contract, 65–66; universal, 59; *see* premonetary society; *see also* charity, Jubilee, redemption
Declaration of Independence, 66
deconstruction, 190–91, 213–14
deism, 90, 136
denarius, 86, 172, 175
deontology, 4, 57
desacralization, ix, 134
discipleship, 161–62, 165–66, 194, 195, 221, 227, 235
dollar, 68, 87, 168

ecology, 78, 144
Economy, the, x, xvi, 13, 14, 76, 79–80, 83, 95, 135
ecosystem, 84, 144
Eden, 88, 108–20, 128, 130, 142, 187, 190, 195, 199, 228–29
egalitarianism, 4, 60, 64, 65, 69, 76–77, 79, 128
Egypt, xii–xiv, xvi, 128, 136, 174, 197–98, 231, 233–34
enlightenment, 40, 44, 45, 75, 76, 80, 123, 145, 206–8
Enlightenment, the, 62, 64, 74, 78
Enoch, 13, 111, 130
environmentalism, 77–78, 84, 101, 139, 190, 213
epic literature, 19, 24, 39, 41, 138
Epicureanism, 146
epistemology, xv, 4–5, 62, 108–9, 126, 140, 144, 149, 190, 192, 210
equality: and debt, 48, 55; estranged, 228–30; and inequality of wealth, 69, 204; myth of, 69, 72; of opportunity, 23, 64, 72, 75, 76, 81; of relationship 55, 58, 62, 229; *see* egalitarianism, hierarchy vs. equality
equilibrium, 2, 48, 58, 59, 69, 77, 160
eschatology, 111, 116, 117
Eskimo culture, 55
espionage, 205
estranged relationship: with creation, 138; with God, 5, 11, 125, 128, 132–37, 147–50, 160, 163, 169, 188–89, 192, 210, 213, 219; with others, 13, 211, 213, 229; with self, 118; subversion of, 156, 195
Estrangement, the, xvi, 108, 121, 124–29, 134–38, 140–48, 160, 186–89, 193, 196, 206–8, 224–29
ethics: and the Bible, x, 151; Christian, 12, 14, 88, 111, 119, 197–231; economic, xv, 57; and estrangement, 123–24, 126, 195; and ontology, 5–6, 91, 92; philosophical, 2–4, 38–39, 44, 57; and relationship, 2–6, 12; subversive, xiv, xvi, 165, 195–96, 197–231; *see also* Adam and Eve, church, cosmos, creation, egalitarianism, equality, rights, universality
etymologies: of barter, 49; of *logos,* 32; of love, 216; of material, 102; of money, 25, 38; of morality, 48, 56; of *ousia,* 34; of property, 34
Eucharist, *see* Communion, sacrament of
eudaimonia, 3, 39
European Union, 73–75

Fall, the, *see* Estrangement, the
festival, 98, 111n48, 171
fictive persons (*persona ficta*), 61–62, 67, 71–72, 82, 87, 177, 188, 220, 221, 225, 233
fiduciarity, 17–18, 21, 26, 35, 39, 40, 45, 70, 85, 92, 134, 175, 189, 221
fines, 16, 18, 28
flourishing, 6, 88
forgiveness: of debt, 53, 58–59, 157, 217; Jesus's teaching on, 175–79, 186, 193–94; *see* Jubilee
Forms, Platonic, 7, 9, 36–37, 42, 43–44
freedom: Christian, 184, 195, 218, 223; and debt forgiveness, 54; of God, 89, 96; and money, 168, 233; and self-sufficiency, 79, 222, 227, 235

genealogy, 14; in literature, 41, 52; Genesis as, 110–11, 134; of

money, 26, 38, 149; of self-interest, 60, 62–63
Gift-Exchange: *see* premonetary society
gifts: and hierarchy, 51, 82–83; to temples, 22, 24, 26
gold: divinity of, 36–37, 43; and money, 16, 17, 21, 25, 68, 192; use of, xiv, 45, 231
golden age, 43, 45, 112–13, 132, 145, 190–91, 208–9
golden mean, 38, 226
Golden Rule, 165–66, 188, 219, 234
good and evil, 122–23, 152, 195, 196, 199–201, 224, 228
gospel: of Jesus Christ, 173–77, 184–85, 191–92, 198–231, 232–35; of monetary society, 42–46, 123; of modern economics, 73–81, 194; of premonetary society, 58–59
government: and economy, 6, 66–68, 168, 170; and justice, x, 28, 62–64, 215; and money, 16–18, 86–87, 189
Greece, x, ch. 2 *passim*

hap, 162
heaven, 59, 132, 149, *see also* kingdom of God
Hebrew Scriptures, ix, xv, 105, 111, 161
heirlooms, 19, 22, 24–26, 52, 82, 143, 173, 174
heroic society, 22–26, 41, 43, 76
hesed, 156
hierarchy, 144; and debt, 48–55, 69, 82, 177; and money, 57, 64; as natural, 38; priestly, 224; subversion of, 180, 195–96, 222; as supposedly premodern, 80; *see also* slavery
hierarchy and equality, x, 55, 57, 72, 82, 228–30
Hinduism, 206
Holy Spirit, 11, 92, 179, 186, 204, 207, 217, 219, 221, 233, 234
homelessness, 211–13, 227
homo economicus, 63, 84, 119

homogeneity of money, 18–21, 23, 24, 26, 37, 40, 52, 53, 57
household management: as human economic role, 20, 40, 45, 52, 87, 114; as not God's role, 92–93, 97–101, 104
human/humanity: ontology/nature, x, 2–6, 44, 56, 62–67, 81, 91–92, 105–6, 124, 126, 149, 187, 193–94, 203, 207; universal, 16, 59–81, 194, 198, 203, 216

image of God: estranged, 137, 158, 219, 229, 234; and ontology, 91, 105, 139, 186, 193; as political representative, 106, 135, 153, 189, 207; reconciled, 154, 187, 207; as relational, 88, 105–7, 115; relation to creation, 106–8, 110, 122, 128, 133, 203; relation to God, 106, 122, 207–8; *see also* Adam and Eve, royal charter
India, 15, 47, 206
individuation, 7, 81
injustice, 27, 38, 72, 74–77, 85, 160, 196, 223
iron spits, 24–26, 169

Jubilee, 53, 156–58
Judas Iscariot, 173, 178
judgment: and estrangement, 123–26, 152, 160, 164–65, 196; of God, 132, 137, 152, 153–54, 160, 184–89, 205; and reconciliation, 164–65, 196, 213, 234
justice: abandonment of, 163–66, 177, 182, 195–96, 219, 223, 234; and debt, 55, 82, 85; equilibrium, 82, 160; of God, 124, 188–89; and government, 18, 68–69, 83, 222–24; and money, 27–28, 38–39, 74, 81, 84, 176; myth of, 69, 72, 77; social, 159–60; *see also* ethics, morality, original sin

Karma/karmic debt, 55–56
kenosis, 219, 229
kesef, ix, 152

kingdom of God, 117, 162, 172, 175, 222, 224, 226

language: condescension of God's, 155, 174, 210, 219, 230; and debt, 55–57, 76, 150, 216; as mediation, 107; and money, 31, 36, 45, 214–15; and ontology, 4, 7–8, 10–11, 149
Levites, 220, 221
lex talionis, 82, 163–64, 165
liberation, 53–54, 59, 80, 81, 157, 181, 198, 212
literature, 19, 23, 41–42, 52, 59, 85, 138, 175, 223
logos, 9, 32–34, 41, 42, 71, 138
Lord's Prayer, 150, 175–76
Lydia, 15, 25, 27, 151n1

magnanimity, 44n52, 89–90, 193
management: of resources, 38, 87, 107, 139, 140; *see* household management
Market, the, 14, 135
Marxism, ix, 74, 80–81, 103, 132, 148, 209n13
mediation: economic, 46, 82, 84, 118, 119, 196; and epistemology, 108–9, 123, 125, 140, 229; relational, 107, 179; religious, 127, 158
Merchant of Venice, 56
metaphysics: and epistemology, 4–5; and ethics, 57, 122–24, 195; and God, 86, 89–91, 230–32; and identity, 193; and the kingdom of God, 175; modern, 60–73, 78–85, 130, 215; and money, xv, 5, 15, 17, 21, 22–46, 145–50, 193, 221; and relationship, xv–xvi, 1–4, 98; and theology, 8–10; *see also* animals, being, coinage, cosmology, ontology, original sin, symbol
Milesians, 27–29
mimetic rivalry, 24n16, 103, 126
Minor Prophets, 159–60
missionaries, 76, 79, 228
moderation, 21, 78, 139, 146, 203, 226

monarchy, 29, 32, 64, 158, 183, 230
monetary society, xv, 32, 39, 42–46, 59–60, 82–84, 138, 151, 173, 176
monism, 28–29, 32, 34, 62, 70, 144
morality: and debt, 48, 59, 218; economic, 55–58, 76, 177, 196; and estrangement, 124, 126, 141, 149, 196, 200; postmonetary, 60–61, 67, 76, 78; *see also* ethics
Moses, xii–xiv, xvi, 156, 159, 231, 233
mystery cult/religion (Orphic), 29, 32–34, 41–42, 43, 45, 149, 206
mysticism, 3, 33, 145

nakedness, 118–19, 125–26, 141, 187, 194–95
natural law, 38–39, 55, 90, 126, 142, 181, 198, 200
Nature (personified), 13, 37–38, 188
Neoclassical economics, 16, 46–47, 74–75, 80–81
Neoplatonism, 27n21, 43, 45, 94, 150
Noah, 13, 132–33, 152, 153–54, 186
non-profit organizations, 215, 225, 227–28
nonviolence, xii, 223
nudism, 119, 195

objectivity: of God, 93, 108, 119, 188, 210; of humans, 91, 106, 142–43; of the world, 102, 133–35, 144–45, 188–89, 194, 207, 215
obol, 25
Old Testament: as premonetary, 16, 137, 151, 194; redemption in, 205; and subversive reconciliation, 153, 161, 165–66, 169
One, the, 3–4, 30, 44–45, 145
ontology, 34; angels and the corporation, 61; and God, 89, 92, 94, 100, 145, 186, 187; and reconciliation, 191–94; and theology, 205–8; *see also* ethics, human, language, original sin, relational ontology
oppression, xiii–xiv, 80, 182, 186–88, 226, 231, 233

original sin, x, xvi, 33–34, 44, 62, 124–26, 129, 149–50, 160, 200, 222
ousia, 34, 37, 162n12

parables: Good Samaritan, 216; Hired Workers, 172; Plato's cave, 40, 44n51; Talents, 173–75, 203, 209n12; Unforgiving Servant, 175–77; Wheat and Tares, 186
Pelagianism, x, 64
penal substitution, 206
Pentecost, 179–80
Persia, 25, 96n19, 151
piracy, 115, 136–37
postmonetary society, xv–xvi, 59–84, 102, 109, 139–40, 143, 185, 194, 198, 211, 215
poverty: absolute, 72, 78–80; and debt, 53; Jesus's teaching on, 164, 178–79; problem of, 75, 81, 104, 160, 213; relative, 72, 80
powers, 88n3, 182
precious metals, 16, 18, 24–26, 68, 107, 151, 220
premonetary society, 5, 15–22, 46–59, 60–62, 67, 70–71, 82–85, 94–95, 193, 206; Hebrew Scriptures and, 122–23, 134, 137–38, 151, 155, 185, 220; and property, 143
priesthood, 71, 96, 108, 127, 157, 171, 219–22, 225
projection mechanism: and cosmos, 46, 125–26, 134–35, 145, 199; and Eden, 113; and God, 89; and debt, 54; and money, 28, 31, 35, 46; and metaphysics, 3, 10, 36; and reconciliation, 191, 199, 209, 214; and religion, xiv, 3, 30, 73, 134, 142; and the self, 73, 92, 118, 131, 141–43; and sin, 149–50; and value, 124, 141, 165
promised land, 59, 154, 155, 156
property: conventionality of, 192, 200, 217; and creation, 100–101; etymology, 34; and God, 93–94; private, 37, 65, 115, 139, 143, 155, 157–58, 168, 188; subversion of, 174, 189, 192
prophets, 151, 159–61, 168, 183
proportionality, 31, 32, 38–39

re-narration, 199–202
reciprocity: crisis of, 22–24, 26; and hierarchy, 51; and justice, 28, 38, 81, 163, 165; and money, 32; subversion by Jesus, 165–66
Reconciler-reconciled relationship, xv, 7, 13, 96, 100, 111, 118, 186–96, 215, 234
redemption, 58–59, 205–8
redistribution, 23–24, 50, 128, 157–58, 178, 218, 221
relational ontology, 3, 5, 7, 90–91
religion: and cosmos, 138, 148, 170; and estrangement, 126–29; money as, 189; postmonetary, 67, 73, 76, 82–85, 217; and reconciliation, 153, 161, 163–64, 171, 188, 218; and the state, 87, 167; *see* mystery cult, projection, sacrifice, temple
responsibility: avoidance of, 61, 126, 158, 177, 187–88, 191, 210, 225, 227, 233; and debt, 50; and God, 126, 137; and the image of God, 106; social and individual, 76, 87, 222; taking, 145, 186–88, 200, 204
rest: Edenic, 114, 127; God's, 96–98; Sabbath, 116–18
restoration (as eschatology), 205–8
revelation: biblical, x, 85, 88, 138, 161, 207, 209; as contextualized, 212, 230; of the kingdom, 202; as relational, 7, 9–11, 198; as source of theology, 9, 235; as subversive, 152, 187, 198, 200, 210; as unique, 199, 232
rights: in Creation, 142; and debt, 49; of God, 106; individual human, 69–72, 74, 81, 222, 235; and reconciliation, 181–82, 219, 222–24; and social contract, 3, 4, 65–66

SUBJECT INDEX 251

ritual, 20, 23, 66, 113, 138, 154–55, 178
royal charter, 106, 136, 158, 189, 207, 234

Sabbath, 116–18, 171
sacred, the, 109, 138, 140, 202
sacrifice: and balance, 2, 23; creating value, 22, 154; and debt, 50, 54, 58, 83, 128, 207; as estrangement, 96, 108, 127–28, 170–71; of Jesus, 207, 218–19, 221; as redistribution, 23–24, 58, 218; ritual, 17, 42; substitution/scapegoat, 218–19, 235; subversion of, 154–55, 162–64, 171, 218–19; and theater, 26, 42; tokens, 25–26, 169
scapegoat, 50, 147, 219
scarcity, 2, 78, 80, 103–5, 115, 119, 140–41, 178
self-expression, 131–32
self-interest, x, 60, 62–66, 73, 75, 222
self-love, 2, 62–64, 89, 222
self-sufficiency, 30, 34, 36, 37, 39, 45–46, 53, 64, 83, 140, 198, 220; as delusional, 72, 79, 81, 94; of God, 93–95
sexuality, 2, 49, 73, 100, 131, 142, 148, 229
shame: *see* clothing, nakedness
silver, ix, xiv, 16, 22n10, 25, 37, 43, 151, 159
sin: Augustine on, x, 63, 150; as creating cosmos, 135–50, 202; and debt, 55, 58–59; and economy, 77, 88, 150, 176; as estrangement, 115, 125–26, 150, 177, 181, 202; as judgment, 164–65; liberation from, 157, 205–7; ontological, 104, 124–26, 150; transmission of, 129; *see* forgiveness, original sin, reconciliation
slavery, xii, 8, 40, 58, 72, 80, 97, 157–58, 168, 175, 204; master-slave dialectic, 100; subversion of, 180–82, 200, 233, 234; and technology, 137, 146, 227

social contract, 60, 65–66, 155, 222–24
social media, 70, 103, 226
social obligation, 16–17, 26, 144
social roles, 142
socialism, x, 84, 148
solipsism, 2, 117, 193, 210
Soviet Union, 54
state theory of money, 18
stewardship, ix, 87, 105, 107, 114, 139, 152, 173, 203–5
subject/object relationship, 9, 10, 44, 93, 107, 142, 144
subjectivity, 2, 8–9, 35, 134, 147
submission in NT, 180–85, 195
subversion: of Christian faith, 87, 205, 233, 235; of *cosmoi*, 156, 158, 160–61, 189–91, 201; ethical action, xvi; NT teachings as, 161–85, 234; reconciliation as, xv, 120, 128, 137, 155, 162, 194–96; re-narrating a subversive gospel, 208–31
sustainability, 75, 84, 103n35, 139
symbol: and coins, 26, 168–70, 214–15; and hierarchy, 51, 168–70; and metaphysics, 36, 43–45, 82; in postmonetary society, 71, 82–88; and sacrifice, 24–25, 132, 218–19; subversion of, 168–71, 175, 189, 214–15, 218–23; and theater, 42
syntax, 7–8

tax: payment of, 76, 86–87, 167–71, 182–83, 195, 203, 233; and the state, 18, 46, 67–68, 158; temple, 23, 170, 233; *see also* tribute
technology: as cosmos, 142, 147–48, 207; and discipline, 104, 141, 146; and economy, 74–82, 103, 113, 127; and estrangement, 125, 137, 139, 203, 229; as formative, 107, 225; as monoculture, 73; as sacred, 140; as structure of meaning, 69–70, 146; subversion of, 227, 235

temple: ancient Near Eastern, 23, 128; in Genesis, 96, 110, 127, 130; Greek, 22–26; Jewish, 159, 167, 171, 202, 219, 221
temptation, 122–24, 185, 199, 207, 209, 226
theological method, xv, 1–14
theology: challenges to specific, 202–8, 214–31; economic influence on, ix–x, 21, 33–34, 50, 57, 176; of relationship, 1–14, 193; relationship to ethics, xvi, 232–35; *see also* estrangement, original sin, reconciliation, self-interest
thrownness, 5
Titanic Fall, 33, 43, 149, 206
tithe, 152, 157, 170, 217, 219–22, 233
tragedy, 41–42, 233
treasure, xiv, 164, 192, 231
tribute, 16, 18, 51, 68, 83, 168, 177, 223
Trinity, 89–94
truth: absolute, 9–10, 108, 142–43, 215; as corporate projection, 36, 191; as correspondence, 9; pragmatic, 75; vs. seeming, 40, 42

universality, 2–4; and economy, 107, 198; and ethics, 195, 209; and God, 90–94, 102, 188, 198, 230; money, 19–21, 26, 29, 39–40, 221, 233; in philosophy, 30–40, 43–44, 84, 145; reconciliation and, 179, 189, 194, 213–14; super-universals, 87, 107, 145, 224; *see also* humanity, perfection, postmonetary society, projection

universe, the, 13, 29, 30, 32–33, 34, 42, 138, 144, 188, 216, 224
Upanishads, 206
utopia, 36, 59, 61, 74, 76, 217; Adam Smith's, 20, 64; and reconciliation, 189, 191, 195, 202; and work, 80, 112

value: conventional, 17–19, 38–39, 192, 203; exchange, 17–18, 21, 38, 92, 97, 98, 101–3, 105, 135; intrinsic, 18; moral, 134, 201; stored, 37, 81, 178, 192, 220, 224; use, xiv, 16–17, 21, 97, 101–3, 105, 115, 118, 124, 139, 220
vengeance, 28, 56, 111, 129, 131, 155, 182
violence: and creativity, 131–32; and debt, 56, 68; and estrangement, 129, 142, 152; ethical method, xiv, 74, 223; and hierarchy, ix, xiii, 51–52, 72; and judgment, 152–53; and money, 28, 57; in myth, 94; reconciliation and, 183–84, 192; solidarity in, 133; and trade, 49–50, 66
virtue, 2–4, 39, 45, 196
vocation, 95, 224–25

Wergild, 56
work-reward relationship, 112–16, 127, 172
world view/*weltanschauung*, 145, 181, 185, 201–2, 206–7, 210, 212, 225, 230, 233

Ancient Document Index

HEBREW SCRIPTURES

Genesis

	52, 94, 97, 105, 110–34, 141–42, 152–54
1–11	105, 121–22, 135, 150
1–3	113, 127, 133, 142, 208, 224
1–2	13, 88, 94, 96, 98, 136, 139, 142, 203, 213
1	91n8, 94n17, 95, 105, 110
1:1	93n15, 130
1:2	89
1:22	104n39
1:26–27	105, 106
1:28	104, 113
1:29–30	106
2	91n8
2:2	97n21
2:4	110
2:18	115n54
2:16	114
2:19–20	110n46
3–11	136
3–5	152
3	13, 34, 104, 114, 121–23, 228
3:5	122
3:15	152
3:24	110n47
4–11	121
4:19–26	111
5:1	110n44
5:24	13n8
6–9	152
6	133
11	224
12	137, 154
15	154, 256
17	154
22	154

Exodus

15:11	90n6
20:2–3	197n1
20:8–11	116n55
21	82n93
32:4	xiv

Leviticus

24	82n93
25	156
25:23	157
27	156

Deuteronomy

19	82n93
33	90n6

Judges

	160, 183

1 Samuel

8:11–17	158n6
16:7	93n14

ANCIENT DOCUMENT INDEX

Kings

	158

1 Kings

10	159n7
21	159n8

2 Chronicles

9	159n7

Nehemiah

5:4	151

Esther

	183

Psalms

35	90n6
71	90n6
113	90n6

Proverbs

25:21–22	166, 182n34

Isaiah

44	90n6
55:1	159n9

Jeremiah

32:9–10	151n1

Daniel

	159

Amos

4	160

Micah

7:18	90n6

Zechariah

1:3	160n10

Malachi

3:7	160n10

NEW TESTAMENT

Matthew

5	163
5:17	165n18
5:23–24	164n16
5:25–26	163n15
6:19–21	192n41
6:24	169n20, 203n7, 231n23
6:24–25	220n17
7:1	164n17
7:12	165
8:22	162n13
17	170
18:21–35	175
20:1–16	172n25
20:25–28	195n43
20:15	172
23:8–12	229n21
25	173n27
25:15	173
26:11	178n32
28:18–20	234n1

Mark

2	211
2:27	116
10:42–25	195n43
14:7	178n32

Luke

9:60	162n13
10:38–42	204n8
12:6	102n30
12:15–31	192n41
14:26	162n13, 194n42
14:33	162n12
16:9	189n37, 226n20, 231n22
16:13	169n20, 203n7, 231n23
17:21	175n30
18:9–14	217
19	173n27
20:24–25	86n1

John

1:1–3	93n15
1:3	102n30
1:18	92n10
4:24	92n9
12:8	178n32
18:36	175n29

Acts

2	209n13, 217

Romans

1	138
1:18	13
4:17	94n17
6:10	196n45
12–13	182
12	182
12:20	182n34
13	169, 182–83
13:7	183
13:8–10	182
13:14	118n58

1 Corinthians

13	216
13:5	160n11
15	111n49

2 Corinthians

5:20	192n40, 199n2

Galatians

	187

Ephesians

5–6	180–81
5:15–16	181n33

Philippians

3:7–8	221n18

Colossians

1:15–16	162n13
2:16–17	171n23
4:5	181

2 Thessalonians

3:10	225n19

1 Timothy

	184–85

2 Timothy

	184–85

Philemon

	180

Hebrews

1:3	208n11
4	116n56
4:12	11
4:13	141n14, 187n35
8–10	171n24
11:3	162n13
11:10	191n39
11:13–16	191n39

Hebrews (continued)

11:13	184
13:5	185
13:8	100n27, 153

1 Peter

2:11–12	184
2:13–17	184

Revelation

119, 183, 195

GRECO-ROMAN WRITINGS

Aesop

Fables

197

Aristotle

Nicomachean Ethics

1133a17–21	19, 38–39, 101
IV.3	44

Politics

1256b	37
1257b	39
1259a	146

Derveni Papyrus

column VII	6–7

Fragment of Anaximander

27n21

Herodotus

24n17

Histories

5.63, 66	52n64

Homer

Iliad

41, 48–49

Isocrates

Antidosis

232	52n64

Josephus

Jewish War

14:70	167

Plato

Euthyphro

14e	172

Laws

918a	37

Republic

	44n51, 57
416e	36–37

Seventh Letter to the Syracusans

342	36

Plutarch

Camillus

7.5–8.2	155

Lysander

17.3	25

Parallel Lives

196

Solon

Frag. 4c.3 21n9

Thucydides

Peloponnesian War

6.53 52n64

5.105 76–77n91

Xenophanes

Frag B25 30

www.ingramcontent.com/pod-product-compliance
Lightning Source LLC
Chambersburg PA
CBHW030615230426
43661CB00053B/1991